Carl Abel

Ilchester Lectures on Comparative Lexicography

Delivered at the Taylor Institution, Oxford

Carl Abel

Ilchester Lectures on Comparative Lexicography
Delivered at the Taylor Institution, Oxford

ISBN/EAN: 9783337221287

Hergestellt in Europa, USA, Kanada, Australien, Japan

Cover: Foto ©Thomas Meinert / pixelio.de

Weitere Bücher finden Sie auf **www.hansebooks.com**

Slavic and Latin.

ILCHESTER LECTURES

ON

COMPARATIVE LEXICOGRAPHY

DELIVERED AT

THE TAYLOR INSTITUTION. OXFORD.

BY

CARL ABEL. Ph.D.

PREFACE.

—o—

DELIVERED before the University of Oxford, these Lectures were intended to serve a double object. Whilst discussing some points of Slavic and Latin philology, I aimed at illustrating Comparative Lexicography, a sister science of Comparative Grammar, whose formation and uses I have repeatedly endeavoured to advocate.

A brief account of the existing discrepancy between the two Russian races and languages opens the book. Of the lexicological details given, and the conceptual estimates taken in these introductory chapters, it may be fairly said that they are an attempt at tilling virgin soil.

An inquiry into Russian, Polish, and Latin synonyms follows. The comparative dissection of a few vocables, indicative of Liberty and Society notions, besides analysing the Slavic mind with the help of the language-test, will, it is hoped, sufficiently demonstrate the method adopted. It cannot be too emphatically asserted, that, on being properly investigated, the words, forms, and constructions of every language are found to display a comprehensive view of the universe, its things, qualities, and transactions, as conceived by each nation after its own peculiar fashion and style.

To complete the systematic analysis of the dictionary, it should, therefore, be supplemented by a corresponding inquiry into grammar, the scrutiny of each verbal notion under conceptual categories being coupled with the examination of synonymous grammatical forms and constructions.

It is by studying grammar exclusively according to parts of speech—at once the most abstract and least instructive method, though the one most indispensable for acquiring rudiments—that we are apt to lose sight of the connection existing between ideas expressed by inflexion, and the same concepts as conveyed in independent words.

As regards the etymologies cited, the reader, should he wish to follow up the subject beyond the details given in the concluding chapter, is referred to the author's Linguistic Essays and Coptic Researches.

Oxford, *February* 15, 1883.

CONTENTS.

—*o*—

I.

THE SLAVIFICATION OF THE FINNISH AREA.

I.

THERE are parts of the earth, uniform on the surface, but concealing a multitude of divers strata disposed at a small depth from the monotonous crust. Wherever the deeper layers are covered with alluvial and diluvial deposits, the surface is rendered homogeneous, while the subsoil retains all its original diversity. As in geology, so it is in ethnology. Not to speak of uncivilised or semicivilised races inhabiting remote quarters of the globe, nearly all European nations include a variety of heterogeneous elements with their former or actual differences hidden from view by fortuitous identity of language.

This remark applies equally to all the principal nationalities of the Continent. Everywhere foreign ingredients have been politically annexed, and linguistically embodied, by physical or intellectual force. Spain, chiefly Arabic in the south, Teuton in the centre, Celtic and Basque in north and east, is nevertheless outwardly Spanish everywhere. France, Roman in the south, Celtic in the centre and west, and Teutonic in considerable portions of the north and north-east, is yet very French

throughout. Germany, with a purely Teutonic
north-west, combines a strong Celtic alloy in the
musical and imaginative south, and a considerable Slavonic and Lithuanian admixture in the
frigid and reasoning north-east. Yet *the one* speech
of Fatherland is uniformly heard in all these various
regions. Neither are the Slav nationalities less
diversified. Of the southern Slavs, the Serbs and
Croats are pre-eminently Slav; but the Bosnian is
semi-Turk, the Montenegrin and Dalmatian is at
least half Albanian, and the Bulgar is a Finno-
Tatar, and a comparatively recent immigrant from
the Ural mountains. Despite their dissimilar origin,
however, Serbs, Croats, Bosnians, Dalmatians and
Montenegrins speak apparently the same tongue,
and the Bulgarian sister dialect closely approxi-
mates the others of the same geographical group.
Farther north the Bohemian Czech has swallowed
up not a few Germans, tinging his speech with
Teutonic idioms. The Pole, too, adds various
foreign elements to his primary Slavonic stock.
Danes, Germans, and Turk-Tatars are with tolerable
distinctness traced as conquerors, who formed the
Poles into the first commonwealth they ever possessed. In Russia the medley is quite as great.
In that country the majority of the people are
actually not of the descent popularly understood
to be indicated by their name. Slavs and Slavdom
being nowadays so much identified with the mighty

name of Rus, this part of our subject would seem to call for a few elucidatory remarks, even were it not intimately connected with the linguistic inquiry in hand.

When Rurik the Swede, towards the end of the ninth century, occupied North-Western Russia from the Baltic to Novgorod and Tver, the people he subjected to his rule were Slavs, seemingly without government, and easily reduced to obedience by the bold and imperious Northmen. Rurik's heir penetrated as far south as Kieff; while his later successors, in less than a century's time, annexed the far-stretching eastern lands down to the river Oka and the ancient town of Susdal. The eastern lands thus added were entirely distinct from the western or Slavonic possessions of the Rurikian dynasty, being Finno-Tataric in point of race and speech ; * but the diversity of the subject elements was hidden under the identity of the ruling nation. Swedes in those days calling themselves Rothrmen, *i.e.*, Ruddermen, or sailors,† the common appellation of Rothr,

* The term Finns is used throughout as a generic appellation of the most westernly branch of the great Finno-Tataric-Mongolian family of speech.

† The inhabitants of the Oestergötland and Upland shores were formerly called Rods-karlar, 'rudder-men,' just as the Norwegian fishermen go to this day by the name of 'Rods-folk' or 'Ross-folk.' Hence 'Ruotsi,' the appellation given to the Swedes by their Finnish neighbours on the opposite shore, and 'Rus,' as pronounced by the Slavs. Cf. Rydquist, 'Svenska Sprakets Lagar;' Aasen, 'Norsk Ordbog;' Wiedemann, 'Estnisches Wörterbuch;' Thomsen, 'Relations between Ancient Russia and Scandinavia;' Ralston, 'Early Russian History.'

Ruothr, Roth, Ruth, was indiscriminately bestowed upon the entire extent of their dominion,
no matter whether the inhabitants were Slavs or
Finns. This is the origin of the promiscuous
denomination of two distinct and, in historical
times, altogether unrelated races by the name of a
third, foreign to both. Still the foreign name did
not attain equal prevalence in both sections of the
Rurikian Empire. The Slavic portion of the Rurikian territory, indeed, was uniformly called Russ
since the ninth century; but the Finnic division,
which soon became politically separated from it,
and probably never received more than a moiety
of Swedish immigrants, for six centuries after the
conquest went chiefly, and indeed almost exclusively, by the more ancient and indigenous names
of Susdal and Muscovy. Not until 250 years ago,
Muscovy, still more than half Finnic at that time,
adopted the appellation of Rus for good. Having
just then conquered from the Poles a portion of the
Slavic country, to which the name more properly
belonged, Muscovy thought it as well to announce
her accession to the western community by dropping
her Finnic designation, and taking that of the more
European and more civilised race. Besides rendering
her European, the style and title of Rus gave Muscovy an apparent right to fresh conquest in the
same desirable quarter. With half the Ukraine
taken from Poland and the title of a Russian

Grand Prince finally appropriated by the ruler of Muscovy, the wish to absorb the Southern Slav seemed to acquire the dignity of a legitimate dynastic claim. In this, it need hardly be said, Russia did neither more nor worse than every other power in those conquering days thought itself entitled to do.

The change of name was productive of characteristic consequences. Directly their Finnic and semi-Finnic neighbours began to don the name of Rus in preference to previous indigenous appellations, the Russians of Slavic descent, by whom the coveted epithet had been formerly all but monopolised, thought it necessary to mark their diversity from their new Finno-Tataric namesakes by pointedly calling themselves Slavic Russians. Up to that time they had, as a rule, contented themselves with the unqualified name of Russians. This reaction of the Muscovite change of name upon the designation of the Kieff Slavo-Russian people is curiously illustrated by the titles of the two oldest Slavo-Russian dictionaries extant. The first dictionary, by Lawrence Sisan, printed at Vilna in 1596, calls the language 'prosti Ruski dialect,' which means 'the Russian vernacular.' Thirty years later, upon a new dictionary being published at Kieff by Berinda, the author deemed it indispensable to describe his language on the title-page as Slaveno-Rosski, *i.e.*, Slavo-Russic, in contradistinction to the Finno-Russian speech prevailing at Moscow. The significant discrimination made is confirmed by a corresponding procedure on the part of the Muscovites themselves. When appropriating the ethnographic title of their western neighbours and recent subjects, the Muscovites did not take it over in its exact form and shape, but significantly altered its mould and general appearance. Slavic Russia always called herself simply Rus; but the princes of the Finnic territory, on espousing the new epithet, adorned it with the classical and eminently European termination of *ia*. What was Rus at Kieff, with a Latin tinge became Russia (Rossiya) at Moscow. Probably the wish to approximate culture by a classical name, and the policy of displaying independence by a distinct appellation, equally contributed to cause Muscovites to change Russ into Russia when dropping their more ancient Finnish patronymic. The political bearing of this cognominal metamorphosis may be traced down to the present day. The reunion of semi-Finnic Muscovy with a portion of Slavic Russia 250 years ago gave the signal for adopting the *denomination* of Russ: the more novel plan to establish Russian hegemony over all Slavs has lately encouraged Muscovite politicians to claim absolute Slavonic *descent*,—a pretension not at all included in the original appropriation of the style and title of Russ.

There is ample indigenous and foreign proof of the national diversity between the two sections of the Russian Empire since the beginning of their recorded history. In the eleventh and twelfth centuries the Rurikian dominion, divided into a number of independent and semi-independent principalities, extended about 700 miles north and south, and 600 miles east and west, comprising about one-fourth of the present area of European Russia. From Nestor, the earliest Russian historiographer, who penned his important chronicles towards the end of the eleventh century, we learn, that at least one-fourth of this original empire, including the principalities of Susdal, Vladimir, and Moscow, was Finnic, not Slavic, in speech. A missionary, scholar, and historian, Nestor carefully separates the Turanic people of Moscow from the Aryans of Kieff, and expressly points out the linguistic diversity of the two. The Nishni Novgorod Chronicler likewise calls the aboriginals of his province 'Finnish heathens.' Six hundred years later, *i.e.*, towards the end of the seventeenth century, barely two hundred years ago, the German traveller Olearius found the eastern portions of Moscow and Susdal still Finnic in speech. The fact is the more notable, as Kutko Khan, the last Finno-Tataric ruler of Moscow and Susdal, was dethroned by Ivan Dolgoruki, a member of the Rurikian family, full five hundred years before Olearius visited those parts. Five

hundred years of Rurikian rule, then, had not suf-
ficed to Slavify Moscow. Towards the middle of
the eighteenth century, L'Abbé Chappe d'Auteroche,
sent to explore Russia in behalf of the French
Government, noted in his diaries the same radical
dissimilarity between Slav and Muscovite. It was
only in the reign of the Empress Elizabeth Petrovna
(1741–1762) that the Mordva Finns of Nishni
Novgorod, Simbirsk, Samara, Pensa, Saratoff, Kasan,
and Astrakhan were forced to adopt Christianity—
a ceremony which did not prevent their adhering
to pagan rites and foreign dialects till thirty or
forty years ago.

The slow progress of Slavification is accounted
for by a variety of geographical and political circumstances. Extending from Novgorod to Muscovy, and farther east across the low ridges of the
Ural, the Finno-Tatar expanse was too large to
be easily dotted with Slavonic settlements. When
the Mongol territory was annexed, being a perfect
wilderness of immense extent, it presented another
obstruction to the progress of Slavonic speech.
There were constantly fresh arrivals from Siberia,
too; while, owing to the long political division
separating the Eastern from the Western, the
Finnic from the Slavonic principalities of the
Rurikian dynasty, comparatively few Slavs (according to Karamsin and other historians) ever
emigrated to the Turanic lands. Neither should

it be overlooked, that the Mongol inroad under
Gingiskhan, though it overran, at the same time
strengthened, the cognate Finno - Tatar element
indigenous in the Eastern territories. In a paper
upon Russian literature in the fourteenth century,
the famous philologist Bouslayeff calls Rurikian
Moscow a semi-Tatar camp, which made war upon
Novgorod, Pskoff, Tver, and the north - western
Slavs generally in the Mongol interest and with
Mongol help. In point of fact, it was this semi-
Tataric character which procured Muscovy the
countenance of the pure and unmitigated Tatar, *i.e.,*
the Mongol, and at the time of the Khanish suze-
rainty, enabled her to begin the subjugation of
the neighbouring Slav, whose speech and name
she subsequently proclaimed as her own. Thus
strengthened in her Finno-Tataric proclivities even
after she had turned the tables upon the common
suzerain, and, with the help of the Slav, whom the
Mongol permitted her to annex, had defeated and
partially annexed the Mongol himself, Muscovy
kept her ancient speech. Like many Asiatic tribes,
Finno-Tatars indeed possess a wonderful facility in
acquiring foreign tongues—a facility which, to a
modern European, is next to unintelligible. Notwithstanding, however, this ready aptitude for linguistic denationalisation, which could hardly occur
if old ideas were cherished and new ones appreciated
in the way they are farther west, the antagonistic

agencies enumerated strongly asserted themselves until within recent times.

Accordingly, Finns, Tatars, and Mongols required a thousand years in the old Rurikian territory, and about half as much in the lands annexed since the overthrow of the Khanates, to attain their present state of more or less advanced Slavification. Passive recipients of everything foreign as they always have been, the Finns, Tatars, and Mongols of European Russia even now largely use their own idiom conjointly with Slav. To this day East Vladimir, the province east of Moscow, and the centre of old Susdal, knows its own Mordva dialect by the side of Slav. Nay, all over the more northern and eastern sections of the ancient Finnish and Tatar area, though the upper classes are Slav in speech, there remain millions of villagers and nomads with a Slavonic smattering and a marked partiality for Turanian word and phrase. As there are only some four hundred towns in the late Finno-Tatar territory, their Russian aspect, accordingly, neither mitigates nor disproves the Turanian descent of the immense majority of the rustics. In many parts the original tribal names of the Finno-Tataric race, Mer, Mordva, Tcheremiss, Tchuwasch, Votyak, Siryan, Teruchan, Karatai, Vogul, Baskhir, Petschenog, &c., are still remembered and in use. The very capital of Moscow derives its name from the Moshka tribe, a subdivision of the Mordva. In

European Russia the total of this wholly or partially Slavified Finno-Tataric population to-day is calculated at 40,000,000 against only 15,000,000 of pure Russo-Slavonic origin.

The political events which contributed to deepen the original national discrepancy between Finno-Russian and Slavo-Russian cannot be too much dwelt upon. In the thirteenth century the semi-Slavified Finns of Muscovy, who had long been struggling with the Polovtsi and other unmitigated Turanians of the southern and eastern area, were absolutely overrun by the Mongolian Tatars, who ruled the country for two hundred years. During these terrible two hundred years, and the hardly less barbarous two hundred years immediately succeeding Mongol rule, Muscovite civilisation, what there had been of it, was tatarised. When revived by Peter the Great, it became European and cosmopolitan, with a decided German and rationalistic tinge. Politically and intellectually the fate of the Slavic Russians was very different. Though likewise suffering from Mongol raids, the Slavic Russians from 1320 to 1680 mainly obeyed Lithuano-Polish masters, who kept them comparatively free from the Turanian scourge, gave them an upper class, converted numbers to the Roman Church, and impregnated their first essays in literary culture with the spirit and the doctrines of the Papal religion. In fact, it was only in consequence of the Poles attempting to force Catholicism upon the southern-most Russian Slavs, that, going over to the Musco-vites, the Ukraine Cossacks paved the way for the subsequent conquest of Slavic Russia by Catherine II. Muscovy's gain in the first division of Poland, broadly speaking, was the annexation of Slavonic Russia by Finno-Tataric Russia, from which it had been estranged since the early days of the Rurikian conquest. Civilisatory despotism in those days forming the Muscovites into powerful armies, while the aristocratic republic of Poland fell a prey to anarchy, the ruin of the weaker, though certainly not the less ambitious state, was rapidly decided in an era of resolute dynastic aggrandisement.

So very heterogeneous are the origin, the history, and the culture of the Slavo-Russians and the Finno-Tataric Russians. Down to the time of Peter the Great, the Finno-Russians never dreamt of concealing the Turanic origin of their race. Only after Peter began to Europeanise his Musco-vites, the notion that they had numerous relations living in Siberia and other Asiatic lands was officially tabooed. Official St. Petersburg in those un-scientific days had not realised the fact that all Europeans are in reality Asiatics, and that the Finns, so far from being the latest, are, on the contrary, the earliest arrivals from the East in these western lands. So the idea of an Asiatic origin was very unnecessarily abhorred and put down with the

strong hand. Dr. Müller, one of the German
scholars summoned to form an Academy of Science
in bran-new St. Petersburg, in 1749 published
a book entitled 'Origines Gentis et Nominis
Russorum.' In this creditable performance the
worthy man, gratefully called to this day the
father of Russian historiography, plainly demonstrated the non-Slavonic extraction of the Muscovites. His arguments were repeated, apparently
without any inkling that he might be giving
offence, by M. Trediakovski, the perpetual Secretary of the new Academy. Upon hearing of these
erudite asseverations, the Empress Elizabeth, the
daughter and third successor of Peter the Great,
was highly incensed, and immediately resolved
upon a most striking description of criticism. Trediakovski was soundly flogged. In fact, he got a
painful hundred for his unpalatable ethnography.
Müller, being a foreigner in a land which wanted
and honoured foreigners in those civilisatory days,
had to be dealt with more leniently. The unlucky
investigator was consigned to durance vile until he
should consent to recant. As the man was too
much of a scholar to like the idea of retracting the
outcome of conscientious research, the Empress, by
way of compromise, adroitly proposed that the in-
discreet doctor should acknowledge the Muscovites
to be the lineal descendants of the Roxolans, a
people of doubtful nationality on the Sea of

Azoff, mentioned by classical writers as fighting
Mithridates in days of yore. Müller, like everybody else, not having the least notion who and
what the Roxolans really were, in the sorry plight
in which he found himself did not object to regard
them as Russians for the nonce. So by an admis-
sion which involved no absolute untruth he hap-
pily got out of jail at last. Twenty years after
this forcible emendation of history, the Empress
Catherine the Great stoutly confirmed her pre-
decessor's verdict. Again it was an unfortun-
ate German scholar whose literary zeal irritated
Majesty. Professor Stritter, a member of the St.
Petersburg Academy, in a book published in 1791,
'Populi Antiquæ Russiæ,' boldly repeated the
Finno-Tatar unpleasantness. Catherine having so
long been a zealous and most generous protectress
of scientific research, the naïve savant thought himself at liberty to proclaim what he regarded as an
incontrovertible fact. But the Empress speedily
disillusioned the confident antiquary. Though
herself a German, the daughter of an Ascanian
prince and Prussian general, the Czarina in this
emergency promptly took the field for the Slavic
theory against Teuton research. In a paper of
instructions to the Russian Schoolbook Department, Catherine forthwith inserted the memorable
words : 'Though the Russians and Slavs are not
of the same origin, there is no ill-will between

them. It would be a scandal to admit Mr. Stritter's opinion that the Russians are Finns. The horror felt at the idea by us all is the best proof that we can have nothing in common with the Finns.' * The better to inculcate her own view of the matter, Catherine subsequently issued a ukase commanding Muscovites to be Europeans. It was with reference to this extraordinary document that Mirabeau, in his 'Liberté de l'Escaut,' indulged in the pert though ethnographically untenable remark, 'Les Russes ne sont Européens, qu'en vertu d'une définition déclaratoire de leur souveraine.' Could he have foreseen the discoveries of modern philology, Mirabeau would not have ventured upon the cutting observation. Albeit partially Finns, the Russians to-day are known to be quite as much European as anybody else, considering that we have all been discovered to be Asiatics by descent. Truth will out. However much deprecated by their Government in those early and comparatively ignorant days, the mixed descent of the Muscovite Russians has been subsequently admitted by almost all the leading writers on Muscovite history, most of them Russians and Slavs. Schlözer, Schnitzler, Schafarik, Soloviev, Saveliev, Karamsin, Pagodine, Castren, all or nearly all of them distinguished members of the St. Petersburg Academy,

* Reprinted in the 'Journal de l'Instruction Publique de l'Empire Russe,' Janvier, 1835.

B

are pretty much in accord upon this pregnant point. Only ten years ago, the famous Kostoma-roff published a learned essay entitled, 'Dve Russkiya Narodnosti,' Anglice, 'The Two Russian Nationalities,' in which some of the realities of the case were set forth with much historical and lin-guistic acumen. Indeed, whatever assertions to the contrary may have been advanced by politicians in the interest of Russian hegemony over the Slav, Russian scholars have never been remiss in acknowledging the conclusive character of the Turanic descent evidence handed down by his-tory.

And why should they have acted otherwise? With so many strong points to give their national character worth and weight, the Muscovite race have no occasion to conceal the elements that have combined to produce them. If neither genuine nor unalloyed Slavs, Muscovites, with all their short-comings, are yet clever, enterprising, enduring, courageous, and, as all the world is aware, have been eminently successful in very many respects. No-thing could be more erroneous than to regard the Muscovite or Finno-Tataric ingredient of the Rus-sian Empire in its present Slavified aspect as inferior to the western or more purely Slavonic portion of the population. Though the two ele-ments differ, either contains highly remarkable traits in its national character.

The Slavo-Russian—to-day called Little Russian,* because his country constitutes only one-fourth of the entire extent of European Russia—is a sensitive, excitable, and musical being, essentially sedentary, agricultural, and domestic. The Slavified Finno-Tatar, on the other hand, formerly called Muscovite, and to-day known as Great Russian, because his race extends over three-fourths of European Russia, is a clever, cold-blooded, calculating individual, who dislikes a settled life, varies agriculture with many an itinerant trade, and dearly loves to rove about as a pedlar or wandering mechanic, with the morrow's bread as uncertain as the road he treads in the pathless steppe. The Slavo-Russian marries for love ; the Finno-Russian is married by his father, with the assistance of the mediating priest. The priest frequently acts as a paid agent, and the father and the priest, in estimating feminine worth, prefer bones that will stand labour to beauty that is only skin-deep. Slavo-Russian family life habitually displays tenderness and mutual consideration and care ; in Finno-Russia the rustic wife and children are obliged to slave for the master of the house, and the sons remaining under the same roof with the father, even when married, the sons' wives too are subject

---

* The names of Great and Little Russia occur for the first time in the Treaty of Pereyaslav, concluded 1654 between the Grand-Duke Alexius of Muscovy and Bogdan Chmelnicki, to enact the incorporation of a portion of the Ukraine. See concluding note of this chapter.

to the dictation of the domestic patriarch. But while the Slavo-Russian is impressible and apt to waver and fret, the Finno-Russian is sturdy, confident, and adventurous; while the Slav sings, the Finno-Muscovite is either silent or indulges in caustical philosophy; while the one glories in innumerable ditties and ballads, the other, besides retaining the epical talent of the Finn, boasts the possession of some ten thousand proverbs, most of them shrewd and pointed, though many of them pessimistic and ill-natured. In the Finn the Slav's feeling is replaced by reasoning power; imagination by plain common-sense; amiable weakness by rough, stern strength. But for the distinctive characteristics of her Muscovite ingredient, Russia would never have attained the might she possesses.

Owing to their innate diversity, there is little love lost between the two Russian races. The Slav dubs the Muscovite 'Katsap,' a term implying something harsh, rough, and at the same time over-politic; the Muscovite, on his part, compliments the Slav as 'Kkokhol,' meaning to denounce him as irresolute, weak, and sly. The Slav every now and then complains that he has been forced by the Muscovites to relinquish the Uniate-Romanist creed, which he accepted under Polish rule, and re-embrace Oriental orthodoxy, from which he was alienated centuries ago. The Slav occasionally grumbles at being placed under Muscovite officials,

with no sympathy for his sensitive temper, and no
pity for his grievances and griefs. Last, not least,
the Slav deplores that his language is officially
tabooed, and may not even be put into print.

This is a sore point. In the centuries marking
the advent of culture to those parts, Slavic Russian,
as a literary language, was stifled by Polish, the
idiom of the then owners of the land; at present,
when Slavic Russia is the property of Finno-Russia,
the linguistic eclipse of the inhabitants continues,
though it emanates from a different quarter. Finno-
Russian being, by the dominating race, declared
the official and literary tongue of the empire,
Slavic Russian, or, to use modern phraseology,
Little Russian, has only at times been allowed to
be printed at all. In the liberal period which in-
augurated the era of Alexander II., the sunshine
of freedom was shed upon Kieff, as upon every
other part of the Empire. Being licensed for print,
the Little Russian language in those days rapidly
produced a promising historical and religious literature. In that halcyon epoch of Russian liberalism,
Little Russian literature witnessed a perfect revival,
and attracted considerable attention at home and
abroad. Not a few of its productions were actually
translated, or recommended for translation, into
Great Russian. Books of sweet and passionate
poetry abounded. Popular songs and tales, the
phantastic heirlooms of a wildly imaginative race,

were numerously collected. Historical, linguistic, and philological inquiries displayed a noble partiality for patriotic and erudite research. But the fates, which had so long obstructed its growth, speedily reasserted their unpropitious influence upon Little Russian literature. In the interest of national unity and Muscovite predominance, the independent literary resurrection of Little Russia was promptly put a stop to by the vigorous statesmen of St. Petersburg. The Slavic or Little Russians showing in their books and papers a decided inclination to assert a distinct nationality and to accentuate their dissimilarity to the Muscovites, the movement had to be stayed, and accordingly *was* stayed with a will. In 1859, in the first blush of the liberal era, M. Lavrovski had been actually permitted to discuss the independent nationality and speech of the Little Russians in the official reports of the Ministry of Public Instruction ; in 1876, fifteen years later, Little or Slavonic Russian, the language from which the Great or Finno-Russian is mainly derived, was absolutely interdicted by Imperial decree. Since then Little or Slavonic Russian may not, as a rule, be printed. Indeed, it may hardly be read or spoken either, except by scholars or boors. Excluded from church, school, and court, it is equally prohibited in the theatre, the concert-room, and the editorial office. For private persons it is scarcely safe to

possess copies of the literature licensed in preceding
reigns; while what little instruction is imparted in
elementary schools is impaired by its delivery to
peasant children in a semi-foreign vernacular. For
an estranged tongue to the Little Russian the Great
Russian idiom has gradually become. Though
chiefly of Little Russian descent, the Great Russian
speech, as we shall have no difficulty in ascertaining,
is very considerably altered from its original type.

As yet, however, the official veto has not suc-
ceeded in silencing the Slavo-Russian tongue. Prohibited in Russia, the ancient idiom is still put
into type by Little Russians inhabiting the eastern
districts of the Austrian province of Galicia, com-
monly called Ruthenes or Russinians. What is
even more remarkable, the Great Russians actually
assist in Galicia what they suppress in Russia.
Unable to put an end to Little Russian literature
on Austrian soil, the Great Russians have made a virtue of necessity, and positively subsidise on Hapsburg territory what they exterminate on their own.
Divers reasons account for this peculiar policy. By
helping him to accentuate his separate nationality,
the Russinian peasant in Galicia is pitted against his
Polish landlord. He is drawn, too, from the Romanist
to the Orthodox Establishment, and he is taught the
Muscovite tongue while he is seemingly treated to his
own. The Russinian speech employed in subsidised
Galician prints is mostly an artificial product made

to order by the writers, very nearly approximating the Great Russian in words, and wholly so in feeling. Thus the idiom persecuted in Russia, where it opposes Great Russian, is fostered, and at the same time Muscovitised, by the Great Russians themselves in Austria, being there administered as an antidote against Polonism, Romanism, and Hapsburg rule.

The struggle between subsidised Russinianism and the Austro-Polish authorities rages fiercely, and every now and then produces strange results. Only a few months ago the Russinian subsidised press in Austria figured largely in a trial for high treason which came off at Lemberg, the capital of Galicia. The prisoners, mostly Austro-Russinian journalists and priests, were charged with the design to betray their sovereign, and hand over Austrian-Russinia to Russia. They were certainly proved to have received money from St. Petersburg; and as leading personages of the St. Petersburg capital were introduced by name in the official *acte d'accusation*, the scene was as sensational as it was painful. Though the punishments inflicted were lenient, the proceedings mark a period in the history of the race. By way of significant epilogue to the trial, the Pope has just deposed the Uniate bishop who countenanced these intrigues, and excommunicated a priest who fostered them. As might have been foreseen, the priest, immediately upon excommunication, embraced Orthodoxy, and addressed a violent letter to the Pope, in which he claimed the Slav, body and soul, for the Czar. The chequered destinies of the Little Russian race are shown in the fact that the priest so signally punished for Muscovitism in 1882, in 1874 achieved notoriety by his loyal devotion to the Austrian Emperor, who protected his countrymen from the Poles. The Polish ascendancy which has since supervened in Galicia has lately reconciled the Little Russians of Austria to the Great Russians, however dissatisfied the Little Russians of Russia may, every now and then, be with their fate. Jammed in between Poles and Great Russians, the Little Russians have ever found it difficult to assert themselves, and are apt to appeal alternately from one neighbour to the other.*

A very different sort of Little Russian literature is produced at Geneva by refugees from Little Russian districts under Great Russian control. Successors of the Ukrainophil poets and politicians, who penned their glowing effusions under Nicholas I. and Alexander II., the gentlemen who have been lately publishing Russinian books, pamphlets, and periodicals on the distant soil of Switzerland aim

---

* In 1770 the Little Russian Cossacks rebelled against the oppression of the Poles. When the Poles failed to suppress the revolt, the Great Russians, finding their own territory threatened, interfered, and by a ruse captured the insurgent chief Gonta, and 8000 men. These 8000 prisoners Field-Marshal Romanzoff handed over to the Poles, who distributed them for execution over their various provinces, when each town killed its quota by the most diverse and ingenious methods.

at the political and literary emancipation of their
countrymen from Great Russian rule. The political
independence of the race, before it became subject
to Muscovites and Poles ; their wars, struggles, and
misfortunes in the last two centuries; their sufferings
at the present period, and their hopes for the future,
are the theme of this modern Helveto-Russinian
literature, as indeed they have been of nearly all
Russinian literature ever since the accession of
Alexander II. To this old programme has been
recently added the propagation of socialist theories,
as a suitable means of rousing the peasant from his
lethargy, and setting him against the Government,
which, in a degree, protects the landlord.

The central figure of Russinian literature is
Schevtchenko,* a poet transported and knouted
under Nicholas I. for the production of objection-
able verse. His last poem, 'Bratskie Poslanie,'
'The Fraternal Mission,' purports to be a satire
upon the notion of some Great Russians to liberate
the Slav from German, Austrian, Hungarian, Rumanian, and Turkish rule, when the two Slavic races
already under the Great Russian sceptre, the Little
Russians and Poles, so frequently complain of the
treatment they receive at their masters' hands. And
thus, though cultivated Slavo-Russians must write

* Cf. K. E. Franzos, 'Die Kleinrussen und ihre Saenger.' Allgem.
Zeitung, 1877, Nos. 164, 165. 'Aus Halb-Asien,' 'Vom Don zur Donau,'
and other Russinian sketches by the same author, are equally remarkable
for brilliancy, depth, and erudition.

Muscovite, or Great Russian, in Russia, if they wish to write at all, the Russinian movement is still continued and a special literature kept alive outside the Czarish territory.*

Curiously enough, modern Russinian is, to a large extent, a foreign-letter paper literature. To facilitate their being smuggled across the Russian frontier, the Geneva volumes and flying-sheets are mostly printed on the thinnest of notepaper. To reduce their bulk, they are made to look wonderfully elegant.†

In my next lecture I shall follow up to-day's historical sketch by some linguistic details respecting the points of contact and difference between the Great Russian and Little Russian idioms.

* Only upon the conquest of Ukraine (1654), Muscovy took to styling herself Great Russia, and conferred the corresponding minor title upon the annexed race. Up to the annexation of Ukraine the only purely Slavic territory possessed by Muscovy was Novgorod and the adjoining north-eastern land, embodied, partially with Mongol help and connivance, in the fourteenth and fifteenth centuries. The Poles never changed the original names of the two countries, but continue to call Russia Muscovy, and Russinia Russ.

† The publication of an illustrated Little Russian periodical, ' Zarya,' was begun and discontinued last year in London. Notwithstanding its Russian bias, it was not admitted in Russia.

II.

THE TWO RUSSIAN LANGUAGES.

II.

If *language* is a test of national character, is not *descent* a matter of indifference? Should not any people be regarded as civilised who speak a cultivated tongue? However primitive their ancestors may have been in times *past*, do not people advance at a leap, do they not reform their entire spiritual self, on adopting a new and more highly developed idiom? Is not a *nation* more particularly raised to the intellectual status of any language it may happen to acquire, no matter whether invented by itself or borrowed from others?

Then, as regards affinity: gauging relationship by an intellectual standard, ought we not to consider races more closely connected with their linguistic congeners than with their ethnographical kindred? If blood is thicker than water, is not the mind even more potent in forming connections than the blood?

No doubt these questions should be answered in the affirmative, provided a qualifying caution is added to the willing consent. There are two ways of adopting a foreign tongue. If it is taken over as it stands, with its phonology, etymology, and

grammar unimpaired, and the significations of its
words unaltered, the recipient certainly allows his
own ideas to be superseded by those of the new
idiom. If, on the contrary, grammar is modified
and the import of words changed in the transmission, then the metamorphosis is limited to the
acquisition of a foreign shell, and the kernel is put
in by the independent exertion, or at least with
the active co-operation, of the linguistic proselyte.
Of these two contingencies, the former occurs, when,
going to a foreign country and staying in it a considerable time, an individual adopts its language to
the entire replacement of his own. Then that part
of a man's intellectual identity which is comprised
in language may be absolutely effaced, and a new
set of standard ideas imprinted upon his mind.
Surrounded by people habitually employing words
and meanings different from his own, a man's mind
in such a case is gradually tinctured with novel
hues, until, having no occasion to air his old
phraseology, he ends by adopting the new one
in the sense and in the meaning in which it is
imposed by the overpowering influences surround-
ing him. The same absolute innovation is witnessed
when a comparatively small number of foreigners
subside in the great mass of another nationality.
It is different, however, when an entire nation takes
to a new tongue. Whether effected by spiritual or
mere military subjugation, the change in this case

cannot be equally complete. Whenever large numbers, bearing the stamp of the same ethnical type, are allowed continued intercourse with each other, their physical and intellectual habits are necessarily preserved to some extent even under the pressure of overwhelming agencies from without. Among other results of their partially victorious resistance, the new words forced upon them in such a case are apt to undergo a change of form and meaning in accord with the peculiarities of the subsiding type. A good, and by its multiplicity perfectly conclusive, example of this linguistic diversification is supplied by the history of colonial Latin. Readily accommodating itself to the different individualities of the different races subjugated, Latin became Italian in Italy, French in France, Spanish in Spain, Portuguese in Portugal, Rumanian in Moldowallachia, and Romaunsch in the south-eastern valleys of Switzerland. Not only was the form of each Latin word specially modified in each of these several lands, but the meaning in most instances was characteristically altered with the form. As one example out of a thousand, take the Latin word 'perdere,' to ruin, to lose. Retaining its general aspect everywhere, it shows very different features nevertheless in each of the several countries to which it emigrated. Its Spanish representative 'perder' includes the signification of 'to bet;' its Rumanian form 'perdu' may mean to execute, to hang and to spoil; while the French reflexive 'se perdre' denotes to disappear, and the Portuguese 'perderse' to capsize. The differentiation of transplanted thought is even greater in the case of abstract ideas. 'Vitium,' defect, deficiency, and guilt in Latin, in Portuguese becomes 'vicio,' which may mean no more than error; in Spanish 'vicio,' which comprises caprice, habit, and pullulation; in Italian 'vizio,' cupidity; in Provençal French, 'vici,' cunning; in Rumanian, 'vichiu,' vice in its most repulsive form. It is clear, the conception of guilt must have been very different in these different nationalities, to have prompted them to metamorphose the Latin 'vitium,' the one into error, the other into caprice, *bad* habit and *mere* habit, the third into cupidity, the fourth into cunning, the fifth into abominable vice.

As similar transformations of intrinsic sense may be observed in most words of what may be called transferred languages, it follows that the mere fact of Finns and Finno-Tatars accepting Slavonic speech does not necessarily imply their acceptance of Slavonic sentiment, but, on the contrary, argues a Turanic remodelling of the original Aryan tongue. Drawn on general linguistic grounds, this conclusion is confirmed by a comparison of the Slavo-Russian and Finno-Russian vocabularies.* The analysis of,

---

* To keep the original national diversity before the reader, I here employ the terms Finno-Russians and Slavo-Russians, in preference to the

comparatively speaking, a very few words will suffice to demonstrate the different turn given to Slavo-
Russian significations upon the acceptance of their
verbal representatives by the Finno-Russians. A
limited number of examples, it is true, in itself proves
not the frequency of the process; but if very ordinary ideas can be shown to have been perverted from
their original Slavo-Russian type by their Finno-
Russian inheritors, the inference will be justified
that many others which cannot be quoted in a
lecture must have shared the same fate.

Ideas of good and bad occupying so prominent a
position in any nation's vocabulary, let us begin
with their comparative dissection in Little Russian
and Great Russian. 'Khoróschi,' probably an etymological development of the root ' kras,' meaning
' red,* coloured,' † in Little Russian mostly keeps to
the sensuous sphere, and getting no farther than a
very slight metaphor will carry it, signifies, 'pleasing,
beautiful;' in Great Russian, on the other hand,
the word at a leap passes from the signification
'pleasing' into that of ' good.' The Little Russians,
as they distinguish between what is merely pleasing
and what is really good, necessarily require a special

accepted names of Great Russians and Little Russians, which refer only
to the extent of their respective geographical areas. In what follows, I
revert to the usual, albeit inappropriate and purely quantitative, terminology.

* See Fourth Chapter.

† *Cf.*, however, the different derivations suggested by the learned
Professor Iagic, in 'Archiv für Slavische Philologie,' vi. 2, p. 282.

word in their language for 'good;' in Great Russian, where the two notions are frequently confounded, one word is apt to cover both. The special Little Russian term for 'good, intrinsically good,' is 'dóber;' and many things in Little Russian are accordingly denoted as 'dóber,' *i.e.*, intrinsically good, which in Great Russian are called 'khoróshi,' *i.e.*, good, because I think they are nice; good, because I like them. The word 'dóber, dóbri,' certainly exists in Great Russian likewise; but as its meaning is mostly usurped by the more arbitrary and capricious 'khoróshi,' 'dóber,' with its respectful recognition of what is really good, of what is good in itself, independently of one's liking it or not, is comparatively neglected. This propensity of the Great Russian to regard as good, not what is good, but what is liked, is emphatically confirmed by a well-known proverb declaring even one's likings to depend upon mere caprice. "Ne po khoróshu mil, a po milu khorósh"—"I do not like a thing because it is nice, but it is nice because I like it."

As a *per contra* proof of what has been stated, the term 'góji,' which in Little Russian means useful, serviceable, and *therefore* good, in Great Russian never gets beyond the meaning of serviceable, and remains for ever removed from the idea of intrinsic worth. The Little Russian dutifully acknowledges the goodness of whatever proves beneficial; the Great Russian, on the contrary, claims the right to regard as good chiefly what he feels himself attracted by, whether serviceable or not. The better to realise the opposite *points de vue* adopted by the two, it may not be amiss to look at the same notion in its English and German garb. Like all the Germanic members of the Aryan family, the English and Germans, in fashioning their notions of goodness, discard the whimsical view taken by the Great or Finno-Russians, and endorse the more reasonable one adopted by the Slav. The English 'good,' the German 'gut,' being derived from the same root as the Slavo or Little Russian 'góji,' equally declare that to be good which is useful.

Again, the term 'blagi,' which in the literary language of Great Russia means good, in the popular tongue of Little Russia (and, to a certain extent, Great Russia too), for reasons which shall be explained in my next lecture, actually signifies *bad*. No more conclusive evidence could be adduced that Slavo-Russian and Great Russian ideas of goodness, though represented by the same words, are wholly distinct. Similarity of term, then, is anything but a guarantee for identity of concept.

There is quite as marked a difference in the conception of badness. 'Chudói,' which in Little Russian indicates nothing worse than a pauper, in Great Russian is degraded to the signification of good for nothing, bad, wicked; a change of meaning which, I am afraid, reflects an opinion extending to other countries than Russia, that a poor man is more apt to be a bad one than a rich man. Again, 'dúrni' in Little Russian denotes a fellow mischievous from stupidity, intoxication, or madness; in Great Russian the word is generalised into signifying anything that is repulsive and ugly, and on these grounds, considered to be very bad. In other words, in Great Russian ugliness is viewed as a sign of badness, just as prettiness, in the case of 'khoróschi' in the same language, is confounded with goodness; whereas in Little Russian the ideas of external elegance and internal worth are, as a rule, religiously kept asunder. Furthermore, in Little Russian we encounter the word 'líchi,' mostly meaning 'wicked,' and occasionally admitting into its principal signification the qualifying *nuance* of 'insolent;' in Great Russian the wicked motives of a man, called 'líchi,' are generally forgotten, while his insolence is raised to the pitch of boldness, resolve, and manly enterprise. 'Líchi,' at Kieff used as 'actively malicious,' at Moscow is connivingly ennobled into the idea of 'enterprising, though, peradventure, wicked.' At Kieff the *malice prepense* is kept in view; at Moscow the daring of the deed is preferably accentuated.

To illustrate other significant changes in the meaning of adjectives, which are legion, a few more instances may be cited. 'Mogútschi,' in Little or Slavo-Russian 'strong and rich,' in Great or Finno-Russian (in the amplified form of 'magúschtschestvenni') becomes 'strong, power-ful, influential;' 'bagáti,' in Little Russian 'copious,' in Great Russian is used for 'rich ;' ' osdóbni,' in Little Russian ' beautiful,' in Great Russian (in the parallel form of ' udóbni ') means 'serviceable, con-venient,' &c.

Passing on to nouns, and comparing a few re-presentative words of this grammatical category, we obtain the like differentiated results. 'Brat,' originally 'brother,' in Little Russian is quite as often employed for 'friend;' in Great Russian it is pretty generally restricted to its primary genea-logical signification. Conversely, 'padrújje, pa-drújka,' literally a 'female *friend*,' in Little Rus-sian is the habitual name of a man's *wife;* in Great Russian it exclusively indicates a girl's girlish playmate. In this last example signification and etymology combine to win the palm for Great Russian ; for as the word 'drugi'—the radical of the words 'padrújje, padrújka'—originally desig-nated nothing more intimate than ' another person,' the derivative term 'padrújje, padrújka,' literally means no more than 'another person, and that a female.' Yet this is the word which in Little or Slavo-Russian suffices to denote ' a wife ;' whereas the same term in Great or Finno-Russian is very

properly confined to the colder notion of 'companion, mate.' The same peculiar confusion of non-
identity with friendship, and of friendship with
wifeship, in Little Russian is carried to the extent
of using the verbal derivatives of 'drug,' 'odrujíty,
odrujítsya,' literally 'to get another,' in the intimate significations of 'to marry' and 'to be married.' In Great Russian, where, it appears, matrimonial ties are taken more *au serieux*, a wife is
never called a friend, and a friend is never styled a
wife. A peculiar exception to the principle of this
rule is the word 'priyátel,' as used by a widow to
designate her defunct husband. 'Priyátel' in Great
Russian originally means 'a well-wisher,' and is
another very common designation for 'friend.' As
long as a husband is alive, the distant term in
this respectful tongue can never apply to him ; but
directly he is dead, his widow is apt to deprive him
of his former more authoritative title, and to content herself with calling the departed one her
'friend.' To wind up, a Little Russian quite com-
monly neglects to discriminate between brother
and male friend, between wife and female friend ;
a Great Russian does make the necessary distinctions, and as he has to use terminology received
from the Little Russian, necessarily narrows its
sense. It need hardly be said that, in consequence
of their greater accuracy in distinguishing between
the various grades of relationship, the Great Rus-

sians have been obliged to appropriate other special words for wife and friend, words rarely used in the same sense by the Little or Slavo-Russians.

Proceeding from matrimonial alliance to friend-ship, we find that the Little Russian has no proper word at all for friend except 'brat,' 'brother;'* the Great Russian has two: 'drug,' 'a constant associate and friend,' and 'priyátel,' 'a pleasant-spoken man, a well-wisher.' Altogether the distinctions drawn by Great Russians in this intellectual category are very nice. From the one word, 'drugi,' meaning 'another man,' which they received from the Little Russians, the Great Russians—to satisfy their desire for exactitude in defining relations between man and man—have evolved no less than five distinct terms: 'drugí,' 'another man ;' 'drúgi,' 'acquaintance ;' 'drug,' 'friend ;' 'drugíe,' 'others ;' 'drusyá,' 'friends.' Little Russian, in its turn, discriminates between 'drugí,' 'another man,' and 'drúgi,' a second man;' while the plural 'drugí' is sometimes used in a loose and rather promiscuous sense for 'friends.'

This does not exhaust the differentiation of the one term 'drug.' Like 'padrújje,' cited above, 'drujína,' another derivative from 'drug,' in Little Russian means 'another party, and she a female, a wife.' In Great Russian, in marked contrast, the

* A distinction is occasionally, but not ordinarily, made between two derivatives of brat: 'bratkó,' 'brother,' and 'brátatsch,' 'friend.'

same word actually signifies 'a company of soldiers.'
Impossible as it at first sight appears, this violent
change of meaning is easily accounted for. The
termination *ina* equally referring to individual
females and to notions classified as feminine by
Russian grammar, what designates a wife in the
one case in the other applies to a collective term of
feminine gender. Thus, from bestowing the wider
signification of 'others' instead of '*one* other
party,' the Great Russian positively uses for an
aggregate of armed men a word which the Little
Russian reserves for the wife of his bosom. The
discrepancy produced by either language giving
the same notion a different turn could not well be
greater.

It is similar with the nomenclature for 'enemy.'
South Slavo-Russian knows only the word 'vrag,'
a foe from innate evil disposition. Finno-Russian
retains the ominous term, but sagaciously supple-
ments it by 'nepriyátel,' an enemy from interest
or other more transient motives; a man, in fact,
who, under altered circumstances, may think fit
to become a friend. At this point of our inquiry,
it may, perhaps, be incidentally observed that
Little or Slavo-Russian, in its modern condition, is
divided into two principal dialects—the Southern or
Ukraina dialect, and the Northern or White Russian speech. Though differing in details, the two
dialects are mainly identical in all the more essen-

tial points of their dictionaries. I chiefly quote from
the Northern or White Russian dialect, without
entirely neglecting the Southern or Ukraina tongue.

Nouns similarly diversified in meaning abound.
' Sláva,' in Little Russian ' talk, rumour,' in the
more ambitious and political Great Russian speech
is exalted into ' glory, honour.' ' Duch,' in simple
Little Russian ' vapour, smoke,' in the literary
development of Great Russia is raised to ' spirit.'
' Slútchai,' in Little Russian ' an unlucky accident,'
in Great Russian, which has a pessimist proclivity,
is used to denote *every* kind of accident, all accidents being in that language regarded as pretty
sure to turn out more or less unlucky. " Vso na
svete slutchai," says a Great Russian proverb
despondingly, — " Everything in this world is
accident, and, as a rule, mischievous accident."
' Mazká,' from ' mazáty,' ' to smear,' in Little Russian is ' blood,' in Great Russian ' ointment.'
' Arúda,' in Little Russian ' a means, an instrument,'
in Finno-Russian becomes ' arúdie,' ' a cannon,'
and ' arújie,' ' a weapon, a musket.' Of the terms
derived from ' arúda, ' arudátsch ' in Little Russian
is ' a man of means, a wealthy man,' whilst ' arujeínik,'
accentuating a more mechanical sort of instrumen-
tality, in Great Russian conveys the very different
notion of ' an armourer, a gunsmith.' Again, ' tchási,'
Little or Slavonic Russian for ' the times,' etymologically accords, whilst it differs from it in point

of signification, with the Finno-Russian 'tchasí,'
'a watch.' To 'pisánka,' in Little Russian 'a painting, a portrait,' in Great Russian corresponds 'pisá-
nie,' meaning 'something *written*, a letter;' while
contrariwise, 'list,' which in Little Russian is
used for a letter, in Great Russian only expresses
'a leaf.' 'Maχ,' in Great Russian 'a blow,' in Little
Russian signifies 'a moment.' It may justly excite
surprise that in the case of the two last words,
'list' and 'maχ,' the primary meanings, 'leaf' and
'blow,' should be preserved in the derived and
younger tongue, the Great or Finno-Russian,
whereas metaphorical meanings, 'letter' and 'moment,' are recorded in the older and more original
Little or Slavo-Russian. The seeming anomaly is
explained by a circumstance which will be subsequently alluded to at greater length. Great or
Finno-Russian is the descendant not only of the
Little or Slavo-Russian, but also of the ancient
Southern or Bulgaro-Slovenian Slavonic, the language in which the Gospel was communicated to
the Northern pagans. Hence primary meanings are
sometimes preserved at Moscow, though superseded
by secondary ones at Kieff.

For completeness' sake, a few verbs may be mentioned, to exemplify the extension to this class of
words of dialectical diversification of meaning. The
names of the senses supply a good example.
'Tchuty,' in Little Russian 'to hear,' in Great

Russian occurs in the enlarged sense of 'to hear, to smell, to scent, to perceive, and to feel.' 'Slúkhaty, slukhátzy,' Little Russian for 'to listen, to obey, in Great Russian is represented by 'slúschaty,' 'to listen,' and 'slúischaty,' 'to hear, to smell, to scent, to understand, to comprehend.' 'Pa ruski slúis-chaty,' literally 'to hear in the Russian tongue,' in Great Russian means 'to hear Russian and comprehend it,' *i.e.*, to be conversant with the Russian idiom. Again, 'divítysya,' in Little Russian 'to see,' in Great Russian, very much at variance with the classical injunction of *nil admirari*, adopts the more spiritual sense of 'to see and admire, to admire.' 'Golosíty,' in Little Russian 'to sob, to groan, to sing the funeral plaint,' and 'to prophecy,' in Great Russian merely denotes 'to talk aloud.' The same root 'glos, glas,' in Little Russian appropriated for expressing the utterance of the human voice, in Great Russian, with its habitual confusion of the senses, applies to the action of the visual organs as well. 'Spravíty,' in Little Russian 'to carry out,' in Great Russian is retained in its primary sense of 'to straighten.' 'Sverschíty,' in Little Russian 'to accomplish,' in Great Russian is diverted into the different meaning of 'to decide.' 'Vóliti,' in Little Russian to *obtain* by earnest solici-tation, in its Great Russian meaning goes no further than to solicit, &c.

Such is the diversity of the Slavo-Russian and

Finno-Russian idioms in the case of words absolutely
transferred from one language to the other. Though
the word is preserved, in all these and other *innumerable* instances a new shade is introduced
into the Little or Slavo-Russian meaning by the
Great or Finno-Russian mind. The shell is the
same; the kernel varies. The sound is taken over;
the signification has been altered.

An analogous, and even more copious, process is
observed in the case of derivations, especially in
the derivation of nouns. As most objects equally
lend themselves to be designated by different
qualities out of the many they have, the two
languages frequently choose to refer the names of
their nouns to different radicals. A cloud in Great
Russian is called ' óblako,' from ' oblekáty,' to cover;
in Little Russian it goes by the name of 'χmara,'
from ' χmúrity,' to darken. Blood, in Great Russian
called ' krov,' from a root designating moisture, in
Little Russian is known as ' mazká,' from ' mazáty,'
to smear. Marriage, which in Great Russian is
described as ' svádba,' meaning probably abduction,
in Little Russian rejoices in the more modern
appellation of ' véssilya,' gladness, frolic. Quantities of such-like examples might be adduced at a
moment's notice. More conclusively than anything else these prove the independent use made
by the Finno-Russians of the roots and stems
handed over to them by the Slav.

Other causes have contributed to enhance the contrast. Change of meaning so often accompanying
preservation of outward form, is even more frequent
when the form is altered likewise. Few languages
more readily admit of such alteration than the
Russian. The extraordinary number of prepositions alternately prefixed to roots; the copious
array of terminations appended in forming derivatives; the facility of creating ever-new compounds,
and applying significant vowel-changes to boot,
allow of roots being used in a hundred different
ways. Each prefix, each affix, each vowel-change
imparts a new shade of meaning; each compound
creates a new term. Now the Slavo-Russian and
Finno-Russian languages by no means always agree
in selecting the same prefixes and affixes for their
roots. On the contrary, they very often couple
their roots with different prefixes, thereby strength-
ening in different ways the different significations
given to the roots; or else they differ in this, that
the one adds a prefix where the other prefers the
naked root, declining to develop the idea contained
in the radical. As an instance, take the root 'kon,'
meaning 'to end, to terminate.' Little or Slavo-
Russian knows the simplest application of the root,
the verb 'konáty,' only in an intransitive aspect,
meaning 'to die.' Great or Finno-Russian, on the
contrary, uses this very verb in a most vehement
transitive signification, meaning 'to drive a man to

the end,' *i.e.*, to the end of his wits, to make him go
to extremes. Again, Little Russian compounds the
simple form 'konáty' with the preposition *vi*,
meaning 'out,' thus creating a verb, 'víkonaty,' 'to
carry out, to accomplish.' Great Russian, on the
other hand, prefixes to the same root the preposition *o*, meaning, among a great many other things,
'through' in a finishing sense, thus producing the
verb 'okontcháty,' with the signification of 'to
finish.' To quote a few other words, the root
'myenáty' in both languages means to change;
but whilst in Great Russian it is associated with
the preposition *ob*, meaning 'about,' and produces
'obmyenáty,' meaning 'to exchange, to mistake,' in
Little Russian it is connected with the preposition
za, meaning 'instead,' and brings forth the verb
'zaminátí,' meaning 'to make up for.' Or the
verb 'pravdíty,' 'to act straightly,' when coupled
with the preposition *s*, in Little Russian engenders
'spravdíti,' 'to amend,' which does not exist at all
in the affiliated tongue. Similarly, the verb 'vólity,'
in Great Russian 'to will, to solicit,' in Little
Russian 'to obtain by solicitation,' in the latter
language, joined with the preposition *v*, meaning
'out,' creates the verb 'vvolíti,' 'to fulfil some-
body else's wish,' for which no analogous term is
found in the related tongue. And so on to the
end of the chapter. I omit to extend these examples to the variations produced by different

terminations, significant vowel-changes, and other similar means. They are equally abundant.

Two other sources of discrepancy deserve to be mentioned. Of many Slavo-Russian roots not a trace is found in Finno-Russian; of not a few Finno-Russian words no vestige can be detected in Slavo-Russian. Slavo-Russian roots lost in Finno-Russian speech were either not presented for acceptance, or else rejected by the recipient race, being altogether at variance with their own original ideas of men and things. The Finno - Russian terms missing in Slavo-Russian are either derived from Southern or Bulgaro-Sloveno-Slavonic, or else are scattered remnants of Finnish or Tatar origin. Finno-Russian, as I observed above, is not exclusively the descendant of Slavo-Russian, but acknowledges a considerable influence of the ancient South Slavonic, or Bulgaro-Sloveno-Slavonic tongue, the ecclesiastical language of the Orthodox Church, formerly spoken by the Slavs between the Euxine and the Adriatic. The first of their race who received Christianity from the neighbouring Greeks, Bulgaro-Slovenian is the idiom in which the new religion was subsequently transmitted farther north. In it the Gospel was preached to Slavo-Russians as well as to Finno-Russians; but while it had little influence upon the cognate tongue of the Slavs, the southern idiom powerfully affected the speech of the Finn, then in the first stage of incipient Slavification.

D

To the Kieff Slav, Bulgarian was a mere variety of his own vernacular, too easily understood and altogether too familiar to derive much additional interest from the religious teaching it conveyed; to the Finn it came clothed with the double dignity of a foreign, more civilised tongue, and of the medium for the inculcation of lofty doctrine and creed. Hence, Finno-Russian retains many more visible traces of the ecclesiastical dialect than the Slavo-Russian, or, to call it from its ancient capitals, the Kieff-Novgorod speech.

As the aggregate result of the various agencies enumerated, we have the existing discrepancy between the Little or Slavo-Russian, and the Great or Finno - Russian idioms. Where such very large sections of the dictionary are entirely distinct; where others, though similar, abound in words used in different senses by either tongue, it is impossible to subordinate the one language to the other as a mere dialect. The few comparisons I have instituted are, I believe, the first attempt ever made at likening the notions of the two kindred idioms. However, as they might be easily augmented by multitudes of similar examples, the instances given are enough to warrant the inference that Little or Slavo - Russian and Great or Finno - Russian are neither identical, nor the one a subordinate dialect of the other, but distinct and independent, though closely related tongues. Only after the two dictionaries shall have been made the subject of a thorough comparative analysis will it be possible to tell to what extent the Finns have been Slavified, or how far they may be said to assert their ancient national character under the cloak of a foreign idiom. A long time will have to elapse before any such complete estimate can be formed. Comparative lexicology is in its infancy in all languages, let alone Russian.

If there are two Russian languages, the number of Russian nationalities extant is far in excess of two. Not to speak of the numerous Caucasian and Asiatic races annexed by the Czars, hosts of Germans, Poles, Lithuanians, Rumanians, &c., have been absorbed in course of time by the mighty Northern Empire. Some of these engulfed nationalities retain their speech; others, on becoming Russianised, imprinted visible vestiges of their previous tongues and types upon the idiom adopted by them.

There is still one other nationality in Russia more important than any of those mentioned. This highly remarkable species of mankind consists of the upper classes of the realm. A mixture of all the various races assembled under the Czarish sceptre, the upper classes form one of the most intelligent, most courageous and enterprising types of humanity ever reared on the face of the earth. In them Finnish common sense mingles with Polish courage; Armenian astuteness blends with German deliberate and methodic thought; while to the patient endurance of the Tatar is added the quick versatility of the Slav. If Russia has accomplished so much in diplomacy and war, she is quite as much indebted for her success to the extraordinary abilities of the mixed race at her head, as to the sturdiness, the submissiveness, and the enduring capacities of her docile millions. In this upper section of Russian society, names are no clue to descent. Owing to long-continued intermarriage between its different ingredients, a Finno-Slavic name may be borne by a man of German extraction, or an Armenian title by one most of whose ancestors were Poles. But whatever their patronymic, whatever their origin and descent, what distinguishes them all alike is the uncommon amount of talent prevailing in the caste. It is one of the most telling facts in the ethnographical and political configuration of Europe, that while the Russian lower orders are further removed from culture than those of any other European land, the Russian upper classes are equal, if not superior, in intelligence, to their peers in most other countries. Thanks to this extraordinary combination of opposite advantages, Russia has attained the enormous power she proudly calls her own.

Neither have the potent upper ten thousand left the national idiom without some very visible traces of their social influence. The literary language and style of Russia has been moulded by the cultured few, chiefly upon the pattern of German and French, the tongues gradually adopted by Russian society since the age of Peter the Great and prevalent down to the Crimean war. The more rapidly to civilise his country, Peter, it is well known, favoured the spread of German as a vehicle of official culture. As to French, this, in its brilliant eighteenth century, found its way aided and unaided to Muscovy, as everywhere else. Things remained in this condition until toward the latter end of Nicholas' reign. Intent upon fanning the pride of race upon the eve of a Panslavonic war, Nicholas discountenanced the foreign idioms (which, moreover, had acquitted themselves of their civilising task in the meantime) and reverted to Russ. But the restoration of the old linguistic régime by the Iron Emperor had no power to obliterate the results of the preceding period. Though he certainly made Slavic again the habitual language of the upper classes, Nicholas neither attempted the extermination of the numberless Russian words framed upon German and French patterns in the preceding cosmopolitan epoch, nor did he propose a patriotic return from the clear and elegant forms of Gallic syntax then adopted to the loose and confused structure of the old Muscovite sentence. The imperative example of the Court easily replaced the use of foreign tongues by the national idiom; but the development Russian had derived from copying foreign speech was wisely preserved as a lasting gain and abiding improvement of the vernacular. Owing to this exotic and partially imitative origin of innumerable Russian words, phrases, and grammatical combinations, the language of culture in its higher uses in no European country differs in so many essential points from the popular speech as in Russia. Nothing can be richer than the Russian dictionary, if not in roots, at least in compounds and derivatives; nothing nicer than the shades root-meanings acquire by etymological modifications; but with unmitigated simplicity the villager still uses one and the same word in a promiscuous sense where a host of differentiated terms is habitually employed by the civilised portion of society. Again, nothing can be more analytical, more strictly logical, and concise than the build of a Russian literary sentence, while incompleteness, allusiveness, and vague metaphorical idiomatism still constitute a leading feature of the peasant's brogue. As the necessary consequence of it all, it is easy enough to read a Russian book on metaphysics, but it is hard to exactly comprehend a Muscovite ploughman discussing any commonplace incident in his indefinite lingo.

Slavonic philology is not altogether without English ramifications. Reverting at a leap from

Russia to Great Britain, we find remnants of Slavonic speech lingering in localities not very far distant from this ancient seat of learning. These relics of a remote linguistic past, it is true, consist only in a few geographical names : Wilton, Wiltshire, Wily. According to early tradition, handed down in Beda's History and vaguely alluded to by Venantius Fortunatus and other chroniclers, the Viltsi, a Slavonic tribe in ancient Pomerania and Brandenburg—the name of Vilt, Wind, Wend formerly applied to many western Slavs—sent colonies from the mouth of the Oder to Holland and England in the fourth and fifth centuries. In England these emigrants from the neighbourhood of Berlin probably founded the town of Wilton ; as regards Holland, it seems certain that they occupied Utrecht, the Ulterius Trajectum of the Romans, then called Wiltaburg. Surviving the vicissitudes of many centuries, a small handful of this race still exist in the region whence their ancestors are related to have set out on their journey to Great Britain fourteen hundred years ago. In the Spreewald, a sequestered locality near Berlin, whither they retreated eight hundred years since before the advance of the colonising German, the Wends to this day are a living reality. To this day this interesting remnant of Brandenburg Slavs retain the national name, together with the knowledge of

their ancient tongue, which they use in familiar converse along with German. The Brandenburg Wends
are a well-to-do and most respectable tribe. Living
in a sort of rustic Venice formed by numberless
channels of the river Spree, their water-bound
settlements remind the startled visitor of the lake-
dwellings of primitive Europe, and highly deserve
inspection by the ethnographer, the painter, and
the excursionist. A few months ago, as I was
navigating with a Cantabrigian fellow-traveller the
endless watercourses of this aquatic region, my
companion expressed no little surprise that so very
peculiar a district should be unknown to the sight-
seers of Europe. Whether threading its way
through primeval forest, steeped in swamp and
lake, or passing along the insulated settlements
of a happy and amiable race, the vistas opened
up by the gliding boat were invariably curious and
picturesque. The inhabitants of these secluded
recesses, quick, wiry, and industrious, are an altogether superior sort of rustics, and very well able
to take care of themselves in the social struggle
of these stirring times. Their women, famous for
attachment to children, are frequently engaged as
a kind of ornamental nurses by wealthy Berliners,
and in their gorgeous national attire, all red,
green, and white, attract the attention of foreigners
in the streets of the German capital. Notwith-

standing the care taken in school and church to preserve their time-honoured nationality,* it is disappearing fast. In Wiltshire, in obedience to the law of linguistic absorption, it has succumbed long ago.

* Wends also survive in the adjoining district of Upper Lusatia, kingdom of Saxony.

III.

THE RUSSIAN LINGUISTIC CONCEPTION OF 'GENTLEMAN' AND 'NOBLEMAN.'

WORDS express what men agree to put into them ; and as there is hardly a notion which cannot be viewed in more ways than one, there is hardly a word which does not differ in signification from its nearest equivalents in other languages. From the most complicated mental operations down to ordinary sensuous objects, things admit of being conceived differently, and in consequence are given names carrying different meanings in the various languages of the world.

Let us take an instance or two. The Latin ' gladius,' being a short sword of peculiar shape, is inaccurately rendered by ' sword,' which may or may not be what the Roman term indicates. The Latin ' cantus,' signifying an articulated clangour, in preference to anything else, is too much honoured in the translation by ' song,' which plainly refers to melody. The Latin ' amicus,' implying a disposition to aid, abet, and confer benefits, cannot be regarded as an exact equivalent of the English ' friend,' a word which lays stress upon affection rather than help. Passing on to more abstract notions, the Roman ' virtus' is properly ' effi-

ciency,' not 'virtue;' the Roman 'vis' more ordinarily imports energy and force than strength;
while the Roman 'ingenium' should be mostly
understood as expressing capacity and disposition,
in preference to intellect and genius.

Differences increase in the case of adjectives and
verbs. Expressing conditions of the nouns to
which they apply, adjectives and verbs are apt to
vary in signification according to the nature of the
subjects they happen to refer to. The wider their
signification, the less likely it is that their compass
should be exactly the same in different tongues.
In the Latin 'magnus' we encounter the three
meanings of 'great,' 'long,' and 'copious,' according to the nouns with which it is coupled. The
Greek quality of 'καλός,' like the English 'hand-
some,' may be fittingly ascribed to persons that
have nothing personally attractive about them;
whilst the English 'nice,' a peculiarly generous
vocable, lends itself to be predicated of a good
many people who would not be awarded similar
praise by its Latin prototype 'nitidus.' Again,
in Latin we discover the verb 'transmittere'
to embrace the several meanings of 'transmit,
transfer, cede, intrust, dedicate, perforate, pass, pass
by, throw across, live through, live down,' all of
which, in English, have to be rendered singly
by their respective equivalents. Greek has its
'λογίζεσθαι' in the cumulated sense of 'to cypher,

calculate, sum up, add, attribute, meditate, consider, judge, and infer.' The German 'scheinen'
unites the notions of 'to shine,' and 'to seem ;' the
Russian 'slagaty' combines the ideas of 'to add'
and to 'wrap up ;' and the Egyptian 'sem, setem,'
is tantamount to both 'hear' and 'listen.' Comparing the foreign words enumerated with their nearest
English equivalents, we have no difficulty in notic-
ing the inherent discrepancy of meaning which
separates original and translation. In some cases,
Latin cannot be accurately rendered at all, there
being no word found in English with exactly the
same conceptual ingredients. In other instances,
where the same ingredients are forthcoming in both
languages, they occur in different proportions, and
accordingly impart different hues to their representative compound in either. In both cases, the
notions compared have been differently viewed by
the men who formed the two languages.

The above remarks hold good when analysis
is coupled with synonymy. Confronting a word
with its closest approximate in another tongue, we
are apt to suppose that what cannot be mutually
rendered by the two limbs of the comparison,
cannot be expressed at all by the language in which
the deficiency happens to occur. When, however,
investigation is extended to the synonyms of the
terms contrasted, we are frequently gratified to
detect the missing shade in some cognate vocable,

mixed up with tints other than those associated to it in the language in which it was first noticed. Comparing, *e.g.*, the English and Russian ideas of zeal, there is no Russian adjective corresponding to 'strenuous.' The ardour in 'strenuous,' it is true, is appropriately expressed by 'révnosti,' anglice 'zealous;' but the boldness, activity, and enter-prise inherent in the British vocable as well, and inseparable from the ardour which forms its primary element, cannot apparently be conveyed by any one Russian adjective bearing upon the notion. In searching, however, a little farther afield, we are agreeably surprised to come upon the noun 'maladyétz,' meaning a young man possess-ing the very combination of qualities for which the English idea of strenuousness is conspicuous. Hence it is clear that to form an idea of any con-cept in any language, it is indispensable to extend observations over groups of words, and eliminate the entire notion from the various individual ex-ponents over which it is scattered.

By way of illustrating this method by a Slavic specimen, let us dissect the Russian terminology for some socially and morally interesting notions,— gentleman, gentlemanly, nobleman, and noble. Of the large number of words coming under this cate-gory, a few principal ones admit of being presented in a brief sketch.

Russian does not possess any single term com-

bining the three constituent qualities of a gentleman : good breeding, liberal education, and high
honour.   Each of these qualities is separately
ascribed by Russian linguistic usage.   Beginning
with the element of honour, there are four principal
terms set apart for its expression as a distinctive
personal trait.   'Nadéjni tchelovék' designates a
trustworthy man ; 'dobrosavéstni tchelovék,' a conscientious man ; 'tchéstni tchelovék,' an honest
honourable, and honoured man ; and 'dóblestvennik,' a moral hero.   Of these four epithets, two
refer each to one particular feature of social morality only, while the two remaining ones include
every commendable quality comprised in the
notion of honour.   'Nadéjni tchelovék,' a trustworthy man, and 'dobrosavéstni tchelovék,' a conscientious man, are one-sided appellations; 'tchéstni
tchelovék,' a man of marked honesty and honour,
and 'dóblestvennik,' moral hero, on the contrary,
indicate an honourable man all round.   There is a
notable distinction made between these four several
terms as regards frequency of application.   Upon ac-
quainting ourselves a little more closely with the position they occupy in the language, we find the one-
sided terms 'nadéjni' and 'dobrosavéstni tchelovék,'
respectively trustworthy and conscientious man,
to be in constant use ; while 'tchéstni tchelovék,' a
man of marked honesty and honour, and 'dóblestvennik,' moral hero, are much more rarely heard.

E

It seems natural expressly to extol trustworthiness and conscientiousness, when found ; while the more comprehensive quality of honour is not so often mentioned, unless, indeed, the possession of positive virtue is intended to be specially emphasised.   As to 'dóblestvennik,' moral hero, it stands altogether too high for everyday parlance.   Accordingly, no term is appropriated to the colloquial ascription of the ordinary, commonplace, and, so to say, matter of course amount of personal honour in all its various aspects at once.   There is not only no one word as comprehensive as the English vocable 'gentleman' in its triple reference to character, culture, and education ; but among the several familiar words relating to character alone, there is not one conveying *all* that is conveyed respecting this *one* quality by the wider English term.

On the other hand, there are several much-used phrases indicative of education.   'Abrasóvanni,' cultivated, and 'prosveschtschénni,' enlightened, are words constantly recurring in Russian conversation.   Everybody in the upper classes claims these qualities as his own, and delights in having them attributed to himself.   A man is 'abrasóvanni,' cultivated, when he knows enough of the world to look upon things in the approved European way, and to converse upon them in customary French phraseology ; he is 'prosveschtschénni,' on the other hand, enlightened, civilised, when he has given up the oppressive superstitions of ancient Muscovy, and has become both intelligent and humane. Significantly enough, this word 'prosveschtschénni,' though primarily referring to intellectual improvement alone, has a decided tendency to include moral amelioration. To be ' prosveschtschénni,' now-a-days, is not only to be well-instructed, but also to recognise the notions of duty, veracity, and philanthropy. Thus it happens that the demands of honour, which, as a mere matter of honour, are not embodied in any commonplace epithet, come to be incorporated in a familiar byname, whose original import refers to civilisation.

Thirdly, as to the good-breeding, which forms an indispensable ingredient in a gentleman's character, its ordinary denominations in Russian are derived from culture possessed, respect paid, or friendliness shown. ' Utschlívi ' means well-taught, and in consequence polite ; ' véjlivi ' signifies well-informed, and in consequence well-mannered ; 'utschtívi,' respectful, and consequently considerate. The other more demonstrative group embraces ' priyátni,' pleasant; ' lubésni,' amiable ; and ' míli,' nice, friendly, and expansive. From which we may safely infer that good manners are supposed to arise chiefly from culture or amiability, from adopted Europeanism, or the innate blandness of the Russian heart.

On summarising the result of this analysis, we find ordinary social morality, as well as culture and manners, represented as often springing from civilisation alone—a curious and yet, considering the circumstances, a very intelligible way of looking upon men and things. Again, such manifestations of ordinary social morality as do not arise from civilisation alone are most frequently represented as trustworthiness, reliability, and absence of deceit. In fact, absence of deceit is found to be the popular interpretation of honour. On the other hand, a word is not wanting which declares high social morality to have its source in a keen sense of personal honour; whereas mere politeness, besides frequently proceeding from culture, is described as the outcome of the supple complaisance and obsequiousness as natural to the Russian character as the extreme reverse. Handled in this wise, the dissection of a few words enables us to extract from the Russian national mind important avowals respecting the origin and nature of some of its most remarkable notions and qualities. From the linguistic evidence elicited it will be seen that the French story of a Russian asking in blank astonishment, 'Tschto eto honor?' ('In the name of goodness, what is honour?') is no more than a disrespectful gibe, instinct with the spirit of international derision, so very common in all lands and times. Had it no object besides helping nations to

form a more correct and equitable estimate of each
other, comparative lexicography would require to
be created.

If there is no *commonplace* name indicating the
possession of personal honour, except as regards
that particular point of honour known as trustworthiness, there are several familiar phrases denoting individuals to whom honour is habitually
rendered. The first word we come across in this
category is ' patchótni.' ' Patchótni secretar,' honorary secretary, exactly corresponds with the English translation, and serves to determine the meaning of the vocable. But ' patchótni grashdanín,' an
honorary citizen, is a wealthy merchant upon whom
the title has been specially conferred by a gracious
Czar. At the top of the peculiar climax there stands
' patchótni tchelovék,' literally an honorary man,
i.e., an individual reverenced for his prominent
position by equals and inferiors, and dubbed honorary in consequence by the voice of the people.
The better to realise the singular meaning of this
term ' patchótni,' honorary, we shall compare it
with ' patchténni,' honoured, which attributes as
a mere temporary possession what ' patchótni,'
honorary, confers as a lasting qualification and as
a sort of inherent dignity. To be honoured on one
occasion or on several occasions is to be ' patchténni ; ' to be habitually honoured is to become an
altogether ' honorary person,' ' patchótni tchelovék.'

A Russian, therefore, may not only be honorary as a secretary or as a member of *a* society, but honorary even as a member of *society* at large.

Passing on to neighbouring ground, we find a remarkable distinction drawn between the several equivalents for the English adjective 'noble.' The adjectives derived from the old and popular words for nobleman have nothing whatever to do with noble in a moral sense. 'Bárin,' 'boyárin' (bar), anglice boyard, originally denoted the master of the slave, that is, in accordance with ancient local institutions, the nobleman; but the adjective derived from this noun, 'bárski,' simply means that which belongs to the master, without any reference to nobility or any other moral or immoral qualities inherent in that individual. The only metaphorical touch added to this adjective refers to imperiousness and the strenuous exercise of masterdom; 'bárski' means not only that which appertains to the master, but also masterful. It is the same with 'dvoryanín,' a more modern word for nobleman. 'Dvoryanín' literally signifies courtier, a man attached to the Czar's cabinet or household, who accordingly ranks as a nobleman.* The adjective 'dvoryánski,' deduced from this noun, has nothing of personal nobility in it; like 'bárski,' it signifies almost exclusively that which is the

---

* There is another etymology, referring the word to the possession of large property.

property of the exalted person mentioned. Not
noble feelings, but the nobleman's house, wife,
and chattels are usually called bárski or dvoryánski. In signal contradistinction to these two
old and historical appellations of the nobility, a
novel word, frequently applied since modern civilisation extended to Russia, includes both meanings in its more comprehensive compass, noble
in position and noble in point of character.
' Blagoródni,' literally well-born, indicates a man of
noble station, and noble sentiments as well. By
the time this aristocratic term came into use, the
moral development of the country had sufficiently
advanced to admit of rank being identified with
virtue. There is a gratifying chapter of Russian
history contained in the rise of this word ; there is
a remarkable trait of modern Muscovy indicated in
the limited use made of the term. The use of this
novel and more commendatory appellation ' blagoródni ' is very much confined to the upper classes.
Originally an official title devised by Government, in
imitation of the German Wohlgeboren, 'blagorodni,'
well-born, was first enforced as the proper style
and phrase in addressing persons included in the
six last classes of the civil and military hierarchy.
In the Europeanising reigns of Peter the Great
and his immediate successors, the decree went
forth that official personages, from the captain and
Government secretary down to the ensign and

Government clerk, should be vouchsafed the style and title of this 'blagorodni,' well-born ; just as colonels, majors, and Government councillors were dubbed 'visokoblagorodni,' high well-born ; State councillors, 'visokorodni,' high-born ; generals, 'prevoskhoditelstvo,' excellency; full generals, 'visokoprevoskhoditelstvo,' high excellency, and so forth, to the top of the ladder. Superior Government employment until very lately conferring nobleman's rank, the lowest class title, applying to all noblemen alike, came to be used for all sections of the nobility, and eventually attracted the higher meaning of noble in feeling and mind. Hence 'blagorodni' is essentially an official and a bookish term, invented by the literate, or what is about the same, the literary portion of society, whose language differs more markedly from that of the lower orders in Russia than anywhere else in Europe. Hence, too, the amalgamation of moral and social import in the term is likewise more or less restricted to the classes who framed the word after a foreign pattern, and lodged in it some of the double meaning which its prototype had abroad.

Besides the historical evidence alleged, there is curious linguistic proof that the lower orders can have had nothing to do with the devising and the determining of this interesting vocable. 'Blagorodni,' well-born, is a compound made up of 'blági,' good, well, and 'rodni,' born. Strange as it may appear, the first word in this compound, the word 'blagi,' which I have just translated by 'good,' 'well,' might with almost equal correctness have been rendered 'bad,' 'evil.' It so happens that this word 'blagi' is one of the comparatively few left in Russian illustrating the primeval linguistic phenomenon of inversion of meaning. On this startling process a few explanatory observations require to be incidentally offered at this place. In my Egyptian Researches* I have shown absolute change of signification to abound in what probably is the most ancient preserved form of human speech, the Hieroglyphic. In several thousand examples I have proved the extraordinary fact and traced its origin to the demonstrable practice of primitive humanity of defining notions by contrasting them with opposites. † If in Egyptian we find it to be quite the practice to put two prepositions of opposite meanings together, in order the more clearly to bring out the signification inherent in *one* of them, the absolute combination of two meanings in one vocable is legitimately explained by analogous reasoning.‡ The more easily to conceive their primary notions, our primitive ancestors very largely had recourse to contrast. To readily under-

---

* Koptische Untersuchungen, Berlin, 1875.   † See Chapter V.
‡ Cf. the author's 'Origin of Language,' in 'Linguistic Essays,' London, 1882. Prof. Bain, in his 'Logic,' i. 54, theoretically discovers the necessity of the process, now confirmed by philological evidence. No happier co-operation of science and science could be imagined.

stand the import of strength, they, on forming the
idea, separated it from weakness; to facilitate the
comprehension of darkness, it was mentally pitted
against light; to realise the notion of 'great,' it
used to be contrasted with 'little.' Once invented
and transmitted for many successive centuries,
these and all other ordinary notions are now-a-days
glibly apprehended, without any, or at least any
conscious, repetition of the original contrasting
process. Directly, however, some entirely novel
idea is submitted for acceptance, we are instinc-
tively driven even now, to imitate the practice of
our early ancestors and facilitate comprehension by
comparison. Whether concrete or abstract, knowledge and its acquisition have ever a tendency to
confront. Hearing a new variety of rose mentioned,
we are apt to desire our informant to describe the
qualities of the unknown flower by likening them
to the similar yet different ones of some familiar
species. Still more surely, whenever introduced to
a new idea in the less popular domain of mathematics, philosophy, or word-signification in a foreign
tongue, shall we be driven to measure the strange
concept by a known opposite, the more readily to
realise its import. The definition of a circle is
easiest taken in by placing it side by side with the
characteristic attributes of another mathematical
figure not a circle. Roman ideas of morality and
immorality being very different from our own, are

best understood through gauging them by ours; and if the peculiar compound of enlightenment and morality which constitutes the distinctive feature of 'prosveschtschénni,' is ever to be fully appreciated by non-Russians, they will have to place it side by side with words of their own language, related yet dissimilar in meaning. The more delicate the linguistic distinction drawn, the more nearly related are the two members of the comparison; the simpler the concept to be grasped, the more complete will the explanatory antithesis require to be made. For a nineteenth-century individual to ascertain the Russian meaning of 'khoróshi,' it is only necessary to discriminate between what is good and what is pleasing; whilst, when our primitive ancestors taxed their reasoning powers to discern the elementary notion of darkness, the exigencies of the desperate situation in which they found themselves compelled the thick-skulled savages to call in the notion of light as *secundum comparationis.* Egyptian words including the two elements of the comparison instituted by prehistoric thinkers, their instructive conservatism luckily reveals the intellectual effort by which the first and most indispensable notions had to be originally achieved. Without the clear and cumulative evidence of the Egyptian language, this unexpected fact in the history of human reason would not, probably, have been discovered; with the aid of Egyptian the process is manifest, and the host of preserved vestiges in other tongues plainly discernible.

The proved diversity of meaning in aboriginal speech apparently compels the conclusion that our antediluvian friends must have experienced some very considerable difficulty in rendering themselves mutually intelligible : that the mental exertion, which enabled them to grasp a thought, by its very laboriousness impeded intercourse. But however hard their case may have been, it was scarcely quite as bad as it is apt to appear to people in the possession of perfect speech. They did not need any very distinct and copious phraseology in those early days. The primitive circumstances in which the speakers were placed ; the rapidly realised nature of the situations in which they used to hold converse ; and, in most instances, the accompanying gestures must have determined the important question, which meaning out of the two possible ones was intended to be vested in each word on a particular occasion. Gossiping in those halting times cannot indeed have been the facile and pleasurable diversion it became in more civilised days, when notions, once fixed, were every one of them snugly put away in a separate term for separate expression. Nevertheless, as primordial mankind had neither very many nor very deep subjects to prattle about, and as the circumstances in which savages are placed are easily judged, and mostly

judged alike by the members of a barbarous household, men probably managed to understand each
other tolerably well from the outset, the imperfec-
tions of their incipient speech notwithstanding.
To this day savages, with little or no inkling of
each other's language, fluently converse by gesture
the moment the subject of the conversation is
apprehended by the interlocutors. Nor should it
be forgotten that, as reasoning developed, the most
indispensable words must have gradually attained
a definite signification—a gratifying process, which,
by the way, admits of being watched in the
Egyptian tongue. The more distinctly each part
of the comparison was realised, the less occasion
could there be to go on comparing.

Remnants of these pristine and, at first sight,
rather perplexing dialectics are scattered even now
over our modern tongues. However incredible it
may appear, even in English, cases of opposite
meanings crammed into the same vocable (comparatively frequent in Saxon) are not altogether
wanting to-day. 'To bid' means 'to demand' as
well as 'to offer.' As a substantive, 'down' designates an elevation ; as a particle, it refers to what is
below. The preposition 'with,' ordinarily conveying
the notion of 'conjointly,' in words like 'withdraw,
withhold, withgo, withsay,' assumes the opposite signification of 'away from' or 'against.' Nay, the compound 'without,' though combining the conflicting

ideas of 'with' and 'out,' conveys the sole notion of 'out' and 'outside,' thus perfectly illustrating the old principle of squeezing antagonistic concepts into a single term. And is not 'better,' though derived from 'bad,' the comparative of 'good'? Is not 'melior,' though derived from 'malus,' the comparative of 'bonus'? Is not 'worse' (Gothic 'wairs,' Icelandic 'ver,' Danish 'vaerre') the opposite of its Sanscrit equivalent 'vara,' meaning 'better,' meaning 'good'? Do not 'dobr,' 'khoroshi' (the latter as 'girsch'), and some other Slavic terms for 'good,' imitate the extraordinary example set them by 'blagi,' and designate 'bad' as well? Do not, in the case of 'dobr,' the two antagonistic meanings, actually and apparently irrationally, occur in the same vocable? While as regards the two others, is not Great Russian 'khoroshi' (good) flatly negatived by its Little Russian representative 'girsch,' importing 'bad'? Even apart from the large amount of corroborative evidence preserved in related idioms, is it possible to look at the following table, and explain the numerous inversions crowding into a single idea within a limited linguistic area as mere accident.

TABLE.

English : Bad, Comparative better.

Latin : Malus (bad), Comparative melior (better).

Sanscrit : Vara (good, better); but Icelandic, ver, worse; Danish, vaerre; Gothic, wairs (wairis *), worse; English, worse.

Great Russian : Blagi (good and bad).
Great Russian : Dobr (good and bad).
Great Russian : Khoroshi (good) ; Little Russian, girsch (bad); Polish, gorsze (worse).

To revert to ' blagi,' its two opposite meanings are placed in peculiar juxtaposition. In Russian literary language this remarkable word bears the sense of 'good,' nay, 'pre-eminently good and superlatively excellent ;' in the language of the people it seems to have always expressed both 'good' and 'bad,' and preferably ' bad.' As in all cases of double meaning, the context decides on the particular signification intended to be expressed by the speaker in each instance. When an educated man says, ' Eto blagói savét,' he means, ' This is excellent advice ;' while when a boor utters, ' Lóschad blagáya,' he wishes to convey, ' This is a miserable old hack,' or ' Blagói tchelovék,' 'That is a *very* wicked fellow.' ' Blagoródni,' as it means 'well-born,' *not* badly born, cannot, accordingly, be of popular origin. To bear the complimentary sense it does, it must have taken birth in good society. The colloquial ascription to the Russian nobility of noble-mindedness, consequently, must have arisen in nobility circles. From these, as culture extended, it gradually spread to the middle and lower orders, creating, it is to be hoped, a wholesome belief in the identity of goodness and might.

Having adverted to primeval inversion of *sense*

as a means of ascertaining the origin and signification of an existing Russian vocable, I may now
appeal to inversion of *sound* for a similar purpose.
Were there no historical evidence to define the
meaning of 'boyard,' the oldest Russian nobility
title, as slaveholder, the testimony of language would
be pretty conclusive on the point. Phonetically
inverting 'bar,' which is the root and oldest recorded
form of 'boyárin,' we obtain the word 'rab.' This
'rab' in Russian signifies 'slave.' Thus by the side
of the word 'bar,' master, we have an inversion in
sound as well as in sense, 'rab,' slave. A brief
inquiry will determine whether we should regard
this peculiar correspondence as purely accidental, or
whether it ought to be recognised as the consequence
of a linguistic process effected for a purpose and
embodying an intellectual result. Let us revert to
Egyptian. Being the most ancient recorded form of
human speech, this language retains primitive features with a freshness, a vividness, and a copious-
ness which, while it clearly displays, fully accounts
for the most extraordinary peculiarities. In this
comparison I take my stand simply upon the fact
that there are etymological phenomena observable,
but wholly unintelligible, in Aryan languages,
which, in Egyptian, a tongue of similar type, a
gender language, and one likewise spoken by people
of Caucasian descent, occur so very frequently, and
are displayed in so many consecutive stages of

their evolutional development, that there they admit of being understood as to origin and purport. Without dwelling upon the demonstrable identity of many radical and formative elements, Egyptian, therefore, is here compared with Aryan on the mere ground that the laws of primitive thought and speech exhibited in the one are found to interpret peculiarities in the constitution of the other, the causes of which, in our Indo-European tongues, have long been obliterated by advance to a higher and more modern stage of logics and phonetics. In Russian, then, as in all Indo-European tongues, inversions of sound and sense, like 'bar' ⌇ 'rab,' master v slave, though much more frequent than would be imagined by the unsuspecting, are yet too rare, and, in consequence, too unintelligible, to have attracted attention prior to the discovery of their copious and absolutely regular occurrence in Egyptian. Only after these topsy-turvy proceedings had been demonstrated as an irrefragable fact by thousands of Egyptian examples (which may be looked for in my "Coptic Researches"), did the numerous cases burst upon sight preserved in existing and highly advanced idioms. Only after the phonetic and intellectual operation involved in the change had been rationally explained by the disinterred laws of Egyptian grammar, could it be lawful to consider the analogous process in European languages as more than mere accident. Inversion of meaning I have already accounted for ;

F

as regards inversion of sound, its why and where-
fore are readily understood upon reference to Egyptian etymology.   In accordance with one of the
best established laws of Hieroglyphic grammar,
Egyptian roots may be enlarged by the repetition
of the initial consonant at the end.   The word
'ker,' for instance, may expand into 'kerk,' the *k*
at the beginning being repeated at the end; the
word 'fes' may swell into 'fesf,' &c.   Monosyllabic
roots being by this process dilated into bisyllabic
ones, either syllable ultimately came to express
the meaning originally vested in the first alone.
'Ker,' 'to turn round,' having developed into
'ker-k,' not only 'ker' and 'ker-rek,' but also 'rek'
eventually denoted 'to revolve,' 'to rotate.'   'Fes,'
'to wash,' bulging out into 'fes-f,' not only 'fes'
and 'fes-sef,' but also 'sef' alone at last meant 'to
moisten, to purify, to clean.'   The added second
syllable, formed by the last letter of the first,
augmented by the first letter of the first, necessarily is the inversion of the first.   'Ker,' augmented by initial *k*, becomes 'kerk, ker-rek,' first
syllable 'ker,' second syllable 'rek.'   Accordingly the second syllable is the inversion of the
first; the accretion is the transposed original.   Of
course, in a primitive state of language, when any
word might mean a thing, and its opposite as
well, this licence of signification extended from the
original root to its inverted form.   Hence, as
regards meaning, the phonetic inversion is as often

identical with the root as it is absolutely opposed
to it. We just discovered 'sef' to signify 'to
wash,' like its primary form 'fes;' but while 'hen'
means 'to bind,' 'neh,' the transposed accretion of
'hen,' signifies 'to separate.'

There are plenty of similar cases extant in English and the Indo-European and Semitic languages
generally. Though they failed to attract attention by themselves, they catch the eye directly
our visual powers are sufficiently sharpened by the
frequent observation of the same phenomenon in
Egyptian. Having no regard to vowel change
(which is subject to special laws), we find, *e.g.*, in
English the tip ◊ the pit, the one referring to what
is above, the other to what is below; the stem ◊ the
mast, the one signifying a tree, the other what is
made of it; to stir ◊ to rest—all inversions of sound
and sense. Again, we come across such words as
'to care' ∧ 'to reck;' 'to tap' ∧ 'to pat;' 'to heal'
∧ 'the leech;' 'to grip' ∧ 'to prig;' 'the boat' ∧ 'the
tub'—all inversions of sound alone. Or admitting
cognate dialects into the inquiry, we discover
numerous parallels like the following : 'to wait' ∧
Lowland German 'taiw,' with exactly the same
meaning as 'to wait;' 'to tear' ∧ Lowland German
'reet,' with precisely the same signification as 'to
tear;' 'the pot,' ∧ equivalent to Lowland German
'top;' 'the hole' ∧ equivalent to Lowland German
'loch;' 'to clash' ∧ equivalent to German 'schlag,'
&c. Again, we are startled to detect that 'to

hurry,' inverted in sound as well as in sense, in German becomes 'ruh,' anglice 'rest;' whereas in Polish this identical 'ruh' (rukh) means 'hurry,' and compared with its English equivalent is inverted only in sound. The 'lug,' scottice that which hears, is found to correspond to the Latin inversion of sense, 'loq-ui,' i.e., the performance which is heard. The Latin 'carp-ere,' to seize, is a phonetic and mental inversion of the Latin 'prec-ari,' of the Polish 'prag-nać,' and of the Lithuanian 'prasz-iti,' 'to desire.' The English 'lief,' Latin 'lib-et,' and German 'lief, lieb,' phonetically metamorphosed in Greek becomes 'φιλ-ός.' The English 'to clamour,' with its relatives, the Latin 'clamare,' and the Slovenic 'kram-lyati,' 'to cry, to bawl, to speak,' inverted in sound and sense in Russian occurs as 'molĕ-aty,' 'to be silent.' This Russian 'molĕ-aty,' again, explains the etymology of Latin 'clam,' 'silently, secretly,' a word which, long investigated in vain, with the aid of these novel tests is determined to be nothing else but the inversion in sense of its cognate 'clamare.' And so forth, especially in the Slavic languages, whose various branches supply a perfectly conclusive multitude of examples.

A few specifically Slavic examples, comprising different idioms of the great eastern division of European speech, may, perhaps, be suitably quoted :

(1.) Inversion of sense: Czech, tem-e, top of a mountain or a tree v Slovenic, tem-en, deep; Slov.

kup, plenty v Czech. chyb-a, dearth; Finno-Russ.
blagi, good and bad; dobri, good and bad; skorbíty,
to strengthen v skorbéty, differently conjugated,
to be ill; Slavo-Russ. dobrischtsche, a great good
or a great evil; Slavo-Russ. χudi, a pauper; χudobá,
poverty, but v χudóba, wealth; prigóda, lucky and
unlucky accident; prigodíty, to be profitable v pri-
godsíty, to be unprofitable; Finno-Russ. slóvo, that
which is communicated, the word v Slavo-Russ.
slóvo, that which is kept back, the secret, &c.

(2.) Inversion of sound, the meaning remaining
the same: Russ. ves ∧ Serv. sev, all; Russ. pol-a
∧ Lith. lap-as, leaf; Russ. χreb-et ∧ Slov. breg, hill;
Russ. palk-a, cudgel ∧ Slov. klep-ati, to cudgel, to
beat; Slov. bol-ši ∧ Polish, lep-szy, better; Russ.
shtshel, gap ∧ Serv. luc-iti, to separate; Lith.
riek-ti, to cut ∧ Polish, s-kier-a, hatchet; Polish,
rość, to grow v Russ. shir-okij, large; Russ. beg-aty,
to go ∧ Slov. na-gib-ati, to move about; Russ. kaz-
aty ∧ Lith. sak-yti, to speak; Serv. ćut-eti, to be
silent ∧ Slov. u-taž-iti, to silence; Czech, sop-titi,
to breathe ∧ Lith. pus-ti, to blow; Lith. laiź-ati ∧
Slov. žul-iti, to lick; Russ. tem-nyi ∧ Slov. mot-en,
dark; Polish, ciem-ni ∧ Slov. mež-av, dark; Polish,
kol-o ∧ luk, circle, ark; Slov. seb-iti, dividere ∧
Russ. bez, without.

(3.) Inversion of sound and sense: Russ. bur-iy,
dark-coloured ◊ Lith. raib-as, particoloured; Russ.
mrač-niy, dark ◊ čerm-nyi, light, shining; Lith.
plik-as, naked ◊ Serv. po-klop-iti, to cover up;

Lith. tam-si, dark ◊ mat-iti, to see ; Lith. rēk-ti, to clamour ◊ kur-o, deaf, &c.

These specimens might be easily multiplied ; but the whole extent of the process will only admit of being measured after the laws of phonetic change shall have been carried back to a period no longer very clearly discernible in the preserved form, and with the unaided etymological resources, of Indo-European speech.

At this point we resume our Russian argument. Inversions on the Egyptian pattern abounding in the various Slavonic languages, these twin seg-ments of a bifurcated root, after what has been said, admit of being, nay, require to be, connected by an intellectual tie in Russian as well as in Ha-mitic. Applying this unavoidable conclusion to the vocable in hand, there is, then, more than mere accidental coincidence between the words ' bar,' master, and ' rab,' slave. There is a phonetic and spiritual bond found to exist between the two. In other words, the master, who, himself being called ' bar,' had a servant called ' rab,' anglice slave, pre-sumably must have been the *master* of a *slave,* a *slaveholder.* What the oldest Russian nobility title was intended to convey is thus etymologically defined. With the linguistic evidence elicited the testimony of history, it is well known, concurs only too fully.

IV.

*THE LINGUISTIC CONCEPTION OF LIBERTY
IN RUSSIAN AND POLISH AS COM-
PARED WITH LATIN.*

IV.

Once or twice a year we are startled by the publication of books and pamphlets recommending the adoption of some universal language. In these periodical addresses to an ungrateful world, nations are admonished to agree upon a common idiom, which shall be spoken from pole to pole, and be equally intelligible in London, Berlin, and Timbuctoo. The grand reform once effected, nations, we are assured by the confident authors, will be speedily connected by the ties of universal brotherhood. As they will perfectly comprehend each-other, they will find it easy to appreciate their mutual qualities, and settle their lingering feuds. The progress of knowledge, too, will be infinitely promoted by there being only one literature equally accessible to all. As to trade, it is clear that it must take an altogether new departure so soon as the red crocodile-hunter on the banks of the Amazon can be daily advised by his correspondent in Cheapside as to the exact article wanted in the market.

To accelerate the realisation of these glowing prophecies, the advocates of linguistic unity either propose the extension of some existing idiom to all the various races of the universe, or else are good enough to invent for the common benefit a new tongue, more simple, and therefore more perfect in their estimation, than any they know. I remember reading a Servian pamphlet several years ago, in which the desired simplicity was actually sought to be attained by reducing every word to a number, and declining and conjugating by appended numerals. No Chinese memory would have been equal to the formidable task of retaining the signification of these cyphered hieroglyphics. If it takes a mandarin ten years to learn to read and to write the literary idiom of his land, twenty must have been consumed in the acquisition of the Servian pasigraphy which was to have developed international relations. So we may congratulate ourselves upon its not having been adopted, except by the inventor.

Supposing, however, the innovation *could* be carried through, its possible effects should not be overrated. They would be infinitely less than their advocates fancy. Pasigraphs and pasilalists are wont to start on the supposition that all languages express the same ideas, and that the only discrepancy between them consists in that they embody their otherwise identical notions in different sounds. The English word 'friend' and the Russian word 'priyátel,' for instance, are assumed to mean exactly the same thing ; their difference being sur-

mised to be limited to the fact that the one is
sounded 'friend,' the other 'priyátel.' Yet nothing
could be more erroneous than this hypothesis.

Words mean what nations put into them, and
the thoughts of nations differing upon most subjects, the significations of their words equally clash.
The Russian conception of 'friendship' varying
from the English, the word ' priyátel,' though it
may be the closest approach to the English 'friend'
the Russian dictionary supplies, should not be mistaken as being identical with the term which it is
of necessity used to render. Names of ordinary
objects excepted, it is the same with most words of
the dictionary. As a rule, every language lends to
every idea a particular shade, a special *nuance*, which
constitutes the national peculiarity of its verbal
representative, and causes it to diverge from similar
notions in other tongues. The greater the importance a language attaches to an idea, the more
carefully, the more specifically will it mould the
signification of the words conveying the same ; the
more indifferent a notion appears, the more general,
the more vague will be its expression.

The introduction of universal language, therefore,
would be far from ensuring uniformity of thought.
Although the sounds might be the same, meanings would be speedily varied according to the
idiosyncrasies of the individual races. Many words
would be dropped by many races, not being needed

or understood by them; nearly all other vocables would have to undergo more or less marked changes of signification before they could convey what each single people might think fit to put into them. It is, perhaps, not too much to say that mutual unintelligibility would be actually augmented by the success of the pasilaletic scheme. When all nations use the same dictionary, but each in a different sense, misunderstandings are more likely to arise than under existing arrangements, when discrepancy of meaning is marked by diversity of words.

There is, however, no fear that existing languages will speedily die out. Though languages are certainly diminishing in number, the survivors gain additional strength from swallowing up the inheritance of the defunct. The weaker die out; the stronger add to the number of their subjects by conquering the orphaned vassals of those that are dead and gone. For the present, then, the knowledge of the national diversity of significations is still facilitated by the palpable disparity of vocables.

In acquiring Russian and Polish more particularly, the strange, though not at all unharmonious, sounds lead us to expect novel ideas. The anticipation is certainly not disappointed by the analysis of significations. The dissection of a few Slavic words bearing upon the notion of freedom will, I hope, prove that the prevailing difference of national

thought extends to the most ordinary ideas, and
that it fairly admits of being traced in the meaning
of representative terms. The more fully to realise
the Slavic hue of the concepts selected, a comparison will be subsequently instituted with Latin, a
highly developed, and at the same time an altogether
heterogeneous tongue. It is through gauging one
language by another that we learn to appreciate
the peculiarity of each.

Poles have long distinguished between personal
and political liberty. Opposite circumstances combined to recommend the distinction. Personal
liberty in matters exempt from political control,
in accordance with the unconstrained character of
the race, has always been unbounded in Poland ;
political liberty, on the contrary, until within
comparatively recent times, was restricted to a
small section of the people, the rest being kept in
a state of absolute, or nearly absolute, subordination.
It would have been absurd to confuse the notions
of personal and political liberty when personal
liberty was less restrained by feeling, custom, and
practice than in most other countries, while political
liberty did not exist, except for the select few.

In keeping with the difference felt and expressed,
the word signifying ' personally free ' originally
means only ' willing, having a will,'—' wolny,'
' willing, having a will,' and accordingly ' free,' a
derivation from ' wola,' ' the will.' The significa-

tion 'willing' is understood in both senses included
in the concept; it *may* mean no more than 'inclined
to do a thing, ready, prepared;' and it *may* mean
'willing and able to *work* one's will,' and in consequence 'free.' 'Mam władzę obrania, albo
jestem wolny,' anglice, 'I have the power of choice,
and accordingly am free,' or more literally 'am a
wilful agent.' 'Nie każdy wolen, który okowów
nie nosi,' 'Not all are free that carry no fetters.'
In this latter sense of having and exercising a
will, the word applies to all the various shades of
freedom in personal and private life. Occasionally
it refers even to political freedom; for as those
who possessed political freedom were no less inclined than their dependants to exercise personal
discretion in private matters as well, the twofold
liberty of the upper classes, the political and the
personal, eventually came to be included in the
term which emphasises the cherished privilege of
free will. 'Wolny' in this case undergoes an
extension rather than an alteration of meaning; it
simply denotes the comprehensive liberty enjoyed
by the lords of the land, in their double capacity
of lords as well as of individuals. The political
shade is especially marked in 'wolność,' 'liberty.'
Wolność lends itself more naturally to the expression of political liberty, which is a *frequent* term,
than to freedom of choice, which—as a noun—is an
abstruse metaphysical notion.

Of the metaphorical applications of 'wolny,' which hardly concern this inquiry into the notion of freedom proper, two are peculiarly characteristic, and would seem to deserve mention. Originally signifying 'free to do a thing,' 'wolny,' at a certain period of its history, came to denote 'free from being done a thing,' *i.e.*, free from something, exempt from something. The stronger the *active* sense inherent in its original meaning, the more easily did it refer to a permanent condition, which, in its turn, admitted of being interpreted in the passive mood. He who always acts freely is in the condition of a freeman, and, being in it, may not be subjected to oppression, is free from, exempt from oppression. Out of this derivative sense of ' free from, exempt from,' there arises the tertiary signification of 'easy,' 'relaxed,' and even 'relaxing.' That a thing which is left to itself, which is not constrained, is apt to become easygoing, loose, and weak, would seem to have appeared a natural conclusion to the Pole. I say a thing, not a man; intent upon asserting its original nobility, and redeeming this falling off from its proud primary sense, 'wolny,' in the meaning of loose, unless it signify licentious, is restricted to inanimate objects. A gown, when it is 'wolny,' is an easy and flowing garment ; a man, being called 'wolny,' is, on the contrary, understood to assert himself as an independent individual. Another and rather discourteous metaphor is that which causes Poles to regard a man, when emphatically designated as 'wolny,' as a bachelor. A free man in Polish may either mean a freeman, or a man, as the Poles uncivilly imply, ' without encumbrance.'

To describe *political* freedom the Poles have the words 'swobodny,' free, and 'swoboda,' freedom. These words, which have been the object of many crude etymological guesses, on reference to the parallel form of 'sloboda' are explained with approximative certainty as 'strong,' 'courageous,' 'self-asserting.' Change of *l* into *v*, under certain circumstances, being a peculiarity of Slavonic phonetics, 'sloboda' (a portion of the historical evidence notwithstanding) should be considered the more ancient form of the two. Due regard being had to the inversion of sense and sound proved in a preceding lecture, the root 'slob,' in the sense of free, upon comparison with 'slabi,' weak, timid, and other cognate vocables, is discovered to point to the original signification of 'strong,' 'courageous.' It is well known that the English word 'free' derives its origin from a root of analogous import, which, toned down to the level of modern civilisation in Great Britain, in Germany to this day retains its primary meaning of 'bold,' 'insolent': 'freoh,' 'frech.' But, whatever its origin, 'swobodny,' in its historical acceptation, plainly bears the sense of politically free. A man, not the born or bought serf of the lord of the manor, was properly designated 'swobodny.' Only a man, who was a *man* and not a slave, was justified in claiming this honorary title: all others might be very 'wolny,' very free in dealing with their wives, children, and chattels, but had no right to call themselves 'swobodny,' freemen and independent members of the community. In the present state of the country, when serfdom is abolished, and freedom, in the sense in which modern Poles are apt to interpret the term, is not conceded, 'swobodny' is a vocable which has almost fallen into disuse. At all times, however, reference to social condition has been so emphatically accentuated in the word as to confine it very much to this one meaning, and almost exclude metaphor. When the word does not mean politically free, it may indicate some peculiarly characteristic qualities of a freeman, such as frank, obstinate, unceremonial, and the like; into the domain of private and undemonstrative freedom it hardly ever emerges.

In the Russian idea of freedom Polish notions run into extremes. With the same general discrimination between political and personal liberty, between servitude and volition, either concept in Russian is carried to a pitch unknown in Polish. As regards personal liberty, it is assumed to be so absolutely identified with the gratification of one's every wish, that the Russian word which means 'liberty' signifies 'will' as well. And not only

G

'will,' but 'wish, desire, hankering, cupidity, contumacy, licence, and licentiousness' too. All these significations, together with those of volition and personal liberty, are contained in the ordinary Russian term for freedom (volya). The striking combination of ideas embodied in this aggregate term, 'volya,' had, perhaps, be better illustrated by a few examples. 'Swetáya vólya bójia' means 'the holy will of God.' 'Kto yemú ne velít : svoya volya,' 'Why should he do this' (or omit to do this, as the case may be), 'when he has liberty to act as he chooses ?' is a passage in which the freedom of choice, the *liberum arbitrium*, is conspicuously apparent. Again, 'Vólnomu vólya, spasénomu rai,' 'Freedom to the free and paradise to the redeemed,' conveys the loftiest conception of liberty. With these exalted shades of will, freedom, and liberty, compare the meaner applications of the same word, such as the following :—'Svóya vólya stráshneye nevóli,' 'To have one's *will* is worse than to be a slave ;' or 'Vólya i dobra mujíka portít,' 'Freedom and its obstinate use' (all this being included in the one word 'vólya') 'deprave even a good man ;' 'Dai dúsche vólyu, zakhótchet i bóle,' 'Indulge in licence, and you will never be sated.' It will be readily conceded that to admit of these various interpretations —will, liberty, and licence—freedom must be conceived by the Russians as the unrestrained exercise

of individual volition, not as the modified and
temperate application of one's independence, which
alone is compatible with the weal of self and of
others.   This peculiar conception of liberty naturally implies not only the power (as every conception of liberty should), but also the disposition (as
no conception of liberty ought) to transgress.   In
a fainter though still sufficiently prominent degree,
the same chequered hue is preserved by the adjective 'volni,' 'free, unbridled, licentious.'   In both
cases the Pole, though similarly disposed, takes a
somewhat different view.   The Polish ' wolny,'
' free,' in the wide extent of its meaning, borders
upon, but does not go the length of, the corresponding Russian term ; in point of fact, whenever it does
not actually mean ' free,' it signifies much more frequently ' easygoing, lax, gentle,' than anything like
' too free, unlawful, or licentious.'   Again, the Polish
' wola,' 'will,' unlike the Russian 'vólya,' has nothing
at all to do with liberty, but is exclusively reserved
for the expression of its primary and more restricted
sense, 'will ; ' while the Polish ' wolność,' 'liberty,'
means nothing but liberty, thus completing the
line the language draws between the abstract freedom of choice and its discreet application, between
personal volition and the use made of it under the
necessary social restraints.   I may here observe
that the Russian likewise possesses the term ' volnost,' 'liberty,' by the side of ' volya,' 'will, caprice,

and liberty ; ' but ' his volnost ' refers to the condition rather than to the quality or the act, and is altogether a more abstract and bookish vocable than ' volya.' When the Russian revolutionary party raised the cry of ' Land and Liberty for the peasant,' it would have been both incorrect and affected for them to ask in their proclamations, for ' Zemya i volnost ; ' to be popular and to accurately define their intention to procure and accord personal independence, they had to demand, not ' volnost,' but ' volya.'

Political liberty, *i.e.*, the liberty which consists in not belonging to the enthralled classes, in Russian, as in Polish, is expressed by the vocables 'svobodni' and 'svoboda,' ' free, freedom.' The proper sense and application are the same in both languages ; but the metaphorical use of the two adjectives, at least, is characteristically different. In Polish, ' wolny,' ' personally free,' diverges into the direction of ' easy, lax, gentle ; ' whereas ' swobódny,' ' politically free,' remains more or less confined to its original sphere. In the sister tongue it is just the reverse, the Russian ' svobódni ' assuming the tropical signification of the Polish ' wolny,' and the Russian ' volni ' remaining shut up in its first more direct sense. How is this ? Why should in Polish the notion of ' personally free,' why should in Russian the opposite idea of ' politically independent,' expand into the cognate concept of laxity ?

The reason may be plainly enough discerned from what has been said, and indeed confirms preceding remarks. Russian personal liberty involves too much self-will and energetic caprice ever to become lax. Polish personal liberty, on the other hand, implying the permanent posssession of freedom in preference to the momentary use of it, its linguistic exponents are apt to refer to the condition rather than the act, and in consequence are liable to decline into a certain quiescence, inertness, and looseness. Accordingly, if they wished to express at all the connection existing between want of restraint and indulgence, the Russians had to embody the idea in their political-liberty vocables, while the Poles, *per contra*, were preferably attracted by the quieter tone of their personal-freedom nomenclature.

A word altogether peculiar to the Russian is 'prostór.' It means originally 'wide and empty space,' and in its figurative signification of 'liberty' is a most significant complement of 'volya,' 'unrestrained will.' As 'volya' indicates 'untrammelled volition,' so 'prostor' expresses 'unbounded scope;' the one is the absolute capacity of a man to work his free will, the other the perfect favour of circumstance, the complete absence of impediment or restraint. The existence of 'prostor,' unnecessary as it would seem to be, when the same idea in a different form is so fully conveyed in another word, supplies interesting evidence in support of the specific tinge of the entire concept in the Russian tongue. 'Smert dúsche prostór,' 'Death is liberty to the soul.' 'Prostóru rebyatám davát isbalú-yutsya,' 'By allowing too much liberty to children, we are sure to spoil them.' In these and many similar instances neither 'volya' nor 'volnost,' respectively denoting 'freedom as an act and possession,' or 'freedom as condition,' suffice to express the wide, vast, and boundless liberty aspired to by the Russian mind. To fully express his yearning for entire absence of restraint, the Russian in these cases is obliged to have recourse to a term actually signifying 'absolute emptiness and infinite scope.' Such are the Russian facts. The moral is easily drawn. Whatever adventitious circumstances may have retarded the growth of political liberty in Russia, the national conception of *personal* freedom is pitched somewhat too high to effectually promote the development of public institutions.

Before proceeding with this inquiry, I may perhaps be permitted to revert to one of the examples quoted, in order to illustrate the peculiar vagueness and abruptness indulged in by Russian colloquial speech. The example referred to is this: 'Kto yemú ne velít : svóya vólya ;' literally, 'Quis ei non jubere : sua voluntas,' or, 'Who to him not to order : his will.' This apparently very deep and unintelligible passage is intended to convey nothing more formidable than the simple phrase, 'Who com-

mands him? He has his own free will.' Strange
as it may appear, the negative in this case is understood not to negative, but, on the contrary, to
strengthen the affirmation contained in the word
'order' to which it belongs. 'Who orders him?'
in this case being intended to convey that nobody
orders him, the Russian, with more regard for the
general sense than the specific logic of his utterance,
boldly asks, 'Who orders him not?' As to the
infinitive 'to order' instead of the present tense
'orders,' and the abrupt statement, 'his will,'
instead of 'he has his free will,' these are national
abbreviations which must be taken into the bargain.
Logical leaps, anticipated meanings, and abrupt
grammar of this nature abound in colloquial Russian,
and sometimes make it hard to follow the gist of
popular confab.

The scene is completely changed on entering
Latin ground. In Latin a single word suffices to
describe the political condition of a freeman, and
the latitude left to all alike to be guided by their
own discretion in the management of their own
private affairs. Though the freeman alone was
called 'liber' in the political sense of the term,
both freeman and slave were equally entitled to
the important designation in respect of their freedom of choice as rational beings, and of the margin
left them by the law of the land. In Rome, freeman and slave alike were wont to say, 'Liberum

habeo aliquid, liberum est mihi,'* though the man
who used the confident phrase was, peradventure,
not a 'liber' himself as regarded the possession of
civil rights.   In Russia civil and personal freedom
until lately were considered two such entirely distinct entities, that the word which applied to the
former was by the very fact disqualified from referring to the latter.   A Russian would have to
strain his language were he to say, 'Svobodno mne'
instead of 'Volno mne,' 'I am politically free to
attend to my own private affairs,' instead of, 'I am
personally free to do so.'   In Latin the distinction
does not exist, and a man is simply and unqualifiedly
free in his own personal concerns.   Of the various
figurative shades of 'liber,' let it suffice to say that
the livid hue of licentiousness, frequently apparent
in the Russian term for 'personally free,' hardly ever
disfigures the noble colouring of the Latin word.
The unconstrainedness of 'liber' is *dégagé*, but
neither flippant nor loose. 'Liber,' which stood
so high that the children in a respectable house
were called 'liberi,' the free, in contradistinction
to the vernæ or domestic slaves, could not well
descend to the low level of excess.

Notwithstanding, however, the care taken in
guarding the perfect purity of the word from metaphorical taint, the Romans could not fail to observe
that there was a difference between 'liber' and

---

* 'I am free to do this.'

' liber.' From an early period they had too many
' liberti,' ' liberated slaves,' among them to be able to
regard all ' liberi ' as essentially alike. All, indeed,
who boasted the name were expected to behave
with the becoming propriety of freemen, as may
be inferred from the dignified limits within which
the signification of the word was wont to keep.
Still, the man born and bred a freeman, early
inured to a noble and intelligent view of the
universe, and exempt from the temptations of a
sordid struggle for life, naturally was a different
being from the upstart who achieved independence
at an advanced age, and could not help carrying
the traces of past disabilities about with him in
his new career. To express their sense of the
innate discrepancy between the two characters, the
Romans called the man born free ' ingenuus,' and
the man set free ' libertus ; ' the former term
implying a noble liberality of thought and act,
the latter admitting a tinge of meanness into its
otherwise creditable sense. So religiously was the
distinction upheld, that down to the fifth century
of the republic the son of a ' libertus ' even had no
right to call himself ' ingenuus,' but had to content
himself with the minor appellation, ' libertinus.'
Only the grandson was considered to have had his
mind sufficiently cleansed from the lingering dregs
of low descent, to deserve the rank and title of
' ingenuus.' Later on, it is true, the sons of the

'liberti' were at once promoted to the dignity of 'ingenui;' still later, under the emperors, the 'liberti' achieved the final stage of becoming 'ingenui' at a leap, and holding high office, and wearing the 'latus clavus,' or broad-bordered vestment, immediately on emerging from servitude. But in those days ancient Rome existed no more. With the decay of the old families, the advent of many cultivated prisoners combined to bridge over the gulf between freeman and serf.

Still, the self-respect of the upper classes, which instituted the original discrimination between 'liber' and 'libertus,' was not wholly extinct even then. In proportion as 'ingenuus' became depreciated, 'liberalis,' a term not formerly in frequent use, acquired additional weight and increased currency. Birth, in those ochlocratic days, being no longer of much account, the worth it formerly tended to ensure, if it existed at all, was found to be the product of individual merit, and, accordingly, was expressed by a vocable denoting a fresh variety of ingenuousness and its beneficent consequences. In accord with its history, this innovating term, 'liberalis,' applied to individual features in a man's character rather than the entire character. The upper class was gone or going when the word attained popularity, and what gentlemanly feeling there remained was bound up with the superior qualities of individuals, not with the uniform distinction and abiding rank of the members of a caste. While the ancients used to delight in the appellations 'ingenuus homo,' 'ingenuus vir,'—noble and free man—their descendants were content to extol the 'mens liberalis,' the 'artes liberales,' the 'studia liberalissima '—the liberal mind, the liberal arts and the liberal knowledge. In one characteristic phrase only 'liberalis' was habitually coupled with the names of individuals. When it described that species of nobility which consists in being free with one's money, it was considered the predominant attribute of a man, not a mere qualification of one of his various attributes, as in all other instances. In that sense, the most desirable in the public opinion of those days, 'liberalis homo '—a liberal man—used to be dubbed in dictatorial and imperial times he who bought influence with cash and handsomely paid for the right to oppress. The 'ingenuus homo' of old was a freeman, and mostly a nobleman, who happened to be a *noble man* as well ; the 'liberalis homo '—the term which replaced the 'ingenuus homo' in the decline of the State—was understood to be a party that hired the mob for his own personal aggrandisement. In the history of their words we discern the landmarks of a nation's moral and intellectual life.

The temperate character of Roman liberty is seen in two words, respectively flanking the grave and the more free-and-easy side of 'liber': 'arbitrium '

and 'licentia.' Themselves repressing what there is
of license in them, both vocables are highly characteristic of the Roman mind and manners. 'Arbitrium' is the absolute exercise of one's judgment
and will, unrestrained by any law. The gods
rule the world by 'arbitrium,' not by their mere
liberty to act as they please : 'Jovis O. M. nutu
et arbitrio cœlum terra mariaque reguntur'—Cic.
Rosc. Am. 45. 131.* The conqueror deals with his
defeated enemy in accordance with his arbitrary
decision : 'Populum Romanum victis non ad
alterius præscriptum sed ad suum arbitrium
imperare consuesse'—Cæs. Bell. Gall. 1. 36.† And
the Equity Judge or arbiter, whether appointed
by the State or selected by the litigants, is equally
entitled to use his own absolute discretion in case
of defective evidence : 'Non sub formula judicat'
—Sen. Clem. 2. 7.‡ 'Ex rebus penitus perspectis
planeque cognitis atque ab opinionis arbitrio se-
junctis'—Cic. de Or. 1. 23. § But this absolute and
discretionary decision is absolute only in respect of
its being untrammelled by law or custom. It is all
the same subject to reason, equity, and humane
feeling. It is, in reality, the reverse of arbitrari-
ness, being the very essence and acme of justice.

---

* Heaven and earth are governed by the will of omnipotent Jove.

† Romans are wont to deal with defeated nations as they please, not
as others may be disposed to prescribe.

‡ His judgment is not restricted by the ordinary judicial limits.

§ Conclusive evidence, exempt from guess or doubt.

It enforces right in spheres inaccessible to statute law, and metes out justice from loftier considerations than the ordinary judge can be allowed to admit. There is a grand passage in Seneca de Benef. 3. 7, thus nobly defining the arbiter's office : ‘Arbitri liberi nullis astricta vinculis religio et detrahere aliquid potest, et adjicere, et sententiam suam non prout lex aut justitia suadet, sed prout humanitas et misericordia impulit regere.’*

Such was the noble use habitually made by Romans of unrestrained decision and volition. It remains to analyse their idea of uncontrolled action as embodied in ‘licentia.’ Like ‘arbitrium,’ ‘licentia,’ in its primary acceptation, is a license *legally* conceded and possessed : it is the elbow-room left to a man by law' or custom in certain less important matters. ‘Licere id dicimus, quod legibus, quod more majorum institutisque conceditur. Neque enim quod quisque potest, id ei licet ; nec si non obstatur, propterea etiam permittitur’—Cic. Orat. Philippicæ xiii. 6.† License, accordingly, *originally* was freedom of choice in minor or other altogether uncontrollable matters. It was the freedom to eat and drink, and indulge

---

* Arbiters are free to extend or restrict the bearings of the case submitted to them, and may judge, not according to the letter of the law, but according to an equitable, humane, and sympathetic view of the matter.

† Only what the laws and the manners and customs of our ancestors allow is permitted. A man may meet with no resistance, and yet commit an unlicensed act.

oneself as much as one liked. It was the margin
left to the father of a family in managing his household. It was the latitude allowed every one in
arranging the lesser details of social intercourse.
It was the warrant, too, bestowed upon dictator
and imperator to act according to circumstances in
a political crisis or in war. In point of fact, it was
liberty, a necessary and most legitimate liberty, and
no licence at all. If it was called 'licentia,' not
'libertas,' the distinction solely arose from the wish
of the Romans to divorce liberty and its accurately
defined privileges from 'licentia,' a condition and
an act somewhat *too* free to admit of being included in the Roman temperate concept of *free*.

However, privilege uncontrolled and affecting
matters which from their very nature *cannot* easily
be controlled, is apt to be overstepped. Hence we
are speedily treated to such phraseology as 'licentia
cupiditatum,' 'licentia juvenum,' 'militum,' 'poeta-
rum.' * When abuse of privilege had perverted
the sense of the word from its primary to this
secondary shade, *licentia* was only too well fitted to
express a greater contrast to liberty than before.
Ancient 'licentia' meant private freedom within the
narrow limits left to it by the well-ordered and
disciplined 'libertas,' which ruled Roman life; *later*
'licentia' signified the political license which in-
vaded the domain of liberty and shattered the State.

* The license of youth, of poets, of soldiery.

'Civitas inter libertatem et licentiam incerta,'* as Tacitus pointedly contrasts the two sister notions (Hist. 2. 10. 1).

We close our synonymical dissection, and proceed to summarise and compare the principal results obtained. Poles, Russians, and Romans alike distinguish between private and public, between personal and political liberty. But the private liberty of the Russians is conceived as identical with the *unfettered* exercise of volition, from will down to whim, cupidity, and caprice. The Pole, on the other hand, though his liberty is a very wide concept too, begins to distinguish between liberty and will, assigning to the former a more restricted province in accord with its recognised intersocial character, and a due respect for the interests of others. In Latin, finally, the domain of private liberty was so effectually restricted by law and custom, 'lex mos et consuetudo,' that, whether it appeared in the guise of the disciplined 'libertas' or the less strictly supervised 'licentia,' freedom was conceded only to an extent compatible with a proper respect for the claims of others.

It is a remark worth making, that the Russian 'volya,' freedom, approaches more closely the Latin 'licentia,' license, than any other term occurring in the Latin nomenclature for 'liberty.' As to 'prostor,' the truly national superlative of the

---

* A State oscillating between liberty and license.

Russian 'volya' and 'volnost,' the Roman mind was incapable of forming the concept.

With his greater self-command, and more active regard for his neighbour's rights and feelings, the Roman, politically, became the freest of the three nationalities reviewed. His cherished designation of 'liber' was not only opposed to the 'servus,' the man positively the property of another; it involved not only the right to dispose of one's time and the fruits of one's labour as one listed; it also included the privilege to participate in the conduct of public affairs. The Russian 'svobodni' never did anything of the kind : its import was always limited to absence of slavery.

The Polish 'swobodny,' in its connection with 'pan, lord,' produced the famous title of 'swobodny pan,' a translation of the medieval Latin 'liber baro,' anglice a baron. Noblemen boasting this epithet were not only freemen, but the masters and governors of the State to a most inordinate degree. It is well known that, at one time, every one of them claimed the right to ratify, or else resist, the enactment of new bills by parliament, and that it was this unreasonable pretension, the so-called *Liberum Veto*, which so effectually contributed to disorganise the Polish Commonwealth.

As regards the transition from slavery to liberty, Russians, Poles, and Latins have special terms designating the man that achieves freedom. But

the Russian 'otpúschtschennik' and the Polish
'wyzwolénicc,' not to speak of other equivalents for
freedman, refer merely to the species of boor that is
no longer attached to the soil ; any further allusion
to social advance, to a rise in the world, to aspira-
tion eked out by vulgarity, such as is plainly heard
in the peculiar ring of the Latin 'libertus,' these
Slavic words do not contain. Persons bearing
these names are, by Russian and Polish institutions,
as a rule, excluded from every chance of entering
society. They are peasants, and either remain
peasants or become tradesmen, and even merchants,
without the hope, or, in many cases, the wish, to
acquire culture or attain rank. The Polish term
'wyzwolenczyk' corresponds indeed to the Latin
'libertinus,' 'a freedman's son,' and might be supposed to refer to a higher round on the social ladder ;
yet this word too is confined to mere rustic use.
As to the natural connection between free station
and liberal disposition, expressed in the language of
aristocratic Rome by 'ingenuus,' and in the ochlocratic Empire by 'liberalis,' neither Russian nor
Polish has lodged this shade in any of its liberty
words. To represent an ingenuous and liberal
mind as the outcome of social station, both languages require to fall back upon the nobility nomenclature. 'Blagoródni' and 'szlachetny,' 'noble
in rank and mind, illustrious and magnanimous,'
however different from the more catholic ·ingenuus'

and 'liberalis,' are yet the nearest equivalents of them.

Is it necessary to observe that in England, where all men have long been freemen, there is no occasion to set a special word apart for political liberty as distinct from personal freedom? Or need it be pointed out that the only appreciable difference between the two nouns, 'freedom' and 'liberty,' is this, that the Saxon word is rather an act than a condition, and the Norman more abstract and constitutional term a condition rather than an act? We *speak* with *freedom*, and we *are* at *liberty* to speak with freedom. We *possess freedom* of will, and *enjoy liberty* of conscience. To grant him a voter's right, one man is presented with the *freedom* of the city, while all citizens rejoice in owning the *liberties* of the burgh. However, I hardly dare enter upon the analysis of English notions at this hour and at this place. I will only observe that the English notion of liberty could not adequately be investigated without calling in words like 'independent,' 'scope,' 'range,' 'latitude,' and others less directly affecting the concept in the languages included in this rapid sketch.

Science is but beginning systematic inquiry into the meaning of related words, forms, and syntactical combinations. A new and promising task is set to philology: so long chiefly clinging to the form, linguistics tend to accentuate the essence of language

as well in the future. To the elementary acquisition
of language according to parts of speech the less
abstract and infinitely more fertile study will be
added according to ideas expressed. The notions of
nations will be accurately realised by an analytical
and comparative study of their dictionaries, and
the lexicon linked to the grammar in a joint elu-
cidation of the ideas common to both. Grammar,
psychology, ethnology, and the history of human
culture will be equally benefited by the gradual
accomplishment of this noble work. I shall deem
myself happy if, whilst discoursing upon the potent
and gifted race of Slav, I am considered to have
not altogether failed in establishing some such
linguistic facts after this novel method. England
and the English-speaking world generally, whose
national dictionary, in its rare completeness and
precision, offers an excellent gauge of less copious
and accurate tongues, seems pre-eminently fitted
to take an active part in developing psychological
linguistics.

V.

EGYPTIAN INVERSION.

V.

THE following tables are appended to illustrate the Egyptian inversion of sound and sense, alluded to in the third chapter. Of the examples selected, few, if any, require a knowledge of Egyptian phonetics to be intelligible at sight. It may not, however, be altogether superfluous to observe, that Egyptian admits of copious vowel-change, and for the enlargement of its roots habitually resorts to the use of a complicated prefix and suffix machinery ; the orthography adopted separates roots from affixes. Further tables and explanations of the extraordinary phenomenon will be found in treatises upon the 'Origin of Language' and 'Coptic Intensification,' included in the author's 'Linguistic Essays,' as well as in his 'Coptic Researches' and 'Egyptian Etymology.'

A.—INVERSION OF SOUND.

ăb ᴧ ba, stone, wall.	ān ᴧ nā, catalogue.
āb ᴧ bă, stone.	ān, to imitate ᴧ na, equally as.
ăbāb ᴧ babe, to vanish.	ān ᴧ nāā, colour.
ăm ᴧ ma, equally.	ăr ᴧ rā, to make.
ăm ᴧ ma, place.	ăs ᴧ sa, beautiful.
ăm ᴧ ma, come.	ăs ᴧ sa, miserable.

at ʌ tu, to give.
àt ʌ tau, toi, to give.
àt ʌ tà, a part.
àat ʌ ta, time.
aχ ʌ χa, to put.
ash, much ʌ sha, thousand.
ah-e ʌ ḥā, time, life, lifetime.
āḥ ʌ ḥā, substance, flesh.
àh ʌ ḥā, to rejoice.
ah-e ʌ ḥā, to stand.
bek ʌ kep, light.
bek ʌ keb-s, tree.
balk-u ʌ kolb-s, vessel.
belj ʌ jarb-s, vessel.
bon, bad ʌ nob-e, a sin.
bas, bis-e ʌ seb, to cut.
bēt ʌ teb, a fig.
bot-s ʌ tob-s, to hurt, to wound.
beh ʌ χeb, to bend.
beh, to bow ʌ hob-e, humble.
beh ʌ χeb, to strike, push.
boh ʌ hep, to cover.
eu-i ʌ ue-i, to recede.
tham-ie ʌ mat-e, to possess.
àh ʌ χa, acre.
āk ʌ ko, to put.
kr-r ʌ rek, to burn.
kolb-s ʌ balk-u, vase.
kul-ol ʌ lik, to draw together.
terp ʌ pordsh, to smash.
kolp ʌ polk, to destroy.
klip-i ʌ plik, to carve.
hēm, hot ʌ meh, to burn.
ken-ken, ken-au ʌ nek, to strike.
konh ʌ ḥank, to blossom.
kap ʌ pok-f, hair, wool.
koor ʌ lok-lek, to tear.
ker ʌ rek, to turn.

kor-h ʌ rak-h, to burn.
kas, to cut ʌ sakh, to carve.
lek, green ʌ hr-r, leaf, flower.
lek, a part ʌ hel, to cut, divide.
lok-s ʌ khōl, to stab, prick.
las ʌ sal, tongue.
rash-e ʌ shair-i, rejoice.
loih-e ʌ hair-e, dirt.
lodj ʌ djol, to desist.
lotj ʌ tjol, to rob.
mà, place ʌ àm, in.
mà ʌ àm, similarly.
ma-i ʌ àm, to love.
mo ʌ am, to catch.
mu v iom, water, sea.
mu ʌ nm, and.
mes-ī, night ʌ sam, darkness.
mes-t ʌ sem-ṭ, to paint.
met-ī ʌ t'am-ā, volume.
māt-n ʌ ṭem, sword.
mash ʌ tshem-tshom, to be able.
mesh-e ʌ tshem-tshom, to seek.
mesh-ā ʌ shem, to travel.
meh, girdle, wreath ʌ hōm-i, to turn round, encircle.
meh ʌ hēm, to burn.
nau ʌ ān, to see.
n-neḥ ʌ ḥen, a string, to tie (also).
nut', to knock down ʌ ton, to kill.
nutsh-s ʌ tshon-t, wrath.
neh, to separate ʌ ḥen, to tie, and (also).
leh ʌ har-h, to care, to work.
neḥ ʌ ḥen-nu, to adore.
osh ʌ sho, much.
oh-e ʌ hā, to stand.

u-bes ∧ u-seb, a heap.

pir ∧ rep-i, to grow.

ush ∧ shu, immense.

pā-t ∧ ap-e, head, beginning.

pa ∧ àb, to jump.

pā-pā ∧ āb, to shine.

beh ∧ χeb-χeb, to strike.

plotsh ∧ dsharb, naked.

peltsh-e ∧ shorp, old.

penh ∧ χenp, to catch.

pursh-a, to break ∧ sōlp, to cut, destroy.

plik, to strike, to do stone-cutter's work ∧ kelp, fist, stick.

nesh ∧ shen, to terrify.

pash-f, net ∧ shop, to catch.

peh ∧ hep, to go.

beh ∧ χab, to incline.

peh ∧ χeb, to cut.

rek, to bend ∧ kel, to bend, kr-os, a ring.

rek, to turn round ∧ kor-ker, to turn about, to fly.

rek, to cut, divide ∧ kār-tī, knife.

rok-h ∧ kor-h, to burn.

rek ∧ kr-r, keial, to burn.

ret ∧ djor-j, to net, to entrap.

reχ-s, to cut ∧ { χer-s, to cut, divide. tshor-te, knife. kkōl, to stab.

reχ-t ∧ χer, to measure.

rōsh-e ∧ dshōr, tshor-tsh, to see.

rosh-resh ∧ shair-i, red.

rash, to cut ∧ shar, to divide.

sa ∧ as, to proceed, progress.

sa v àis, sarcophagus.

sab ∧ besh, to wash.

seb ∧ besh-t, bad, enemy.

seb ∧ bas, to cut.

s-bek ∧ s-keb, thigh.

s-ben∧ s-neb, tie.

s-reχ ∧ s-χer, throne, raised seat.

tep, tap-t, to eat ∧ pāt, food.

sol, sāl, lux ∧ resh, to see.

sem-tt ∧ mes-tm, antimony.

se-t ∧ as-t, the soil.

s-tu χ ∧ hāt, to cover.

seχ, sōh ∧ hes-k, deaf.

sesh ∧ shes, becoming.

sōsh ∧ shōs, unbecoming.

sef ∧ fes, to wash, to clean.

sakh ∧ kas, to carve.

soph (sof), beverage ∧ pos, water.

ta ∧ àat-t, unclean.

toi ∧ àat, seat, dwelling.

teb ∧ à-pet, hippopotamus.

tōb-i ∧ pet, vessel.

tik, to hurl ∧ kat-o, arrow.

t'ek-ā, to divide ∧ ket, a morsel.

tek-t, food ∧ ket-ti, corn.

tem ∧ met-n, sword.

ton ∧ nut', to cut down, smash.

ten-nu, to grow ∧ natsh, great.

t'en-nut ∧ net'-a, wrath.

t'ep ∧ à-pt, ship.

tep ∧ à-pt, goose.

ter ∧ à-redj, term, end, border.

t'ar ∧ rodj, to see.

tes, to divide ∧ shet, amputate.

teχ, to irrigate ∧ χet, to flow.

teχ ∧ χet, to cut down.

teh ∧ χet, to proceed.

teh-u ∧ hat, to bawl, hurrah.

tef ∧ fotsh, to leap.

tadj ∧ shōt-i, substance, mass.

χa, rope ∧ ho-k, to tie, bind.

χā ∧ aχ. to put, place, fling.

χa-u ∧ āχ, altar.

χau ∧ uχ-a, night.

χeb ∧ beh, to bend.

χeb ∧ beh, to strike.

χeb ∧ beh, to cut.

kheib-i ∧ beh-t, shade.

ōt ∧ t'e-ṭa, fat.

sha ∧ esh-she, becoming.

sho ∧ osh, much.

shuä ∧ ansh, the wind, to blow.

shen-t ∧ nesh-ṭ, to smash, strike down, break to pieces.

shep ∧ ä-pesh, splendour.

shap ∧ pesh, to divide.

shōp, to move ∧ pōsh-s, to remove.

üa ∧ au, to carry, bear.

khōl ∧ lok-s, to prick, stab.

kher ∧ pōkh-t, reχ-s, to strike, smash.

hou, more ∧ uoh, also, and.

ḥā ∧ oh-i, heap, multitude.

ḥeb-s ∧ beh-n, to cover.

ḥob-s, to go round ∧ bik-i, girdle.

ḥam ∧ meḥ-i, a fish.

ḥem ∧ ä-meḥ, to see.

ḥen ∧ neḥ, to adore.

ḥan ∧ a-uχ, a plant, vegetable.

ḥank ∧ konh, to grow, blossom.

ḥep ∧ peḥ, to move, go.

djorb ∧ pordj, to break.

pert' ∧ torp, to smash, break.

her-sh ∧ rokh-t, to smash.

djau, to chew ∧ uadj-i, the jaw.

tsheu ∧ uesh, narrow.

djom, dshom, force ∧ mash, to be able.

tshol, to rob ∧ latsh, to exact.

tshōlp, to reveal ∧ bredsh, lightning.

B.—Inversion of Sense.

bāḥ, full ∨ empty.

meχ, empty ∨ meḥ, full.

ṭem, to sunder ∨ ṭem, ṭem-i, tōm, to join.

nāsh, small, weak ∨ nesh-ṭ, big, strong.

neh, to cut, sunder, separate ∨ noh, rope.

tauf, to burn ∨ djaf, cold.

χer-s, to divide ∨ χer-sh, to join.

sam, darkness ∨ sem, to become visible.

sat, to throw away ∨ set, to recover.

sesh, becoming ∨ sōsh, unbecoming.

tes, to sunder ∨ teshtesh, to mix.

äfṭ, to jump ∨ to rest quiet.

kef, to take up ∨ to let lie.

ken, strong ∨ weak.

men, to stand ∨ menmen, to move.

tūa, to honour ∨ to despise.

terp, to take ∨ to give.

χen, to stand ∨ to go.

C.—INVERSION OF SOUND AND SENSE.

ben, to be absent, nothing ◇ neb, nib, all.

bredsh, splendour ◇ χreb, darkness.

kar, wise ◇ rak-a, stupid.

mer, left hand ◇ rem, right hand.

meh, full ◇ χem, empty.

noh, to run ◇ χen, to stand still.

nāsh, weak, feeble ◇ tshn-e, strong.

ot, to tie ◇ tä, to cut.

pir, fire, light ◇ reb, dark.

pert', to tear ◇ t'erp, to sow.

peχ, to cut, divide ◇ hop-t, to tie, join.

pesh, to divide ◇ sheb, to join, mix.

pesh, to destroy ◇ säp, to create, shape.

pah, to divide ◇ hop-t, to join.

lōk, ardere, lucere ◇ hlo-l, dark.

mes-î, darkness ◇ sem, to become visible.

sem-ä, to show ◇ mesh-e, to seek.

χen-st, knot ⎫
hen, to tie. ⎭ ◇ nek, to cut.

sōsh, unbecoming ◇ shes, becoming.

tä, to cut, divide ◇ ot, to tie up, join, connect.

tem, to sunder ◇ modj-t, to connect.

toh, to consolidate ◇ het, to destroy.

teh, to run ◇ ket, to stand still, rest.

χen, to rest ◇ noh, to run, leap.

χreb, darkness ◇ bredsh, brightness.

χerr-sh, to connect ◇ rek, to separate.

o-djep, cold ◇ u-bet, to glow.

hel-hōl, to extend ◇ lik, to draw together.

neh, to separate ◇ hn, to tie.

hōp-t, to join ◇ pah, to cut, divide.

These tables include Hieroglyphic, Demotic, and Coptic words promiscuously. Attention is directed to the occurrence of the same words in the three tables, showing roots to have undergone the three metamorphoses simultaneously.

PRINTED BY BALLANTYNE, HANSON AND CO.
EDINBURGH AND LONDON.

Prospectus.

———o———

Post 8vo, pp. viii.—266, cloth, price 9s.

LINGUISTIC ESSAYS.

By CARL ABEL, Ph.D.

———◆———

CONTENTS.

Language as the Expression of National Modes of Thought.
The Conception of Love in some Ancient and Modern Languages.
The English Verbs of Command.
The Discrimination of Synonyms.
Philological Methods.

The Connection between Dictionary and Grammar.
The Possibility of a Common Literary Language for all Slavs.
The Order and Position of Words in the Latin Sentence.
Coptic Intensification.

The Origin of Language.

Proving the signification of words and forms to reflect a nation's general view of the universe, the Author advocates a psychological study of language, to supplement the prevailing formalism of ordinary grammar. To this end English and other familiar linguistic notions are tested by a new method of national and international analysis, which combines the dictionary and the grammar; the origin of language and the primitive significance of sounds are unravelled in essays, containing striking results of etymological research; while in the connection between philology, psychology, and politics, the bearing of linguistic lore upon the general concerns of mankind is conclusively evidenced. The most enjoyable faculty in the exercise, but, frequently, the one least enjoyed in the study, speech, in these treatises is shown to constitute at once the most faithful and the most attractive record of the history of the human, and more especially the national, mind.

———

Opinions of the Press.

" Dr. Abel maintains, with justice, that sounds do not constitute a language until sense and meaning are breathed into them, and that, consequently, in linguistic investigation we must have regard quite as much to psychology as to phonology. Language is the mirror in which the ideas and beliefs of a people are reflected, and in dealing with it we cannot afford to forget this fact. Dr. Abel's views on the origin and growth of speech are best exemplified in an essay which is now published for the first time. . . . The attractive style and admirable English of Dr. Abel, give his views an unusually good chance of being heard."—*Academy*.

" No doubt it is to the discovery that all phonetic changes are regulated by strict law that modern linguistic science owes its origin ; no doubt, too, the chief progress hitherto made in the scientific study of language has been upon the physiological rather than upon the psychological side of speech ; but this ought not to blind us to the importance of a psychological investigation of the words we utter, and the necessity of discovering the laws which regulate the development of ideas and significations. This is the task to which Dr. Abel has devoted himself, and carried out in the series of works prefixed to this article. The student of comparative philo-

logy will welcome the presence of so honest and learned a labourer in a field which has been generally left to the poet or the untrained *dilettante.*"
—A. H. SAYCE in *Academy.*

"Comparative philology has not only solved some curious problems as to the origin and development of certain words, but it has proved an invaluable aid to ethnology, by indicating prominent stages in the history of individual races. Dr. Abel, in the volume before us, has carried the investigation a step further, and discussed the subject from an ethical point of view. His method is to point out how far language is an embodiment of a nation's views of men and things. While grammar deals only with the form and arrangement of words, he aims at appreciating the meaning conveyed in the substance as well as the form—in short, at advocating a psychological study of language instead of the ordinary unintelligent and mechanical method of learning."—Professor PALMER in *Standard.*

" Dr. Abel's Essays are representative of psychological linguistics, and the English public may be congratulated upon receiving so valuable a book on what in reality is the most conclusive account of the intellectual history of mankind. Max Müller, indeed, notwithstanding the different basis he starts from, adopts a similar method in some of his spirited inquiries; but he speedily leaves the psychological region and goes off in a different direction. Dr. Abel's Essays embrace the entire domain of linguistics. Inquiring into the origin of language by the light of the history of the Egypto-Coptic tongue, he analyses existing languages as the expression of distinct national individualities. The most delicate gradations of thought and feeling, as displayed in the notion of Love by Hebrews, Romans, English, and Russians, are accurately set forth by this learned and most intellectual investigator : vowels are proved to supply a peculiar means of varying significations; the order and position of Latin words in the sentence, an intricate and not easily-controlled subject, is reduced to fundamental laws ; the Slav languages, so little known to any except specialists, are discussed to show the expediency of making Russian the common literary medium of the race, were any such medium ever introduced, &c. . . . Synonymical, grammatical, lexicographical, and psychological, the wealth of these inquiries is as great as the instruction they convey, and the suggestive charm they exercise upon the student."—Dr. BRUCHMANN in *Steinthal's Zeitschrift für Völkerpsychologie und Sprachwissenschaft*, Band xiv., Heft 2, 1882.

" Die allgemeine Grammatik beabsichtigt nur den allgemeinen Sinn der fremden Sprache zum Zwecke ungefähren Uebersetzens zu lehren, oder, wo sie tiefer greift, isolirte Punkte der Etymologie, Synonymik oder Syntax zu erklären, ohne den das Geistige erst recht aufdeckenden Zusammenhang mit allem verwandten Geistigen zur Geltung zu bringen. Abel dagegen verlangt, und eben hierin ist er, so viel ich sehe, bahnbrechend, dass wir uns über dies mehr formale Verfahren erheben und durch Vereinigung des Wörterbuchs und einer umfassenden Synonymik mit der Grammatik vor allem den sachlichen Bedeutungsgehalt der Wörter ins Auge fassen. Er will die in einer Sprache niedergelegten Anschauungen eines Volkes nach ihrem Inhalte gruppiren, den Bedeutungen der selbstständigen Worte eine umfassende Bearbeitung zukommen lassen, von der Vergleichung einiger weniger Synonyma auf die gemeinsame Behandlung der Wörter ganzer Gedankenklassen übergehen, gleichviel welchem Redetheile sie angehören, hierauf endlich mehrere Sprachen in derselben Weise behandeln und zuletzt die Ergebnisse unter einander vergleichen. Ueberall erweitert sich die Sprachkenntniss zur Sachkenntniss ; wir erhalten neue Aufschlüsse über die Veränderungen der Gedanken und Gesinnungen, wir bereichern unsere eigene Anschauungen."—Professor NERLICH in *National Zeitung*, December 13, 1882.

"Dieses Buch gehört zur Literatur des In- und des Auslandes; denn es hat einen deutschen Verfasser, ist zum Teil aus dem Deutschen übersetzt und wird eine Zierde der englischen wissenschaftlichen Literatur sein. Wir kennen den Dr. Abel längst als einen der Seltenen, welche zugleich durch Strenge der wissenschaftlichen Methode und Sicherheit des empirischen Takts, wie durch Feinheit des Sprachgefühls, in das Wesen einzelner Sprachen mit der Absicht und mit dem Erfolge eindringen, das Wesen menschlicher Sprache überhaupt tiefer zu erkennen. Denn auch von dem grösseren Werke des Verfassers über das Koptische abgesehen, durch welches er sich eine Stelle in der vordersten Reihe der deutschen Sprachforscher eworben hat, dessen Würdigung aber über die Grenzen dieses Magazins wie über den sprachlichen Horizont des Referenten hinausgeht, hat sich Dr. Abel, dem deutschen gebildeten Publikum durch einige deutsch geschriebene Abhandlungen, welche in dem vorliegenden Buche englisch wieder erscheinen, als ein Meister in der Erweiterung und Vertiefung der Bedeutungslehre bekannt gemacht."—Professor LAZARUS in *Magazin f. d. Literatur d. In- und Auslandes*, Nov. 3, 1883.

"Messrs. Trübner & Co., of London, have just published a volume of Linguistic Essays, by Dr. Carl Abel, of Berlin, who has rapidly taken rank among the first philologists of our time. Language, as not merely the expression, but the embodiment of a nation's general views of men and things, is the theme of the first six Essays. In the seventh Essay he discusses the possibility of a common literary language for the Slav nations. The eighth Essay, on 'Coptic Intensification,' and the ninth, 'On the Origin of Language,' discuss the most mystical problem of the philologist by the latest historical light of Egyptian philology. The tenth and last Essay, 'On the Order and Position of Words in the Latin Sentence,' treats very ingeniously and learnedly of the intellectual principles of laws which determine the arrangement of words in a sentence. Dr. Abel is a leader of the 'Junggrammatische Schule' fast growing up in Germany, which is endeavouring to promote the growth of psychological linguistics, in contradistinction to the prevailing formalism of elementary and abstract grammar. No one would suspect from reading these Essays that he was a Prussian, and not a born Englishman."—*The Critic*, New York, Sept. 23, 1882.

"This book is a somewhat miscellaneous collection of essays by a German scholar, who enjoys considerable reputation as a writer on language in general, and Egyptian philology in particular. His point of view is the psychological side of speech, a field in which Professors Lazarus and Steinthal have worked with distinguished ability. The author lays down, as the basis of his studies, the proposition that a nation's language is an embodiment of its general views of men and things; hence a comparative survey of the significations of words in the idioms of different races is a ready means of estimating their relative moral and intellectual qualities. It must be conceded that Dr. Abel has introduced us to a field which promises exceedingly important discoveries, but of which scholars are as yet scarcely beyond the border."—*Literary World*, Boston, Sept. 9, 1882.

"Dr. Abel, the author of a new German treatise upon Language, recently published in London, is one of the first philologists in Germany. Though still comparatively a young man, he is a leader of the Junggrammatische Schule, now rapidly recruiting in Germany, the aim of which is to promote the growth of psychological linguistics in contradistinction to the prevalent formalism of elementary and abstract grammar; in other words, to make philology yield fruit as well as leaves. . . . Dr. Abel is one of the few German writers of eminence whose English style never betrays his Teutonic origin. No Englishman writes more faultless or idiomatic English. We see it announced that he is to deliver a course of lectures this season at Oxford, where he will renew his efforts to 'emancipate philology from the thrall of conventionalism, and to make its waste places blossom as the rose.'"—*Harper's Magazine*, October 1882.

"It is because Dr. Abel believes that the signification of words and forms reflects a nation's general view of mind and life, and carries on his researches on the basis of national and international linguistic analysis, that we gladly recommend these thoughtful and attractive Essays to the readers of *Mind*. Students of English especially may be congratulated upon a contribution to their branch of knowledge which combines no ordinary amount of empirical tact with a degree of *sprachgefühl* unusual even in the Germans themselves."—HERBERT MORTON BAYNES, in *Mind*, April 1883.

"This is an extremely interesting volume. . . . The author's ultimate object is to render philology a comparative conceptology of nations ; and all his essays are so thoughtful, so full of happy illustrations, and so admirably put together, that we hardly know to which we should specially turn to select for our readers a sample of his workmanship. His first Essay, on ' Language as the Expression of National Modes of Thought,' is quite a model of sound and suggestive criticism ; and not less admirable is the third Essay, which deals with the English verbs of command. Very striking, too, is the Essay on the ' Conception of Love in some Ancient and Modern Languages.'"—*The Tablet*, July 29, 1882.

"Dr. Abel's philological essays are very interesting and suggestive studies of certain aspects of the use of language, and are characterised by thoroughness, clearness, and philosophical acumen. Popular in style, they contain a great many fresh, brilliant, and learned observations from the point of view of a philosophical student of language. Archbishop Trench has taught us how fruitful such themes may be when approached with adequate skill and scholarship : this is a pleasant glimpse of another excursion into the same field."—*The Literary World*.

"Dr. Abel has published an exceedingly subtle and delicate discrimination of the words expressive of love in several ancient and modern languages. . . . The different shades and modes of the very variable sentiment are fully set forth in this instructive treatise."—Professor POTT, *Wurzelwörterbuch*, v. 379, lxvii.

"Dr. Abel's treatise on the Latin order of words is a thoughtful essay, based upon ample and deep observation. Conceived from a thoroughly psychological point of view, it is uncommonly calculated to inculcate correct and discerning notions of Latin linguistic phenomena."—Prof. SCHWEIZER-SIDLER, in *Kühn's Zeitschrift für verzleichende Sprachforschung*, xxi. 1.

"Dr. Abel, honourably known for his contributions to Coptic philology, has published very interesting and ingenious lectures on language as an index to national character. The English, Latin, Hebrew, and Russian languages are principally analysed, and the vocabulary of each, in the crucial examples selected, is shown to be very copious."—*Saturday Review*.

"A psychological analysis of language carried out with all the author's well-known refinement and subtlety."—Professor BASTIAN in *Ethnographische Zeitschrift*, 1882.

"A philologist equally famous for scholarship and intellectual appreciation of linguistic peculiarities has presented us with a most accurate and refined delineation of the English concept of command."—*Cologne Gazette*.

"In dissecting words, Dr. Abel is writing a history of civilisation and culture. While the substance of his essays is equally commendable for philosophical and linguistic subtlety, the form in which he communicates the result of his learned researches is a pattern of attractive and lucid style."—*St. Petersburg Gazette*.

LONDON : TRÜBNER & CO., 57 AND 59 LUDGATE HILL.

A

CATALOGUE OF IMPORTANT WORKS,

PUBLISHED BY

TRÜBNER & CO.

57 AND 59 LUDGATE HILL.

ABEL.—LINGUISTIC ESSAYS. By Carl Abel. CONTENTS: Language as the Expression of National Modes of Thought—The Conception of Love in some Ancient and Modern Languages—The English Verbs of Command—The Discrimination of Synonyms—Philological Methods—The Connection between Dictionary and Grammar—The Possibility of a Common Literary Language for the Slav Nations—Coptic Intensification—The Origin of Language—The Order and Position of Words in the Latin Sentence. Post 8vo, pp. xii. and 282, cloth. 1882. 9s.

ABRAHAMS.—A MANUAL OF SCRIPTURE HISTORY FOR USE IN JEWISH SCHOOLS AND FAMILIES. By L. B. Abrahams, B.A., Principal Assistant Master, Jews' Free School. With Map and Appendices. Third Edition. Crown 8vo, pp. viii. and 152, cloth. 1883. 1s. 6d.

AGASSIZ — AN ESSAY ON CLASSIFICATION. By Louis Agassiz. 8vo, pp. vii. and 381, cloth. 1859. 12s.

AHLWARDT.—THE DIVANS OF THE SIX ANCIENT ARABIC POETS, ENNĀBIGA, 'ANTARA, THARAFA, ZUHAIR, 'ALQAMA, and IMRUULQUAIS; chiefly according to the MSS. of Paris, Gotha, and Leyden, and the Collection of their Fragments, with a List of the various Readings of the Text. Edited by W. Ahlwardt, Professor of Oriental Languages at the University of Greifswald. Demy 8vo, pp. xxx. and 340, sewed. 1870. 12s.

AHN.—PRACTICAL GRAMMAR OF THE GERMAN LANGUAGE. By Dr. F. Ahn. A New Edition. By Dr. Dawson Turner, and Prof. F. L. Weinmann. Crown 8vo, pp. cxii. and 430, cloth. 1878. 3s. 6d.

AHN.—NEW, PRACTICAL, AND EASY METHOD OF LEARNING THE GERMAN LANGUAGE. By Dr. F. Ahn. First and Second Course. Bound in 1 vol. 12mo, pp. 86 and 120, cloth. 1866. 3s.

AHN.—KEY to Ditto. 12mo, pp. 40, sewed. 8d.

AHN.—MANUAL OF GERMAN AND ENGLISH CONVERSATIONS, or Vade Mecum for English Travellers. 12mo, pp. x. and 137, cloth. 1875. 1s. 6d.

AHN.—GERMAN COMMERCIAL LETTER WRITER, with Explanatory Introductions in English, and an Index of Words in French and English. By Dr. F. Ahn. 12mo, pp. 248, cloth. 1861. 4s. 6d.

AHN.—NEW, PRACTICAL, AND EASY METHOD OF LEARNING THE FRENCH LANGUAGE. By Dr. F. Ahn. First Course and Second Course. 12mo, cloth. Each 1s. 6d. The Two Courses in 1 vol. 12mo, pp. 114 and 170, cloth. 1865. 3s.

AHN.—NEW, PRACTICAL, AND EASY METHOD OF LEARNING THE FRENCH LANGUAGE. Third Course, containing a French Reader, with Notes and Vocabulary. By H. W. Ehrlich. 12mo, pp. viii. and 125, cloth. 1866. 1s. 6d.

AHN.—MANUAL OF FRENCH AND ENGLISH CONVERSATIONS FOR THE USE OF SCHOOLS AND TRAVELLERS. By Dr. F. Ahn. 12mo, pp. viii. and 200, cloth. 1862. 2s. 6d.

A

AHN. FRENCH COMMERCIAL LETTER WRITER. By Dr. F. Ahn. Second Edition. 12mo, pp. 228. cloth. 1866. 4s. 6d.

AHN.—NEW, PRACTICAL, AND EASY METHOD OF LEARNING THE ITALIAN LANGUAGE. By Dr. F. Ahn. First and Second Course. 12mo, pp. 198, cloth. 1872. 3s. 6d.

AHN.—KEY to Ditto. 12mo, pp. 22, sewed. 1865. 1s.

AHN. NEW, PRACTICAL, AND EASY METHOD OF LEARNING THE DUTCH LANGUAGE, being a complete Grammar. with Selections. By Dr. F. Ahn. 12mo, pp. viii. and 166, cloth. 1862. 3s. 6d.

AHN.—AHN'S COURSE. Latin Grammar for Beginners. By W. Ihne, Ph.D. 12mo, pp. vi. and 184, cloth. 1864. 3s.

ALABASTER.—THE WHEEL OF THE LAW : Buddhism illustrated from Siamese Sources by the Modern Buddhist, a Life of Buddha, and an Account of the Phra Bat. By Henry Alabaster, Esq., Interpreter of Her Majesty's Consulate-General in Siam, Member of the Royal Asiatic Society. Demy 8vo, pp. lviii. and 324, cloth. 1871. 14s.

ALLEN.—THE COLOUR SENSE. See English and Foreign Philosophical Library, Vol. X.

ALLIBONE.—A CRITICAL DICTIONARY OF ENGLISH LITERATURE AND BRITISH AND AMERICAN AUTHORS (LIVING AND DECEASED). From the Earliest Accounts to the latter half of the 19th century. Containing over 46,000 Articles (Authors), with 40 Indexes of subjects. By S. Austin Allibone. In 3 vols. royal 8vo, cloth. £5, 8s.

ALTHAUS.—THE SPAS OF EUROPE. By Julius Althaus, M.D. 8vo, pp. 516, cloth. 1862. 7s. 6d.

AMATEUR MECHANIC'S WORKSHOP (THE). A Treatise containing Plain and Concise Directions for the Manipulation of Wood and Metals ; including Casting, Forging, Brazing, Soldering, and Carpentry. By the Author of " The Lathe and its Uses." Sixth Edition. Demy 8vo, pp. vi. and 148, with Two Full-Page Illustrations, on toned paper and numerous Woodcuts, cloth. 1880. 6s.

AMATEUR MECHANICAL SOCIETY.—JOURNAL OF THE AMATEUR MECHANICAL SOCIETY. 8vo. Vol. i. pp. 344 cloth. 1871 72. 12s. Vol. ii. pp. vi. and 290, cloth. 1873-77. 12s. Vol. iii. pp. iv. and 246, cloth. 1878-79. 12s. 6d.

AMERICAN ALMANAC AND TREASURY OF FACTS, STATISTICAL, FINANCIAL, AND POLITICAL. Edited by Ainsworth R. Spofford, Librarian of Congress. Crown 8vo, cloth. 1878, 1879, 1880, 1881, 1882. 7s. 6d. each.

AMERY.—NOTES ON FORESTRY. By C. F. Amery, Deputy Conservator N. W. Provinces, India. Crown 8vo, pp. viii. and 120, cloth. 1875. 5s.

AMBERLEY.—AN ANALYSIS OF RELIGIOUS BELIEF. By Viscount Amberley. 2 vols. demy 8vo, pp. xvi. and 496 and 512, cloth. 1876. 30s

AMONGST MACHINES. A Description of Various Mechanical Appliances used in the Manufacture of Wood, Metal, and other Substances. A Book for Boys, copiously Illustrated. By the Author of " The Young Mechanic." Second Edition. Imperial 16mo, pp. viii. and 336, cloth. 1878. 7s. 6d.

ANDERSON.—PRACTICAL MERCANTILE CORRESPONDENCE. A Collection of Modern Letters of Business, with Notes, Critical and Explanatory, and an Appendix, containing a Dictionary of Commercial Technicalities, pro forma Invoices, Account Sales, Bills of Lading, and Bills of Exchange ; also an Explanation of the German Chain Rule. 24th Edition, revised and enlarged. By William Anderson. 12mo, pp. 288, cloth. 5s.

ANDERSON and TUGMAN.—MERCANTILE CORRESPONDENCE, containing a Collection of Commercial Letters in Portuguese and English, with their translation on opposite pages, for the use of Business Men and of Students in either of the Languages, treating in modern style of the system of Business in the principal Commercial Cities of the World. Accompanied by pro forma Accounts, Sales, Invoices, Bills of Lading, Drafts, &c. With an Introduction and copious Notes. By William Anderson and James E. Tugman. 12mo, pp. xi. and 193, cloth. 1867. 6s.

APEL.—PROSE SPECIMENS FOR TRANSLATION INTO GERMAN, with copious Vocabularies and Explanations. By H. Apel. 12mo, pp. viii. and 246, cloth. 1862. 4s. 6d.

APPLETON (Dr.)—LIFE AND LITERARY RELICS. See English and Foreign Philosophical Library, Vol. XIII.

ARAGO.—LES ARISTOCRATIES. A Comedy in Verse. By Etienne Arago. Edited, with English Notes and Notice on Etienne Arago, by the Rev. E. P. H. Brette, B.D., Head Master of the French School, Christ's Hospital, Examiner in the University of London. Fcap. 8vo, pp. 244, cloth. 1868. 4s.

ARMITAGE.—LECTURES ON PAINTING : Delivered to the Students of the Royal Academy. By Edward Armitage, R.A. Crown 8vo, pp. 256, with 29 Illustrations, cloth. 1883. 7s. 6d.

ARNOLD.—PEARLS OF THE FAITH ; or, Islam's Rosary : being the Ninety-nine beautiful names of Allah. With Comments in Verse from various Oriental sources as made by an Indian Mussulman. By Edwin Arnold, M.A., C.S.I., &c. Crown 8vo, pp. xvi. and 320, cloth. 1883. 7s. 6d.

ARNOLD.—THE LIGHT OF ASIA ; or, THE GREAT RENUNCIATION (Mahábhinishkramana). Being the Life and Teaching of Gautama, Prince of India, and Founder of Buddhism (as told in verse by an Indian Buddhist). By Edwin Arnold, M.A., C.S.I., &c. Tenth Edition. Cr. 8vo, pp. xiii. and 238, limp parchment. 1883. 2s. 6d.

ARNOLD.—THE ILIAD AND ODYSSEY OF INDIA. By Edwin Arnold, M.A., F.R.G.S., &c., &c. Fcap. 8vo, pp. 24, sewed. 1s.

ARNOLD.—A SIMPLE TRANSLITERAL GRAMMAR OF THE TURKISH LANGUAGE. Compiled from Various Sources. With Dialogues and Vocabulary. By Edwin Arnold, M.A., C.S.I., F.R.G.S. Post 8vo, pp. 80, cloth. 1877. 2s. 6d.

ARNOLD.—INDIAN POETRY. See Trübner's Oriental Series.

ARTOM.—SERMONS. By the Rev. B. Artom, Chief Rabbi of the Spanish and Portuguese Congregations of England. First Series. Second Edition. Crown 8vo, pp. viii. and 314, cloth. 1876. 6s.

ASHER.—ON THE STUDY OF MODERN LANGUAGES in general, and of the English Language in particular. An Essay. By David Asher, Ph.D. 12mo, pp. viii. and 80, cloth. 1859. 2s.

ASIATIC SOCIETY OF BENGAL. List of Publications on application.

ASIATIC SOCIETY.—JOURNAL OF THE ROYAL ASIATIC SOCIETY OF GREAT BRITAIN AND IRELAND, from the Commencement to 1863. First Series, complete in 20 Vols. 8vo, with many Plates. £10, or in parts from 4s. to 6s. each.

ASIATIC SOCIETY.—JOURNAL OF THE ROYAL ASIATIC SOCIETY OF GREAT BRITAIN AND IRELAND. New Series. 8vo. Stitched in wrapper. 1864-82.

Vol. I., 2 Parts, pp. iv. and 490, 16s.—Vol. II., 2 Parts, pp. 522, 16s.—Vol. III. 2 Parts, pp. 516, with Photograph, 22s.—Vol. IV, 2 Parts, pp. 521, 18s.—Vol. V. 2 Parts, pp. 463, with 10 full-page and folding Plates, 18s.—Vol. VI., Part 1, pp. 212, with 2 Plates and a Map, 8s.—

Vol. VI. Part 2, pp. 272, with Plate and Map, 8s.—Vol. VII., Part 1, pp. 194, with a Pla'e, 8s.—Vol. VII., Part 2, pp. 204, with 7 Plates and a Map, 8s.—Vol. VIII., Part 1, pp. 156, with 3 Plates and a Plan, 8s.—Vol VIII., Part 2, pp. 152, 8s.—Vol. IX., Part 1, pp. 154, with a P ate, 8s.—Vol. IX., Part 2, pp. 202, with 3 Plates, 10s. 6d.—Vol. X., Part 1, pp. 156, with 2 Plates and a Map, 8s.—Vol. X., Part 2, pp. 146, 6s.—Vol. X., Part 3, pp. 204, 8s —Vol. XI., Part 1, pp 128, 5s.—Vol XI , Part 2, pp. 158, with 2 Plates, 7s, 6d —Vol. XI., Part 3, pp. 250, 8s.—Vol. XII., Part 1, pp. 152, 5s.—Vol. XII., Part 2, pp. 182, with 2 Plates and Map, 6s.—Vol. XII., Part 3, pp. 100, 4s.—Vol. XII., Part 4, pp. x., 152., cxx , 16, 8s.—Vol. XIII., Part 1, pp. 120, 5s.- Vol. XIII., Part 2, pp. 170, with a Map, 8s.—Vol. XIII., Part 3, pp. 178, with a Table, 7s. 6d.—Vol. XIII., Part 4, pp. 282, with a Plate and Table, 10s. 6d.—Vol. XIV., Part 1, pp. 124, with a Table and 2 Plates, 5s.—Vol. XIV., Part 2, pp. 164. with 1 Table, 7s. 6d.—Vol. XIV., Part 3, pp. 206, with 6 Plates, 8s.—Vol. XIV., Part 4, pp. 492, with 1 Plate, 14s.—Vol. XV., Part 1, pp. 136, 6s.

ASPLET.—The Complete French Course. Part II. Containing all the Rules of French Syntax, &c., &c. By Georges C. Asplet, French Master, Frome. Fcap. 8vo, pp. xx. and 276, cloth. 1880. 2s. 6d.

ASTON.—A Short Grammar of the Japanese Spoken Language. By W. G. Aston, M.A. Third Edition. Crown 8vo, pp. 96, cloth. 1873. 12s.

ASTON.—A Grammar of the Japanese Written Language. By W. G. Aston, M.A., Assistant Japanese Secretary H.B.M.'s Legation, Yedo, Japan. Second Edition. 8vo, pp. 306, cloth. 1877. 28s.

ASTONISHED AT AMERICA Being Cursory Deductions, &c., &c. By Zigzag. Fcap. 8vo, pp. xvi.–108, boards. 1880. 1s.

AUCTORES SANSCRITI.
Vol. I. The Jaiminíya-Nyáya-Málá-Vistara. Edited for the Sanskrit Text Society, under the supervision of Theodor Goldstücker. Large 4to, pp. 582, cloth. £3. 13s. 6d.
Vol. II. The Institutes of Gautama. Edited, with an Index of Words, by A. F. Stenzler, Ph.D., Prof. of Oriental Languages in the University of Breslau. 8vo. pp. iv. and 78, cloth. 1876. 4s. 6d. Stitched, 3s. 6d.
Vol. III. Vaitána Sútra : The Ritual of the Atharva Veda. Edited, with Critical Notes and Indices, by Dr. R. Garbe. 8vo, pp. viii. and 120, sewed. 1878. 5s.
Vols. IV. and V.—Vardhamana's Ganaratnamahodadhi, with the Author's Commentary. Edited, with Critical Notes and Indices, by Julius Eggeling, Ph.D. 8vo. Part I., pp. xii. and 240, wrapper. 1879. 6s. Part II., pp. 240, wrapper. 1881. 6s.

AUGIER.—Diane. A Drama in Verse. By Émile Augier. Edited with English Notes and Notice on Augier. By Theodore Karcher, LL.B., of the Royal Military Academy and the University of London. 12mo, pp. xiii. and 146, cloth. 1867. 2s. 6d.

AUSTIN.—A Practical Treatise on the Preparation, Combination, and Application of Calcareous and Hydraulic Limes and Cements. To which is added many useful Recipes for various Scientific, Mercantile, and Domestic Purposes. By James G. Austin, Architect. 12mo, pp. 192, cloth. 1862. 5s.

AXON.—The Mechanic's Friend. A collection of Receipts and Practical Suggestions relating to Aquaria, Bronzing, Cements, Drawing, Dyes, Electricity, Gilding, Glass-working, &c. Numerous Woodcuts. Edited by W. E. A. Axon, M.R.S.I., F.S.S. Crown 8vo, pp. xii. and 339, cloth. 1875. 4s. 6d.

BABA.—An Elementary Grammar of the Japanese Language, with easy progressive Exercises. By Tatui Baba. Crown 8vo, pp. xiv. and 92, cloth. 1873. 5s.

BACON.—The Life and Times of Francis Bacon. Extracted from the Edition of his Occasional Writings by James Spedding. 2 vols. post 8vo, pp. xx., 710, and xiv., 708, cloth. 1878. 21s.

BADEN-POWELL —PROTECTION AND BAD TIMES, with Special Reference to the Political Economy of English Colonisation. By George Baden-Powell, M.A., F.R.A.S., F.S.S., Author of "New Homes for the Old Country," &c., &c. 8vo, pp. xii.-376, cloth. 1879. 6s. 6d.

BADER.—THE NATURAL AND MORBID CHANGES OF THE HUMAN EYE, AND THEIR TREATMENT. By C. Bader. Medium 8vo, pp. viii. and 506, cloth. 1868. 16s.

BADER.—PLATES ILLUSTRATING THE NATURAL AND MORBID CHANGES OF THE HUMAN EYE. By C. Bader. Six chromo-lithographic Plates, each containing the figures of six Eyes, and four lithographed Plates, with figures of Instruments. With an Explanatory Text of 32 pages. Medium 8vo, in a portfolio. 21s. Price for Text and Atlas taken together, £1, 12s.

BADLEY.—INDIAN MISSIONARY RECORD AND MEMORIAL VOLUME. By the Rev. B. H. Badley, of the American Methodist Mission. 8vo, pp. xii. and 280, cloth. 1876. 10s. 6d.

BALFOUR.—WAIFS AND STRAYS FROM THE FAR EAST; being a Series of Disconnected Essays on Matters relating to China. By Frederick Henry Balfour. 1 vol. demy 8vo, pp. 224, cloth. 1876. 10s. 6d.

BALFOUR.—THE DIVINE CLASSIC OF NAN-HUA; being the Works of Chuang Tsze, Taoist Philosopher. With an Excursus, and Copious Annotations in English and Chinese. By F. H Balfour, F.R.G.S , Author of "Waifs and Strays from the Far East," &c. Demy 8vo, pp. xlviii. and 426, cloth. 1881. 14s.

BALL.—THE DIAMONDS, COAL, AND GOLD OF INDIA; their Mode of Occurrence and Distribution. By V. Ball, M.A., F.G.S., of the Geological Survey of India. Fcap. 8vo, pp. viii. and 136, cloth. 1881. 5s.

BALL.—A MANUAL OF THE GEOLOGY OF INDIA. Part III. Economic Geology. By V. Ball, M.A., F.G.S. Royal 8vo, pp. xx. and 640, with 6 Maps and 10 Plates, cloth. 1881. 10s. (For Parts I. and II. see MEDLICOTT.)

BALLAD SOCIETY—Subscriptions, small paper, one guinea; large paper, two guineas per annum. List of publications on application.

BALLANTYNE.—ELEMENTS OF HINDI AND BRAJ BHAKHA GRAMMAR. Compiled for the use of the East India College at Haileybury. By James R. Ballantyne. Second Edition. Crown 8vo, pp. 38, cloth. 1868. 5s.

BALLANTYNE.—FIRST LESSONS IN SANSKRIT GRAMMAR; together with an Introduction to the Hitopadeśa. New Edition. By James R. Ballantyne, LL.D., Librarian of the India Office. 8vo, pp. viii. and 110, cloth. 1873. 3s. 6d.

BARANOWSKI.—VADE MECUM DE LA LANGUE FRANÇAISE, rédigé d'après les Dictionnaires classiques avec les Exemples de Bonnes Locutions que donne l'Académie Française, on qu'on trouve dans les ouvrages des plus célèbres auteurs. Par J. J. Baranowski, avec l'approbation de M. E. Littré, Sénateur, &c. 32mo, pp. 224. 1879. Cloth, 2s. 6d. ; morocco, 3s. 6d. ; morocco tuck, 4s.

BARENTS' RELICS.—Recovered in the summer of 1876 by Charles L. W. Gardiner, Esq., and presented to the Dutch Government. Described and explained by J. K. J. de Jonge, Deputy Royal Architect at the Hague. Published by command of His Excellency, W. F. Van F.R.P. Taelman Kip, Minister of Marine. Translated, with a Preface, by S R. Van Campen. With a Map, Illustrations, and a fac-simile of the Scroll. 8vo, pp. 70, cloth. 1877. 5s.

BARRIERE and CAPENDU.— LES FAUX BONSHOMMES, a Comedy. By Théodore Barrière and Ernest Capendu. Edited, with English Notes and Notice on Barrière, by Professor Ch. Cassal, LL.D., of University College, London. 12mo, pp. xvi. and 304, cloth. 1868. 4s.

BARTH.— THE RELIGIONS OF INDIA. See Trübner's Oriental Series.

BARTLETT.— DICTIONARY OF AMERICANISMS. A Glossary of Words and Phrases colloquially used in the United States. By John Russell Bartlett. Fourth Edition, considerably enlarged and improved. 8vo, pp. xlvi. and 814, cloth. 1877. 20s.

BATTYE.— WHAT IS VITAL FORCE? or, a Short and Comprehensive Sketch, including Vital Physics, Animal Morphology, and Epidemics; to which is added an Appendix upon Geology, IS THE DENTRITAL THEORY OF GEOLOGY TENABLE? By Richard Fawcett Battye. 8vo, pp. iv. and 336, cloth. 1877. 7s. 6d.

BAZLEY. NOTES ON THE EPICYCLOIDAL CUTTING FRAME of Messrs. Holtzapffel & Co. With special reference to its Compensation Adjustment, and with numerous Illustrations of its Capabilities. By Thomas Sebastian Bazley, M.A. 8vo pp vi and 192 cloth. Illustrated. 1872. 10s. 6d.

BAZLEY.— THE STARS IN THEIR COURSES: A Twofold Series of Maps, with a Catalogue, showing how to identify, at any time of the year, all stars down to the 5.6 magnitude, inclusive of Heis, which are clearly visible in English latitudes. By T. S Bazley, M.A., Author of "Notes on the Epicycloidal Cutting Frame." Atlas folio, pp. 46 and 24, Folding Plates, cloth. 1878. 15s.

BEAL.— TRAVELS OF FAH-HIAN AND SUNG-YUN, Buddhist Pilgrims, from China to India (400 A.D. and 518 A.D.) Translated from the Chinese. By Samuel Beal, B.A., Trin. Coll., Cam., &c. Crown 8vo, pp. lxxiii. and 210, with a coloured Map, cloth, ornamental. 1869. 10s. 6d.

BEAL.— A CATENA OF BUDDHIST SCRIPTURES FROM THE CHINESE. By S. Beal, B.A., Trinity College, Cambridge; a Chaplain in Her Majesty's Fleet, &c. 8vo, pp. xiv. and 436, cloth. 1871. 15s.

BEAL.— THE ROMANTIC LEGEND OF SAKYA BUDDHA. From the Chinese-Sanskrit. By the Rev. Samuel Beal. Crown 8vo., pp. 408, cloth. 1875. 12s.

BEAL.— DHAMMAPADA. See Trübner's Oriental Series.

BEAL.— BUDDHIST LITERATURE IN CHINA : Abstract of Four Lectures, Delivered by Samuel Beal, B.A., Professor of Chinese at University College, London. Demy 8vo, pp. xx. and 186, cloth. 1882. 10s. 6d.

BEAMES.— OUTLINES OF INDIAN PHILOLOGY. With a Map showing the Distribution of Indian Languages. By John Beames, M.R.A.S., Bengal Civil Service, Member of the Asiatic Society of Bengal, the Philological Society of London, and the Société Asiatique of Paris. Second enlarged and revised Edition. Crown 8vo, pp. viii. and 96, cloth. 1868. 5s.

BEAMES.— A COMPARATIVE GRAMMAR OF THE MODERN ARYAN LANGUAGES OF INDIA, to wit, Hindi, Panjabi, Sindhi, Gujarati, Marathi, Oriya, and Bengali. By John Beames, Bengal Civil Service, M R.A.S., &c., &c. Demy 8vo. Vol. I. On Sounds. Pp. xvi. and 360, cloth. 1872. 16s.—Vol. II. The Noun and the Pronoun. Pp. xii. and 348, cloth. 1875. 16s.—Vol. III. The Verb. Pp. xii. and 316, cloth. 1879. 16s.

BELLEW.— FROM THE INDUS TO THE TIGRIS. A Narrative of a Journey through the Countries of Balochistan, Afghanistan, Khorassan, and Iran in 1872; together with a complete Synoptical Grammar and Vocabulary of the Brahoe Language, and a Record of the Meteorological Observations and Altitudes on the March from the Indus to the Tigris. By Henry Walter Bellew, C.S.I., Surgeon, Bengal Staff Corps. Demy 8vo, pp. viii. and 496, cloth. 1874. 14s.

BELLEW.— KASHMIR AND KASHGHAR : a Narrative of the Journey of the Embassy to Kashghar in 1873-74. By H. W. Bellew, C.S.I. Demy 8vo, pp. xxxii. and 420, cloth. 1875. 16s.

BELLEW.—THE RACES OF AFGHANISTAN. Being a Brief Account of the Principal Nations Inhabiting that Country. By Surgeon-Major H. W. Bellew, C.S.I., late on Special Political Duty at Kabul. 8vo, pp. 124, cloth. 1880. 7s. 6d.

BELLOWS.—ENGLISH OUTLINE VOCABULARY for the use of Students of the Chinese, Japanese, and other Languages. Arranged by John Bellows. With Notes on the Writing of Chinese with Roman Letters, by Professor Summers, King's College, London. Crown 8vo, pp. vi. and 368, cloth. 1867. 6s.

BELLOWS.—OUTLINE DICTIONARY FOR THE USE OF MISSIONARIES, EXPLORERS, AND STUDENTS OF LANGUAGE. By Max Müller, M.A., Taylorian Professor in the University of Oxford. With an Introduction on the proper use of the ordinary English Alphabet in transcribing Foreign Languages. The Vocabulary compiled by John Bellows. Crown 8vo, pp. xxxi. and 368, limp morocco. 1867. 7s. 6d.

BELLOWS.—TOUS LES VERBES. Conjugations of all the Verbs in the French and English Languages. By John Bellows. Revised by Professor Beljame, B.A., LL.B., of the University of Paris, and Official Interpreter to the Imperial Court, and George B. Strickland, late Assistant French Master, Royal Naval School, London. Also a New Table of Equivalent Values of French and English Money, Weights, and Measures. 32mo, 76 Tables, sewed. 1867. 1s.

BELLOWS.—FRENCH AND ENGLISH DICTIONARY FOR THE POCKET. By John Bellows. Containing the French-English and English-French divisions on the same page ; conjugating all the verbs ; distinguishing the genders by different types; giving numerous aids to pronunciation ; indicating the *liaison* or *non-liaison* of terminal consonants ; and translating units of weight, measure, and value, by a series of tables differing entirely from any hitherto published. The new edition, which is but six ounces in weight, has been remodelled, and contains many thousands of additional words and renderings. Miniature maps of France, the British Isles, Paris, and London, are added to the Geographical Section. Second Edition. 32mo, pp. 608, roan tuck, or persian without tuck. 1877. 10s. 6d. ; morocco tuck, 12s. 6d.

BENEDIX.—DER VETTER. Comedy in Three Acts. By Roderich Benedix. With Grammatical and Explanatory Notes by F. Weinmann, German Master at the Royal Institution School, Liverpool, and G. Zimmermann, Teacher of Modern Languages. 12mo, pp. 128, cloth. 1863. 2s. 6d.

BENFEY.—A PRACTICAL GRAMMAR OF THE SANSKRIT LANGUAGE, for the use of Early Students. By Theodor Benfey, Professor of Sanskrit in the University of Göttingen. Second, revised, and enlarged Edition. Royal 8vo, pp. viii. and 296, cloth. 1868. 10s. 6d.

BENTHAM.—THEORY OF LEGISLATION. By Jeremy Bentham. Translated from the French of Etienne Dumont by R. Hildreth. Fourth Edition. Post 8vo, pp. xv. and 472, cloth. 1882. 7s. 6d.

BETTS.—See VALDES.

BEVERIDGE.—THE DISTRICT OF BAKARGANJ. Its History and Statistics. By H. Beveridge, B.C.S., Magistrate and Collector of Bakarganj. 8vo, pp. xx. and 460, cloth. 1876. 21s.

BICKNELL.—See HAFIZ.

BIERBAUM.—HISTORY OF THE ENGLISH LANGUAGE AND LITERATURE.—By F. J. Bierbaum, Ph.D. Crown 8vo, pp. viii. and 270, cloth. 1883. 3s.

BIGANDET. THE LIFE OF GAUDAMA. See Trübner's Oriental Series.

BIRCH.—Fasti Monastici Aevi Saxonici ; or, An Alphabetical List of the Heads of Religious Houses in England previous to the Norman Conquest, to which is prefixed a Chronological Catalogue of Contemporary Foundations. By Walter de Gray Birch. 8vo, pp. vii. and 114, cloth. 1873. 5s.

BIRD.—Physiological Essays. Drink Craving, Differences in Men, Idiosyncrasy, and the Origin of Disease. By Robert Bird, M.D. demy 8vo, pp. 246, cloth. 1870. 7s. 6d.

BLACK.—Young Japan, Yokohama and Yedo. A Narrative of the Settlement and the City, from the Signing of the Treaties in 1858 to the Close of the Year 1879; with a Glance at the Progress of Japan during a Period of Twenty-one Years. By John R. Black, formerly Editor of the "Japan Herald" and the "Japan Gazette." Editor of the "Far East." 2 vols. demy 8vo, pp. xviii. and 418 ; xiv. and 522, cloth. 1881. £2, 2s.

BLADES.—Shakspere and Typography. Being an Attempt to show Shakspere's Personal Connection with, and Technical Knowledge of, the Art of Printing ; also Remarks upon some common Typographical Errors, with especial reference to the Text of Shakspere. By William Blades. 8vo, pp. viii. and 78, with an Illustration, cloth. 1872. 3s.

BLADES.—The Biography and Typography of William Caxton, England's First Printer. By William Blades. Founded to a great extent upon the Author's "Life and Typography of William Caxton." Brought up to the Present Date, and including all Discoveries since made. Elegantly and appropriately printed in demy 8vo, on hand-made paper, imitation old bevelled binding. 1877. £1, 1s. Cheap Edition. Crown 8vo, cloth. 1881. 5s.

BLADES.—The Enemies of Books. By William Blades, Typograph. Crown 8vo, pp. xvi. and 112, parchment wrapper. 1880. 5s.

BLAKEY.—Memoirs of Dr. Robert Blakey, Professor of Logic and Metaphysics, Queen's College, Belfast, Author of "Historical Sketch of Moral Science," &c., &c. Edited by the Rev. Henry Miller, of St. Andrews (Presbyterian Church of England), Hammersmith. Crown 8vo, pp. and 252, cloth. 1879. 5s.

BLEEK.—Reynard the Fox in South Africa ; or, Hottentot Fables and Tales, chiefly Translated from Original Manuscripts in the Library of His Excellency Sir George Grey, K.C.B. By W. H. I. Bleek, Ph.D. Post 8vo, pp. xxvi. and 94, cloth. 1864. 3s. 6d.

BLEEK.—A Brief Account of Bushman Folk Lore, and other Texts. By W. H. I. Bleek, Ph.D. Folio, pp. 21, paper. 2s. 6d.

BOEHMER.—Spanish Reformers of Two Centuries, from 1520, their Lives and Writings. Described by E. Boehmer, D.D., Ph.D. Vol. i. royal 8vo, pp. 232, cloth. 1874. 12s. 6d. Roxburghe, 15s.

BOEHMER.—*See* Valdes.

BOJESEN.—A Guide to the Danish Language. Designed for English Students. By Mrs. Maria Bojesen. 12mo, pp. 250, cloth. 1863. 5s.

BOLIA.—The German Caligraphist : Copies for German Handwriting. By C. Bolia. Oblong 4to, sewed. 1s.

BOOLE.—Message of Psychic Science to Mothers and Nurses. By Mary Boole. Crown 8vo, pp. xiv and 266, cloth. 1883. 5s.

BOY ENGINEERS.—See under Lukin.

BOYD.—Nágánanda ; or, the Joy of the Snake World. A Buddhist Drama in Five Acts. Translated into English Prose, with Explanatory Notes, from the Sanskrit of Sá-Harsha-Deva. By Palmer Boyd, B.A., Sanskrit Scholar of Trinity College, Cambridge. With an Introduction by Professor Cowell. Crown 8vo, pp. xvi. and 100, cloth. 1872. 4s. 6d.

BRAMSEN.—Japanese Chronological Tables, showing the Date, according to the Julian or Gregorian Calendar, of the First Day of each Japanese Month. From Tai-Kwa, 1st year, to Mei-ji, 6th year (645 A.D. to 1873 A.D.). With an Introductory Essay on "Japanese Chronology and Calendars. By W. Bramsen. Oblong fcap. 4to, pp. 50 84, cloth. 1880. 14s.

BRAMSEN—The Coins of Japan. By W. Bramsen. Part I. The Copper, Lead, and Iron Coins issued by the Central Government. 4to, pp. 10, with Plates of 74 Coins, boards. 1880. 5s.

BRAMSEN.—Japanese Weights, with their Equivalents in French and English Weights. Compiled by W. Bramsen. Fcap. folio sheet. 1877. 1s.

BRAMSEN.—Japanese Lineal Measures, with their Equivalents in French and English Measures. Compiled by W. Bramsen. Fcap. folio sheet. 1877. 1s.

BRENTANO.—On the History and Development of Gilds, and the Origin of Trade-Unions. By Lujo Brentano, of Aschaffenburg, Bavaria, Doctor Juris Utriusque et Philosophiæ. 1. The Origin of Gilds. 2. Religious (or Social) Gilds. 3. Town-Gilds or Gild-Merchants. 4. Craft-Gilds. 5. Trade-Unions. 8vo, pp. xvi. and 136, cloth. 1870. 3s. 6d.

BRETSCHNEIDER.—Early European Researches into the Flora of China. By E. Bretschneider, M.D., Physician of the Russian Legation at Peking. Demy 8vo, pp. iv. and 194, sewed. 1881. 7s. 6d.

BRETSCHNEIDER.—Botanicon Sinicum. Notes on Chinese Botany, from Native and Western Sources. By E. Bretschneider, M.D. Crown 8vo, pp. 228, wrapper. 1882. 10s. 6d.

BRETTE.—French Examination Papers set at the University of London from 1839 to 1871. Arranged and edited by the Rev. P. H. Ernest Brette, B.D. Crown 8vo, pp. viii. and 278, cloth. 3s. 6d.; interleaved, 4s. 6d.

BRITISH MUSEUM.—List of Publications of the Trustees of the British Museum, on application.

BROWN.—The Dervishes; or, Oriental Spiritualism. By John P. Brown, Secretary and Dragoman of the Legation of the United States of America at Constantinople. Crown 8vo, pp. viii. and 416, cloth, with 24 Illustrations. 1868. 14s.

BROWN.—Sanskrit Prosody and Numerical Symbols Explained. By Charles Philip Brown, M.R.A.S., Author of a Telugu Dictionary, Grammar, &c., Professor of Telugu in the University of London. 8vo, pp. viii. and 56, cloth. 1869. 3s. 6d.

BROWNE.—How to use the Ophthalmoscope; being Elementary Instruction in Ophthalmoscopy. Arranged for the use of Students. By Edgar A. Browne, Surgeon to the Liverpool Eye and Ear Infirmary, &c. Crown 8vo, pp. xi. and 108, with 35 Figures, cloth. 1876. 3s. 6d.

BROWNE.—A Bángáli Primer, in Roman Character. By J. F. Browne, B.C.S. Crown 8vo, pp. 32, cloth. 1881. 2s.

BROWNE.—A Hindi Primer in Roman Character. By J. F. Browne, B.C.S. Crown 8vo, pp. 36, cloth. 1882. 2s. 6d.

BROWNE.—An Uriyá Primer in Roman Character. By J. F. Browne, B.C.S. Crown 8vo, pp. 32, cloth. 1882. 2s. 6d.

BROWNING SOCIETY'S PAPERS.—Demy 8vo, wrappers. 1881-84. Part I., pp. 116. 10s. Bibliography of Robert Browning from 1833-81. Part II., pp. 142. 10s. Part III., pp. 168. 10s.

BRUNNOW.—*See* Schieffel.

BRUNTON.—Map of Japan. See under Japan.

BUDGE.— Archaic Classics. Assyrian Texts ; being Extracts from the Annals of Shalmaneser II., Sennacherib, and Assur-Bani-Pal. With Philological Notes. By Ernest A. Budge, B.A., M.R.A.S., Assyrian Exhibitioner, Christ's College, Cambridge. Small 4to, pp. viii. and 44, cloth. 1880. 7s. 6d.

BUDGE.—History of Esarhaddon. See Trübner's Oriental Series.

BUNYAN.—Scenes from the Pilgrim's Progress. By. R. B. Rutter. 4to, pp. 142, boards, leather back. 1882. 5s.

BURGESS : —

Archæological Survey of Western India :—

Report of the First Season's Operations in the Belgâm and Kaladi Districts, January to May 1874. By James Burgess, F.R.G.S. With 56 Photographs and Lithographic Plates. Royal 4to, pp. viii. and 45 ; half bound. 1875. £2, 2s.

Report on the Antiquities of Kâthiâwâd and Kachh, being the result of the Second Season's Operations of the Archæological Survey of Western India, 1874-75. By James Burgess, F.R.G.S. Royal 4to, pp. x. and 242, with 74 Plates ; half bound. 1876. £3, 3s.

Report on the Antiquities in the Bidar and Aurangabad Districts, in the Territories of His Highness the Nizam of Haiderabad, being the result of the Third Season's Operations of the Archæological Survey of Western India, 1875-76. By James Burgess, F.R.G.S., M.R.A.S., Archæological Surveyor and Reporter to Government, Western India. Royal 4to, pp. viii. and 138, with 63 Photographic Plates ; half bound. 1878. £2, 2s.

Report on the Buddhist Cave Temples and their Inscriptions ; containing Views, Plans, Sections, and Elevation of Façades of Cave Temples ; Drawings of Architectural and Mythological Sculptures ; Facsimiles of Inscriptions, &c. ; with Descriptive and Explanatory Text, and Translations of Inscriptions, &c., &c. By } 2 Vols. 1883. £6, 6s.
James Burgess, LL.D., F.R.G.S., &c. Royal 4to, pp. x. and 140, with 86 Plates and Woodcuts ; half-bound.

Report on Elura Cave Temples, and the Brahmanical and Jaina Caves in Western India. By James Burgess, LL.D, F.R.G.S., &c. Royal 4to, pp. viii. and 90, with 66 Plates and Woodcuts ; half-bound.

BURMA.—The British Burma Gazetteer. Compiled by Major H. R. Spearman, under the direction of the Government of India. 2 vols. 8vo, pp. 764 and 878, with 11 Photographs, cloth. 1880. £2, 10s.

BURNELL.—Elements of South Indian Palæography, from the Fourth to the Seventeenth Century A.D., being an Introduction to the Study of South Indian Inscriptions and MSS. By A. C. Burnell. Second enlarged and improved Edition. 4to, pp. xiv. and 148, Map and 35 Plates, cloth. 1878. £2, 12s. 6d.

BURNELL.—A Classified Index to the Sanskrit MSS. in the Palace at Tanjore. Prepared for the Madras Government. By A. C. Burnell, Ph.D., &c., &c. 4to, stiff wrapper. Part I., pp. iv.-80, Vedic and Technical Literature. Part II., pp iv.-80, Philosophy and Law. Part III., Drama, Epics, Purânas, and Tantras ; Indices. 1879. 10s. each.

BURNEY.—The Boys' Manual of Seamanship and Gunnery, compiled for the use of the Training-Ships of the Royal Navy. By Commander C. Burney, R.N., F.R.G.S., Superintendent of Greenwich Hospital School. Seventh Edition. Approved by the Lords Commissioners of the Admiralty to be used in the Training-Ships of the Royal Navy. Crown 8vo, pp. xxii. and 352, with numerous Illustrations, cloth. 1879. 6s.

BURNEY.—The Young Seaman's Manual and Rigger's Guide. By Commander C. Burney, R.N., F.R.G.S. Sixth Edition. Revised and corrected. Approved by the Lords Commissioners of the Admiralty. Crown 8vo, pp. xxxviii. and 592, cloth. With 200 Illustrations and 16 Sheets of Signals. 1878. 7s. 6d.

BURTON.—Captain Richard F. Burton's Handbook for Overland Expeditions; being an English Edition of the "Prairie Traveller," a Handbook for Overland Expeditions. With Illustrations and Itineraries of the Principal Routes between the Mississippi and the Pacific, and a Map. By Captain Randolph B Marcy (now General and Chief of the Staff, Army of the Potomac). Edited, with Notes, by Captain Richard F. Burton. Crown 8vo, pp. 270, numerous Woodcuts, Itineraries, and Map, cloth. 1863. 6s. 6d.

BUTLER.—The Spanish Teacher and Colloquial Phrase-Book. An easy and agreeable method of acquiring a Speaking Knowledge of the Spanish Language. By Francis Butler. Fcap. 8vo, pp. xviii. and 240, half-roan. 2s. 6d.

BUTLER.—Hungarian Poems and Fables for English Readers. Selected and Translated by E. D. Butler, of the British Museum; with Illustrations by A. G. Butler. Foolscap, pp. vi. and 88, limp cloth. 1877. 2s.

BUTLER.—The Legend of the Wondrous Hunt. By John Arany. With a few Miscellaneous Pieces and Folk-Songs. Translated from the Magyar by E. D. Butler, F.R.G.S. Crown 8vo, pp. viii. and 70. Limp cloth. 2s. 6d.

CAITHNESS.—Serious Letters to Serious Friends. By the Countess of Caithness, Authoress of "Old Truths in a New Light." Crown 8vo, pp. viii. and 352, cloth. 1877. 7s. 6d.

CAITHNESS.—Lectures on Popular and Scientific Subjects. By the Earl of Caithness, F.R.S. Delivered at various times and places. Second enlarged Edition. Crown 8vo, pp. 174, cloth. 1879. 2s. 6d.

CALCUTTA REVIEW.—Selections from Nos. I.–XVII. 5s. each.

CALDER.—The Coming Era. By Alexander Calder, Officer of the Legion of Honour, and Author of "The Man of the Future." 8vo, pp. 422, cloth. 1879. 10s. 6d.

CALDWELL.—A Comparative Grammar of the Dravidian or South Indian Family of Languages. By the Rev. R. Caldwell, LL.D. A second, corrected, and enlarged Edition. Demy 8vo, pp. 804, cloth. 1875. 28s.

CALENDARS OF STATE PAPERS. List on application.

CALL.—Reverberations. Revised. With a chapter from My Autobiography. By W. M. W. Call, M.A., Cambridge, Author of "Lyra Hellenica" and "Golden Histories." Crown 8vo, pp. viii. and 200, cloth. 1875. 4s. 6d.

CALLAWAY.—Nursery Tales, Traditions, and Histories of the Zulus. In their own words, with a Translation into English, and Notes. By the Rev. Canon Callaway, M.D. Vol. I., 8vo, pp. xiv. and 378, cloth. 1868. 16s.

CALLAWAY.—The Religious System of the Amazulu.

Part I.—Unkulunkulu; or, The Tradition of Creation as existing among the Amazulu and other Tribes of South Africa, in their own words, with a Translation into English, and Notes. By the Rev. Canon Callaway, M.D. 8vo, pp. 128, sewed. 1868. 4s.

Part II.—Amatongo; or, Ancestor-Worship as existing among the Amazulu, in their own words, with a Translation into English, and Notes. By the Rev. Canon Callaway, M.D. 8vo, pp. 127, sewed. 1869. 4s.

Part III.—Izinyanga Zokubula; or, Divination, as existing among the Amazulu, in their own words, with a Translation into English, and Notes. By the Rev. Canon Callaway, M.D. 8vo, pp. 150, sewed. 1870. 4s.

Part IV.—On Medical Magic and Witchcraft. 8vo, pp. 40, sewed, 1s. 6d.

CAMERINI.—L'Eco Italiano ; a Practical Guide to Italian Conversation. By E. Camerini. With a Vocabulary. 12mo, pp. 98, cloth. 1860. 4s. 6d.

CAMPBELL.—The Gospel of the World's Divine Order. By Douglas Campbell. New Edition. Revised. Crown 8vo, pp. viii. and 364, cloth. 1877. 4s. 6d.

CANDID Examination of Theism. By Physicus. Post 8vo, pp. xviii. and 198, cloth. 1878. 7s. 6d.

CANTICUM CANTICORUM, reproduced in facsimile, from the Scriverius copy in the British Museum. With an Historical and Bibliographical Introduction by I. Ph. Berjean. Folio, pp. 36, with 16 Tables of Illustrations, vellum. 1860. £2, 2s.

CAREY.—The Past, the Present, and the Future. By H. C. Carey. Second Edition. 8vo, pp. 474, cloth. 1856. 10s. 6d.

CARLETTI.—History of the Conquest of Tunis. Translated by J. T. Carletti. Crown 8vo, pp. 40, cloth. 1883. 2s. 6d.

CARNEGY.—Notes on the Land Tenures and Revenue Assessments of Upper India. By P. Carnegy. Crown 8vo, pp. viii. and 136, and forms, cloth. 1874. 6s.

CATHERINE II., Memoirs of the Empress. Written by herself. With a Preface by A. Herzen. Trans. from the French. 12mo, pp. xvi. and 352, bds. 1859. 7s. 6d.

CATLIN.—O-Kee-Pa. A Religious Ceremony ; and other Customs of the Mandans. By George Catlin. With 13 coloured Illustrations. Small 4to, pp. vi. and 52, cloth. 1867. 14s.

CATLIN.—The Lifted and Subsided Rocks of America, with their Influence on the Oceanic, Atmospheric, and Land Currents, and the Distribution of Races. By George Catlin. With 2 Maps. Cr. 8vo, pp. xii. and 238, cloth. 1870. 6s. 6d.

CATLIN.—Shut your Mouth and Save your Life. By George Catlin, Author of "Notes of Travels amongst the North American Indians," &c., &c. With 29 Illustrations from Drawings by the Author. Eighth Edition, considerably enlarged. Crown 8vo, pp. 106, cloth. 1882. 2s. 6d.

CAXTON.—The Biography and Typography of. See Blades.

CAXTON CELEBRATION, 1877.—Catalogue of the Loan Collection of Antiquities, Curiosities, and Appliances Connected with the Art of Printing. Edited by G. Bullen, F.S.A. Post 8vo, pp. xx. and 472, cloth, 3s. 6d.

CAZELLES.—Outline of the Evolution Philosophy. By Dr. W. E. Cazelles. Translated from the French by the Rev. O. B. Frothingham. Crown 8vo, pp. 156, cloth. 1875. 3s. 6d.

CESNOLA.—Salaminia (Cyprus). The History, Treasures, and Antiquities of Salamis in the Island of Cyprus. By A. Palma di Cesnola, F.S.A., &c. With an Introduction by S. Birch, Esq., D.C.L., LL.D., Keeper of the Egyptian and Oriental Antiquities in the British Museum. Royal 8vo, pp. xlviii. and 325, with upwards of 700 Illustrations and Map of Ancient Cyprus, cloth. 1882. 31s. 6d.

CHALMERS.—The Speculations on Metaphysics, Polity, and Morality of "The Old Philosopher," Lau-tsze. Translated from the Chinese, with an Introduction by John Chalmers, M.A. Fcap. 8vo, pp. xx. and 62, cloth. 1868. 4s. 6d.

CHALMERS.—Structure of Chinese Characters, under 300 Primary Forms ; after the Shwoh-wan, 100 A.D., and the Phonetic Shwoh-wan, 1833. By J. Chalmers, M.A., LL.D., A.B. Demy 8vo, pp. x. and 200, with two plates, limp cloth. 1882. 12s. 6d.

CHAMBERLAIN.—The Classical Poetry of the Japanese. By Basil Hall Chamberlain, Author of "Yeigo Henkaku, Ichiran." Post 8vo, pp. xii. and 228, cloth. 1880. 7s. 6d.

CHAPMAN.—CHLOROFORM AND OTHER ANÆSTHETICS : Their History and Use during Childbirth. By John Chapman, M.D. 8vo, pp. 51, sewed. 1859. 1s.

CHAPMAN.—DIARRHŒA AND CHOLERA : Their Nature, Origin, and Treatment through the Agency of the Nervous System. By John Chapman, M.D., M.R.C.P., M.R.C.S. 8vo, pp. xix. and 248, cloth. 7s. 6d.

CHAPMAN.—MEDICAL CHARITY : its Abuses, and how to Remedy them. By John Chapman, M.D. 8vo, pp. viii. and 108, cloth. 1874. 2s. 6d.

CHAPMAN.—SEA-SICKNESS, AND HOW TO PREVENT IT. An Explanation of its Nature and Successful Treatment, through the Agency of the Nervous System, by means of the Spinal Ice Bag ; with an Introduction on the General Principles of Neuro-Therapeutics. By John Chapman, M.D., M.R.C.P., M.R.C.S. Second Edition. 8vo, pp. viii. and 112, cloth. 1868. 3s.

CHAPTERS ON CHRISTIAN CATHOLICITY. By a Clergyman. 8vo, pp. 282, cloth. 1878. 5s.

CHARNOCK.—A GLOSSARY OF THE ESSEX DIALECT. By Richard Stephen Charnock, Ph.D., F.S.A. Fcap., pp. xii. and 64, cloth. 1880. 3s. 6d.

CHARNOCK.—PRŒNOMINA ; or, The Etymology of the Principal Christian Names of Great Britain and Ireland. By R. S. Charnock, Ph.D., F.S.A. Crown 8vo. pp. xvi. and 128, cloth. 1882. 6s.

CHATTOPADHYAYA.—THE YATRÁS ; or, The Popular Dramas of Bengal. By N. Chattopadhyaya. Post 8vo, pp. 50, wrapper. 1882. 2s.

CHAUCER SOCIETY.—Subscription, two guineas per annum. List of Publications on application.

CHILDERS.—A PALI-ENGLISH DICTIONARY, with Sanskrit Equivalents, and with numerous Quotations, Extracts, and References. Compiled by Robert Cæsar Childers, late of the Ceylon Civil Service. Imperial 8vo, double columns, pp. 648, cloth. 1875. £3, 3s.

CHILDERS.—THE MAHAPARINIBBANASUTTA OF THE SUTTA PITAKA. The Pali Text. Edited by the late Professor R. C. Childers. 8vo, pp. 72, limp cloth. 1878. 5s.

CHINTAMON.—A COMMENTARY ON THE TEXT OF THE BHAGAVAD-GITÁ ; or, the Discourse between Khrishna and Arjuna of Divine Matters. A Sanskrit Philosophical Poem. With a few Introductory Papers. By Hurrychund Chintamon, Political Agent to H. H. the Guicowar Mulhar Rao Maharajah of Baroda. Post 8vo, pp. 118, cloth. 1874. 6s.

CHRONICLES AND MEMORIALS OF GREAT BRITAIN AND IRELAND DURING THE MIDDLE AGES. List on application.

CLARK.—MEGHADUTA, THE CLOUD MESSENGER. Poem of Kalidasa. Translated by the late Rev. T. Clark, M.A. Fcap. 8vo, pp. 64, wrapper. 1882. 1s.

CLARK.—A FORECAST OF THE RELIGION OF THE FUTURE. Being Short Essays on some important Questions in Religious Philosophy. By W. W. Clark. Post 8vo, pp. xii. and 238, cloth. 1879. 3s. 6d.

CLARKE.—THE EARLY HISTORY OF THE MEDITERRANEAN POPULATIONS, &c., in their Migrations and Settlements. Illustrated from Autonomous Coins, Gems, Inscriptions, &c. By Hyde Clarke. 8vo, pp. 80, cloth. 1882. 5s.

CLAUSEWITZ.—ON WAR. By General Carl von Clausewitz. Translated by Colonel J. J. Graham, from the third German Edition. Three volumes complete in one. Fcap 4to, double columns, pp. xx. and 564, with Portrait of the author, cloth. 1873. £1, 1s.

CLEMENT AND HUTTON.—Artists of the Nineteenth Century and their Works. A Handbook containing Two Thousand and Fifty Biographical Sketches. By Clara Erskine Clement and Lawrence Hutton. 2 vols. crown 8vo, pp. lxxxvii. 386 and 44, and lvii. 374 and 44, cloth. 1879. 21s.

COLEBROOKE.—The Life and Miscellaneous Essays of Henry Thomas Colebrooke. The Biography by his Son, Sir T. E. Colebrooke, Bart., M.P. 3 vols. Vol. I. The Life. Demy 8vo, pp. xii. and 492, with Portrait and Map, cloth. 1873. 14s. Vols. II. and III. The Essays. A new Edition, with Notes by E. B. Cowell, Professor of Sanskrit in the University of Cambridge. Demy 8vo, pp. xvi. and 544, and x. and 520, cloth. 1873. 28s.

COLENSO.—Natal Sermons. A Series of Discourses Preached in the Cathedral Church of St Peter's, Maritzburg. By the Right Rev. John William Colenso, D.D., Bishop of Natal. 8vo, pp. viii. and 373, cloth. 1866. 7s. 6d. The Second Series. Crown 8vo, cloth. 1868. 5s.

COLLINS.—A Grammar and Lexicon of the Hebrew Language, Entitled Sefer Hassoham. By Rabbi Mosch Ben Yitshak, of England. Edited from a MS. in the Bodleian Library of Oxford, and collated with a MS. in the Imperial Library of St. Petersburg, with Additions and Corrections, by G. W. Collins, M.A. Demy 4to, pp. viii. and 20, wrapper. 1882. 3s.

COLYMBIA.—Crown 8vo, pp. 260, cloth. 1873. 5s.
"The book is amusing as well as clever."—*Athenæum.* "Many exceedingly humorous passages"—*Public Opinion.* "Deserves to be read."—*Scotsman.* "Neatly done."—*Graphic.* "Very amusing."—*Examiner.*

COMTE.—A General View of Positivism. By Auguste Comte. Translated by Dr. J. H. Bridges. 12mo, pp. xi. and 426, cloth. 1865. 8s. 6d.

COMTE.—The Catechism of Positive Religion : Translated from the French of Auguste Comte. By Richard Congreve. 18mo, pp. 428, cloth. 1858. 6s. 6d.

COMTE.—The Eight Circulars of Auguste Comte. Translated from the French, under the auspices of R. Congreve. Fcap. 8vo, pp. iv. and, 90 cloth. 1882. 1s. 6d.

COMTE.—The Positive Philosophy of Auguste Comte. Translated and condensed by Harriet Martineau. 2 vols. Second Edition. 8vo, cloth. Vol. I., pp. xxiv. and 400 ; Vol. II., pp. xiv. and 468. 1875. 25s.

CONGREVE.—The Roman Empire of the West. Four Lectures delivered at the Philosophical Institution, Edinburgh, February 1855, by Richard Congreve, M.A. 8vo, pp. 176, cloth. 1855. 4s.

CONGREVE.—Elizabeth of England. Two Lectures delivered at the Philosophical Institution, Edinburgh, January 1862. By Richard Congreve. 18mo, pp. 114, sewed. 1862. 2s. 6d.

CONTOPOULOS.—A Lexicon of Modern Greek-English and English Modern Greek. By N. Contopoulos. Part I. Modern Greek-English. Part II. English Modern Greek. 8vo, pp. 460 and 582, cloth. 1877. 27s.

CONWAY.—The Sacred Anthology : A Book of Ethnical Scriptures. Collected and Edited by Moncure D. Conway. Fifth Edition. Demy 8vo, pp. viii. and 480, cloth. 1876. 12s.

CONWAY.—Idols and Ideals. With an Essay on Christianity. By Moncure D. Conway, M.A., Author of "The Eastern Pilgrimage," &c. Crown 8vo, pp. 352, cloth. 1877. 5s.

CONWAY.—EMERSON AT HOME AND ABROAD. See English and Foreign Philosophical Library.

CONWAY.—TRAVELS IN SOUTH KENSINGTON. By M. D. Conway. Illustrated. 8vo, pp. 234, cloth. 1882. 12s.

CONTENTS.—The South Kensington Museum—Decorative Art and Architecture in England—Bedford Park.

COOMARA SWAMY.—THE DATHAVANSA; or, The History of the Tooth Relic of Gotama Buddha, in Pali verse. Edited, with an English Translation, by Mutu Coomara Swamy, F.R.A.S. Demy 8vo, pp. 174, cloth. 1874. 10s. 6d. English Translation. With Notes. pp. 100. 6s.

COOMARA SWAMY.—SUTTA NIPATA; or, Dialogues and Discourses of Gotama Buddha (2500 years old). Translated from the original Pali. With Notes and Introduction. By Mutu Coomara Swamy, F.R.A.S. Crown 8vo, pp. xxxvi. and 160, cloth. 1874. 6s.

CORNELIA. A Novel. Post 8vo, pp. 250, boards. 1863. 1s. 6d.

COTTA.—GEOLOGY AND HISTORY. A popular Exposition of all that is known of the Earth and its Inhabitants in Pre-historic Times. By Bernhard Von Cotta, Professor of Geology at the Academy of Mining, Freiberg, in Saxony. 12mo, pp. iv. and 84, cloth. 1865. 2s.

COUSIN.—THE PHILOSOPHY OF KANT. Lectures by Victor Cousin. Translated from the French. To which is added a Biographical and Critical Sketch of Kant's Life and Writings. By A. G. Henderson. Large post 8vo, pp. xciv. and 194, cloth. 1864. 6s.

COUSIN.—ELEMENTS OF PSYCHOLOGY: included in a Critical Examination of Locke's Essay on the Human Understanding, and in additional pieces. Translated from the French of Victor Cousin, with an Introduction and Notes. By Caleb S. Henry, D.D. Fourth improved Edition, revised according to the Author's last corrections. Crown 8vo, pp. 568, cloth. 1871. 8s.

COWELL.—PRAKRITA-PRAKASA; or, The Prakrit Grammar of Vararuchi, with the Commentary (Manorama) of Bhamaha; the first complete Edition of the Original Text, with various Readings from a collection of Six MSS. in the Bodleian Library at Oxford, and the Libraries of the Royal Asiatic Society and the East India House; with Copious Notes, an English Translation, and Index of Prakrit Words, to which is prefixed an Easy Introduction to Prakrit Grammar. By Edward Byles Cowell, of Magdalen Hall, Oxford, Professor of Sanskrit at Cambridge. New Edition, with New Preface, Additions, and Corrections. Second Issue. 8vo, pp. xxxi. and 204, cloth. 1868. 14s.

COWELL.—A SHORT INTRODUCTION TO THE ORDINARY PRAKRIT OF THE SANSKRIT DRAMAS. With a List of Common Irregular Prákrit Words. By E. B. Cowell, Professor of Sanskrit in the University of Cambridge, and Hon. LL.D. of the University of Edinburgh. Crown 8vo, pp. 40, limp cloth. 1875. 3s. 6d.

COWELL.—THE SARVADARSANA SAMGRAHA. See Trübner's Oriental Series.

COWLEY.—POEMS. By Percy Tunnicliff Cowley. Demy 8vo, pp. 104, cloth. 1881. 5s.

CRAIG.—THE IRISH LAND LABOUR QUESTION, Illustrated in the History of Ralahine and Co-operative Farming. By E. T. Craig. Crown 8vo, pp. xii. and 202, cloth. 1882. 2s. 6d. Wrappers, 2s.

CRANBROOK.—CREDIBILIA; or, Discourses on Questions of Christian Faith. By the Rev. James Cranbrook, Edinburgh. Reissue. Post 8vo, pp. iv. and 190, cloth. 1868. 3s. 6d.

CRANBROOK.—THE FOUNDERS OF CHRISTIANITY; or, Discourses upon the Origin of the Christian Religion. By the Rev. James Cranbrook, Edinburgh. Post 8vo, pp. xii. and 324. 1868. 6s.

CRAVEN.—THE POPULAR DICTIONARY IN ENGLISH AND HINDUSTANI, AND HINDUSTANI AND ENGLISH. With a Number of Useful Tables. Compiled by the Rev. T. Craven, M.A. 18mo, pp. 430, cloth. 1881. 3s. 6d.

CRAWFORD.—RECOLLECTIONS OF TRAVEL IN NEW ZEALAND AND AUSTRALIA. By James Coutts Crawford, F.G.S., Resident Magistrate, Wellington, &c., &c. With Maps and Illustrations. 8vo, pp. xvi. and 468, cloth. 1880. 18s.

CROSLAND.—APPARITIONS; An Essay explanatory of Old Facts and a New Theory. To which are added Sketches and Adventures. By Newton Crosland. Crown 8vo, pp. viii. and 166, cloth. 1873. 2s. 6d.

CROSLAND.—PITH: ESSAYS AND SKETCHES GRAVE AND GAY, with some Verses and Illustrations. By Newton Crosland. Crown 8vo, pp. 310, cloth. 1881. 5s.

CUBAS.—THE REPUBLIC OF MEXICO IN 1876. A Political and Ethnographical Division of the Population, Character, Habits, Costumes, and Vocations of its Inhabitants. Written in Spanish by A. G. Cubas. Translated into English by G. E. Henderson. Illustrated with Plates of the Principal Types of the Ethnographic Families, and several Specimens of Popular Music. 8vo, pp. 130, cloth. 1881. 5s.

CUMMINS.—A GRAMMAR OF THE OLD FRIESIC LANGUAGE. By A. H. Cummins, A.M. Crown 8vo, pp. x. and 76, cloth. 1881. 3s. 6d.

CUNNINGHAM.—THE ANCIENT GEOGRAPHY OF INDIA. I. The Buddhist Period, including the Campaigns of Alexander and the Travels of Hwen-Thsang. By Alexander Cunningham, Major-General, Royal Engineers (Bengal Retired). With 13 Maps. 8vo, pp. xx. and 590, cloth. 1870. £1, 8s.

CUNNINGHAM.—THE STUPA OF BHARHUT: A Buddhist Monument ornamented with numerous Sculptures illustrative of Buddhist Legend and History in the Third Century B.C. By Alexander Cunningham, C.S.I., C.I.E., Maj.-Gen., R.E. (B.R.), Dir.-Gen. Archæol. Survey of India. Royal 8vo, pp. viii. and 144, with 57 Plates, cloth. 1879. £3, 3s.

CUNNINGHAM.—ARCHÆOLOGICAL SURVEY OF INDIA, Reports from 1862-79. By A. Cunningham, C.S.I., C.I.E., Major-General, R.E. (Bengal Retired), Director-General, Archæological Survey of India. With numerous Plates, cloth, Vols. I.-XII. 10s. each. (Except Vols. VII., VIII., and IX., and also Vols. XIII. and XIV., which are 12s. each.)

CUSHMAN.—CHARLOTTE CUSHMAN: Her Letters and Memories of her Life. Edited by her friend, Emma Stebbins. Square 8vo, pp. viii. and 308, cloth. With Portrait and Illustrations. 1879. 12s. 6d.

CUST.—LANGUAGES OF THE EAST INDIES. See Trübner's Oriental Series.

CUST.—LINGUISTIC AND ORIENTAL ESSAYS. See Trübner's Oriental Series.

CUST.—PICTURES OF INDIAN LIFE, Sketched with the Pen from 1852 to 1881. By R. N. Cust, late I.C.S., Hon. Sec. Royal Asiatic Society. Crown 8vo, pp. x. and 346, cloth. With Maps. 1881. 7s. 6d.

DANA.—A TEXT-BOOK OF GEOLOGY, designed for Schools and Academies. By James D. Dana, LL.D., Professor of Geology, &c., at Yale College. Illustrated. Crown 8vo, pp. vi. and 354, cloth. 1876. 10s.

DANA.—MANUAL OF GEOLOGY, treating of the Principles of the Science, with special Reference to American Geological History; for the use of Colleges, Academies, and Schools of Science. By James D. Dana, LL.D. Illustrated by a Chart of the World, and over One Thousand Figures. 8vo, pp. xvi. and 800, and Chart, cl. 21s.

DANA.—THE GEOLOGICAL STORY BRIEFLY TOLD. An Introduction to Geology for the General Reader and for Beginners in the Science. By J. D. Dana, LL.D. Illustrated. 12mo, pp. xii. and 264, cloth. 7s. 6d.

DANA.—A SYSTEM OF MINERALOGY. Descriptive Mineralogy, comprising the most Recent Discoveries. By J. D. Dana, aided by G. J. Brush. Fifth Edition, rewritten and enlarged, and illustrated with upwards of 600 Woodcuts, with two Appendixes and Corrections. Royal 8vo, pp. xlviii. and 892, cloth. £2, 2s.

DANA.—A TEXT BOOK OF MINERALOGY. With an Extended Treatise on Crystallography and Physical Mineralogy. By E. S. Dana, on the Plan and with the Co-operation of Professor J. D. Dana. Third Edition, revised. Over 800 Woodcuts and 1 Coloured Plate. 8vo, pp. viii. and 486, cloth. 1879. 18s.

DANA.—MANUAL OF MINERALOGY AND LITHOLOGY; Containing the Elements of the Science of Minerals and Rocks, for the Use of the Practical Mineralogist and Geologist, and for Instruction in Schools and Colleges. By J. D. Dana. Fourth Edition, rearranged and rewritten. Illustrated by numerous Woodcuts. Crown 8vo, pp. viii. and 474, cloth. 1882. 7s. 6d.

DATES AND DATA RELATING TO RELIGIOUS ANTHROPOLOGY AND BIBLICAL ARCHÆOLOGY. (Primæval Period.) 8vo, pp. viii. and 106, cloth. 1876. 5s.

DAUDET.—LETTERS FROM MY MILL. From the French of Alphonse Daudet, by Mary Corey. Fcap. 8vo, pp. 160. 1880. Cloth, 3s.; boards, 2s.

DAVIDS.—BUDDHIST BIRTH STORIES. See Trübner's Oriental Series.

DAVIES.—HINDU PHILOSOPHY. 2 vols. See Trübner's Oriental Series.

DAVIS.—NARRATIVE OF THE NORTH POLAR EXPEDITION, U.S. SHIP *Polaris*, Captain Charles Francis Hall Commanding. Edited under the direction of the Hon. G. M. Robeson, Secretary of the Navy, by Rear-Admiral C. H. Davis, U.S.N. Third Edition. With numerous Steel and Wood Engravings, Photolithographs, and Maps. 4to, pp. 696, cloth. 1881. £1, 8s.

DAY.—THE PREHISTORIC USE OF IRON AND STEEL; with Observations on certain matter ancillary thereto. By St. John V. Day, C.E., F.R.S.E., &c. 8vo, pp. xxiv. and 278, cloth. 1877. 12s.

DE FLANDRE.—MONOGRAMS OF THREE OR MORE LETTERS, DESIGNED AND DRAWN ON STONE. By C. De Flandre, F.S.A. Scot., Edinburgh. With Indices, showing the place and style or period of every Monogram, and of each individual Letter. 4to, 42 Plates, cloth. 1880. Large paper, £7, 7s.; small paper, £3, 3s.

DELEPIERRE.—HISTOIRE LITTERAIRE DES FOUS. Par Octave Delepierre. Crown 8vo, pp. 184, cloth. 1860. 5s.

DELEPIERRE.—MACARONEANA ANDRA; overum Nouveaux Mélanges de Litterature Macaronique. Par Octave Delepierre. Small 4to, pp. 180, printed by Whittingham, and handsomely bound in the Roxburghe style. 1862. 10s. 6d.

DELEPIERRE.—ANALYSE DES TRAVAUX DE LA SOCIETE DES PHILOBIBLON DE LONDRES. Par Octave Delepierre. Small 4to, pp. viii. and 134, bound in the Roxburghe style. 1862. 10s. 6d.

B

DELEPIERRE. —Revue Analytique des Ouvrages Écrits en Centons, depuis les Temps Anciens, jusqu'au xix.ème Siècle. Par un Bibliophile Belge. Small 4to, pp. 508, stiff covers. 1868. £1, 10s.

DELEPIERRE. —Tableau de la Littérature du Centon, chez les Anciens et chez les Modernes. Par Octave Delepierre. 2 vols, small 4to, pp. 324 and 318. Paper cover. 1875. £1, 1s.

DELEPIERRE. —L'Enfer : Essai Philosophique et Historique sur les Légendes de la Vie Future. Par Octave Delepierre. Crown 8vo, pp. 160, paper wrapper. 1876. 6s. Only 250 copies printed.

DENNYS. —A Handbook of the Canton Vernacular of the Chinese Language. Being a Series of Introductory Lessons for Domestic and Business Purposes. By N. B. Dennys, M.R.A.S., &c. Royal 8vo, pp. iv. and 228, cloth. 1874. 30s.

DENNYS. —A Handbook of Malay Colloquial, as spoken in Singapore, being a Series of Introductory Lessons for Domestic and Business Purposes. By N. B. Dennys, Ph.D., F.R.G.S., M.R.A.S. Impl. 8vo, pp. vi. and 204, cloth. 1878. 21s.

DENNYS. —The Folk-Lore of China, and its Affinities with that of the Aryan and Semitic Races. By N. B. Dennys, Ph.D., F.R.G.S., M.R.A.S. 8vo, pp. 166, cloth. 1876. 10s. 6d.

DE VALDES. —See Valdes.

DE VERE. —Studies in English : or, Glimpses of the Inner Life of our Language. By M. Schele de Vere, LL.D. 8vo, pp. vi. and 365, cloth. 1867. 10s. 6d.

DE VERE. —Americanisms : The English of the New World. By M. Schele de Vere, LL.D. 8vo, pp. 685, cloth. 1872. 20s.

DE VINNE. —The Invention of Printing : A Collection of Texts and Opinions. Description of Early Prints and Playing Cards, the Block-Books of the Fifteenth Century, the Legend of Lourens Janszoon Coster of Haarlem, and the Works of John Gutenberg and his Associates. Illustrated with Fac-similes of Early Types and Woodcuts. By Theo. L. De Vinne. Second Edition. In royal 8vo, elegantly printed, and bound in cloth, with embossed portraits, and a multitude of Fac-similes and Illustrations. 1877. £1, 1s.

DEWEY. —Classification and Subject Index for cataloguing and arranging the books and pamphlets of a Library. By Melvil Dewey. 8vo, pp. 42, boards. 1876. 5s.

DICKSON. —Who was Scotland's first Printer? Ane Compendious and breue Tractate, in Commendation of Andrew Myllar. Compylit be Robert Dickson, F.S.A. Scot. Fcap. 8vo, pp. 24, parchment wrapper. 1881. 1s.

DOBSON. —Monograph of the Asiatic Chiroptera, and Catalogue of the Species of Bats in the Collection of the Indian Museum, Calcutta. By G. E. Dobson, M.A., M.B., F.L.S., &c. 8vo, pp. viii. and 228, cloth. 1876. 12s.

D'ORSEY. —A Practical Grammar of Portuguese and English, exhibiting in a Series of Exercises, in Double Translation, the Idiomatic Structure of both Languages, as now written and spoken. Adapted to Ollendorff's System by the Rev. Alexander J. D. D'Orsey, of Corpus Christi College, Cambridge, and Lecturer on Public Reading and Speaking at King's College, London. Third Edition. 12mo, pp. viii. and 298, cloth. 1868. 7s.

D'ORSEY.—COLLOQUIAL PORTUGUESE; or, Words and Phrases of Every-day Life. Compiled from Dictation and Conversation. For the Use of English Tourists in Portugal, Brazil, Madeira, &c. By the Rev. A. J. D. D'Orsey. Third Edition, enlarged. 12mo, pp. viii. and 126, cloth. 1868. 3s. 6d.

DOUGLAS.—CHINESE-ENGLISH DICTIONARY OF THE VERNACULAR OR SPOKEN LANGUAGE OF AMOY, with the principal variations of the Chang-Chew and Chin-Chew Dialects. By the Rev. Carstairs Douglas, M.A., LL.D., Glasg., Missionary of the Presbyterian Church in England. High quarto, double columns, pp. 632, cloth. 1873. £3, 3s.

DOUGLAS.—CHINESE LANGUAGE AND LITERATURE. Two Lectures delivered at the Royal Institution, by R. K. Douglas, of the British Museum, and Professor of Chinese at King's College. Crown 8vo, pp. 118, cloth. 1875. 5s.

DOUGLAS.—THE LIFE OF JENGHIZ KHAN. Translated from the Chinese. With an Introduction. By Robert K. Douglas, of the British Museum, and Professor of Chinese at King's College. Crown 8vo, pp. xxxvi. and 106, cloth. 1877. 5s.

DOUSE.—GRIMM'S LAW. A Study; or, Hints towards an Explanation of the so-called "Lautverschiebung;" to which are added some Remarks on the Primitive Indo-European K, and several Appendices. By T. Le Marchant Douse. 8vo, pp. xvi. and 232, cloth. 1876. 10s. 6d.

DOWSON.—DICTIONARY OF HINDU MYTHOLOGY, &c. See Trübner's Oriental Series.

DOWSON.—A GRAMMAR OF THE URDŪ OR HINDŪSTĀNĪ LANGUAGE. By John Dowson, M.R.A.S., Professor of Hindūstānī, Staff College, Sandhurst. Crown 8vo, pp. xvi. and 264, with 8 Plates, cloth. 1872. 10s. 6d.

DOWSON.—A HINDŪSTĀNĪ EXERCISE BOOK; containing a Series of Passages and Extracts adapted for Translation into Hindūstānī. By John Dowson, M.R.A.S., Professor of Hindūstānī, Staff College, Sandhurst. Crown 8vo, pp. 100, limp cloth. 1872. 2s. 6d.

DUNCAN.—GEOGRAPHY OF INDIA, comprising a Descriptive Outline of all India, and a Detailed Geographical, Commercial, Social, and Political Account of each of its Provinces. With Historical Notes. By George Duncan. Tenth Edition (Revised and Corrected to date from the latest Official Information). 18mo, pp. viii. and 182, limp cloth. 1880. 1s. 6d.

DUSAR.—A GRAMMAR OF THE GERMAN LANGUAGE; with Exercises. By P. Friedrich Dusar, First German Master in the Military Department of Cheltenham College. Second Edition. Crown 8vo, pp. viii. and 208, cloth. 1879. 4s. 6d.

EARLY ENGLISH TEXT SOCIETY.—Subscription, one guinea per annum. *Extra Series.* Subscriptions—Small paper, one guinea; large paper, two guineas, per annum. List of publications on application.

EASTWICK.—KHIRAD AFROZ (the Illuminator of the Understanding). By Maulaví Hafízu'd-dín. A New Edition of the Hindūstānī Text, carefully revised. with Notes, Critical and Explanatory. By Edward B. Eastwick, F.R.S., F.S.A., M.R.A.S., Professor of Hindūstānī at Haileybury College. Imperial 8vo, pp. xiv. and 319, cloth. Reissue, 1867. 18s.

EASTWICK.—THE GULISTAN. See Trübner's Oriental Series.

ECHO (DEUTSCHES). THE GERMAN ECHO. A Faithful Mirror of German Conversation. By Ludwig Wolfram. With a Vocabulary. By Henry P. Skelton. Post 8vo, pp. 130 and 70, cloth. 1863. 3s.

ECHO FRANÇAIS. A Practical Guide to Conversation. By Fr. de la Fruston. With a complete Vocabulary. By Anthony Maw Border. Post 8vo, pp. 120 and 72, cloth. 1860. 3s.

ECO ITALIANO (L'). A Practical Guide to Italian Conversation. By Eugene Camerlui. With a complete Vocabulary. By Henry P. Skelton. Post 8vo, pp. vi., 128, and 98, cloth. 1860. 4s. 6d.

ECO DE MADRID. The Echo of Madrid. A Practical Guide to Spanish Conversation. By J. E. Hartzenbusch and Henry Lemming. With a complete Vocabulary, containing copious Explanatory Remarks. By Henry Lemming. Post 8vo, pp. xii., 144, and 83, cloth. 1860. 5s.

EDDA Sæmundar Hinns Froda. The Edda of Sæmund the Learned. Translated from the Old Norse, by Benjamin Thorpe. Complete in 1 vol. fcap. 8vo, pp. viii. and 152, and pp. viii. and 170, cloth. 1866. 7s. 6d.

EDKINS.—China's Place in Philology. An attempt to show that the Languages of Europe and Asia have a common origin. By the Rev. Joseph Edkins. Crown 8vo, pp. xxiii. and 403, cloth. 1871. 10s. 6d.

EDKINS.—Introduction to the Study of the Chinese Characters. By J. Edkins, D.D., Peking, China. Royal 8vo, pp. 340, paper boards. 1876. 18s.

EDKINS.— Religion in China. See English and Foreign Philosophical Library, Vol. XIII.

EDKINS.—Chinese Buddhism. See Trübner's Oriental Series.

EDWARDS.—Memoirs of Libraries, together with a Practical Handbook of Library Economy. By Edward Edwards. Numerous Illustrations. 2 vols. royal 8vo, cloth. Vol. i. pp. xxviii. and 841 ; Vol. ii. pp. xxxvi. and 1104. 1859. £2, 8s. Ditto, large paper, imperial 8vo, cloth. £4, 4s.

EDWARDS.—Chapters of the Biographical History of the French Academy. 1629-1863. With an Appendix relating to the Unpublished Chronicle " Liber de Hyda." By Edward Edwards. 8vo, pp. 180, cloth. 1864. 6s. Ditto, large paper, royal 8vo. 10s. 6d.

EDWARDS.—Libraries and Founders of Libraries. By Edward Edwards. 8vo. pp. xix. and 506, cloth. 1865. 18s. Ditto, large paper, imperial 8vo, cloth. £1, 10s.

EDWARDS.—Free Town Libraries, their Formation, Management, and History in Britain, France, Germany, and America. Together with Brief Notices of Book Collectors, and of the respective Places of Deposit of their Surviving Collections. By Edward Edwards. 8vo, pp. xvi. and 634, cloth. 1869. 21s.

EDWARDS.—Lives of the Founders of the British Museum, with Notices of its Chief Augmentors and other Benefactors. 1570-1870. By Edward Edwards. With Illustrations and Plans. 2 vols. 8vo, pp. xii. and 780, cloth. 1870. 30s.

EDWARDES.—See English and Foreign Philosophical Library, Vol. XVII.

EGER AND GRIME.—An Early English Romance. Edited from Bishop Percy's Folio Manuscripts, about 1650 A.D. By John W. Hales, M.A., Fellow and late Assistant Tutor of Christ's College, Cambridge, and Frederick J. Furnivall, M.A., of Trinity Hall, Cambridge. 4to, large paper, half bound, Roxburghe style, pp. 64. 1867. 10s. 6d.

EGGELING.—See Auctores Sanskriti, Vols. IV. and V.

EGYPTIAN GENERAL STAFF PUBLICATIONS :—

PROVINCES OF THE EQUATOR: Summary of Letters and Reports of the Governor-General. Part I. 1874. Royal 8vo, pp. viii. and 90, stitched, with Map. 1877. 5s.

GENERAL REPORT ON THE PROVINCE OF KORDOFAN. Submitted to General C. P. Stone, Chief of the General Staff Egyptian Army. By Major H. G. Prout, Corps of Enginers, Commanding Expedition of Reconnaissance. Made at El-Obeiyad (Kordofan), March 12th, 1876. Royal 8vo, pp. 232, stitched, with 6 Maps. 1877. 10s. 6d.

REPORT ON THE SEIZURE BY THE ABYSSINIANS of the Geological and Mineralogical Reconnaissance Expedition attached to the General Staff of the Egyptian Army. By L. H. Mitchell, Chief of the Expedition. Containing an Account of the subsequent Treatment of the Prisoners and Final Release of the Commander. Royal 8vo, pp. xii. and 126, stitched, with a Map. 1878. 7s. 6d.

EGYPTIAN CALENDAR for the year 1295 A.H. (1878 A.D.) : Corresponding with the years 1594, 1595 of the Koptic Era. 8vo, pp. 98, sewed. 1878. 2s. 6d.

EHRLICH.—FRENCH READER : With Notes and Vocabulary. By H. W. Ehrlich. 12mo, pp. viii. and 125, limp cloth. 1877. 1s. 6d.

EITEL.—BUDDHISM : Its Historical, Theoretical, and Popular Aspects. In Three Lectures. By E. J. Eitel, M.A., Ph.D. Second Edition. Demy 8vo, pp. 130. 1873. 5s.

EITEL.—FENG-SHUI ; or, The Rudiments of Natural Science in China. By E. J. Eitel, M.A., Ph.D. Royal 8vo, pp. vi. and 84, sewed. 1873. 6s.

EITEL.— HANDBOOK FOR THE STUDENT OF CHINESE BUDDHISM. By the Rev. E. J. Eitel, of the London Missionary Society. Crown 8vo, pp. viii. and 224, cloth. 1870. 18s.

ELLIOT.—MEMOIRS ON THE HISTORY, FOLK-LORE, AND DISTRIBUTION OF THE RACES OF THE NORTH-WESTERN PROVINCES OF INDIA. By the late Sir Henry M. Elliot, K.C.B. Edited, revised, and rearranged by John Beames, M.R.A.S., &c., &c. In 2 vols. demy 8vo, pp. xx., 370, and 396, with 3 large coloured folding Maps, cloth. 1869. £1, 16s.

ELLIOT.—THE HISTORY OF INDIA, as told by its own Historians. The Muhammadan Period. Edited from the Posthumous Papers of the late Sir H. M. Elliot, K.C.B., East India Company's Bengal Civil Service. Revised and continued by Professor John Dowson, M.R.A.S., Staff College, Sandhurst. 8vo. Vol. I. o.p.—Vol. II., pp. x. and 580, cloth. 18s.—Vol. III., pp. xii. and 627, cloth. 24s.—Vol. IV., pp. xii. and 564, cloth. 1872. 21s.— Vol. V., pp. x. and 576, cloth. 1873. 21s.—Vol. VI., pp. viii. 574, cloth. 21s.—Vol. VII., pp. viii.-574. 1877. 21s. Vol. VIII., pp. xxxii.-444. With Biographical, Geographical, and General Index. 1877. 24s.

ELLIS.—ETRUSCAN NUMERALS. By Robert Ellis, B.D., late Fellow of St. John's College, Cambridge. 8vo, pp. 52, sewed. 1876. 2s. 6d.

ENGLISH DIALECT SOCIETY.—Subscription, 10s. 6d. per annum. List of publications on application.

ENGLISH AND FOREIGN PHILOSOPHICAL LIBRARY (THE).

Post 8vo, cloth, uniformly bound.

I. to III.—A HISTORY OF MATERIALISM, and Criticism of its present Importance. By Professor F. A. Lange. Authorised Translation from the German by Ernest C. Thomas. In three volumes. Vol. I. Second Edition, pp. 350. 1878. 10s. 6d.—Vol. II., pp. viii. and 298. 1880. 10s. 6d. —Vol. III., pp. viii. and 376. 1881. 10s. 6d.

ENGLISH AND FOREIGN PHILOSOPHICAL LIBRARY—*continued.*

IV.—NATURAL LAW: an Essay in Ethics. By Edith Simcox. Second Edition. Pp. 366. 1878. 10s. 6d.

V. and VI.—THE CREED OF CHRISTENDOM; its Foundations contrasted with Superstructure. By W. R. Greg. Eighth Edition, with a New Introduction. In two volumes, pp. 280 and 290. 1883. 15s.

VII.—OUTLINES OF THE HISTORY OF RELIGION TO THE SPREAD OF THE UNIVERSAL RELIGIONS. By Prof. C. P. Tiele. Translated from the Dutch by J. Estlin Carpenter, M.A., with the author's assistance. Second Edition. Pp. xx. and 250. 1880. 7s. 6d.

VIII.—RELIGION IN CHINA; containing a brief Account of the Three Religions of the Chinese; with Observations on the Prospects of Christian Conversion amongst that People. By Joseph Edkins, D.D., Peking. Second Edition. Pp. xvi. and 260. 1878. 7s. 6d.

IX.—A CANDID EXAMINATION OF THEISM. By Physicus. Pp. 216. 1878. 7s. 6d.

X.—THE COLOUR-SENSE; its Origin and Development; an Essay in Comparative Psychology. By Grant Allen, B.A., author of "Physiological Æsthetics." Pp. xii. and 282. 1879. 10s. 6d

XI.—THE PHILOSOPHY OF MUSIC; being the substance of a Course of Lectures delivered at the Royal Institution of Great Britain in February and March 1877. By William Pole, F.R.S., F.R.S.E., Mus. Doc., Oxon. Pp. 336. 1879. 10s. 6d.

XII.—CONTRIBUTIONS TO THE HISTORY OF THE DEVELOPMENT OF THE HUMAN RACE: Lectures and Dissertations, by Lazarus Geiger. Translated from the Second German Edition, by David Asher, Ph.D. Pp. x. and 156. 1880. 6s.

XIII.—DR. APPLETON: his Life and Literary Relics. By J. H. Appleton, M.A., and A. H. Sayce, M.A. Pp. 350. 1881. 10s. 6d.

XIV.—EDGAR QUINET: His Early Life and Writings. By Richard Heath. With Portraits, Illustrations, and an Autograph Letter. Pp. xxiii. and 370. 1881. 12s. 6d.

XV.—THE ESSENCE OF CHRISTIANITY. By Ludwig Feuerbach. Translated from the Second German Edition by Marian Evans, translator of Strauss's "Life of Jesus." Second English Edition. Pp. xx. and 340. 1881. 7s. 6d.

XVI.—AUGUSTE COMTE AND POSITIVISM. By the late John Stuart Mill, M.P. Third Edition. Pp. 200. 1882. 3s. 6d.

XVII.—ESSAYS AND DIALOGUES OF GIACOMO LEOPARDI. Translated by Charles Edwardes. With Biographical Sketch. Pp. xliv. and 216. 1882. 7s. 6d.

XVIII.—RELIGION AND PHILOSOPHY IN GERMANY: A Fragment. By Heinrich Heine. Translated by J. Snodgrass. Pp. xii. and 178, cloth. 1882. 6s.

XIX.—EMERSON AT HOME AND ABROAD. By M. D. Conway. Pp. viii. and 310. With Portrait. 1883. 10s. 6d.

XX.—ENIGMAS OF LIFE. By W. R. Greg. Fifteenth Edition, with a Postscript. CONTENTS: Realisable Ideals—Malthus Notwithstanding—Non-Survival of the Fittest—Limits and Directions of Human Development—The Significance of Life—De Profundis—Elsewhere—Appendix. Pp. xx. and 314, cloth. 1883. 10s. 6d.

Extra Series.

I. and II.—LESSING: His Life and Writings. By James Sime, M.A. Second Edition. 2 vols., pp. xxii. and 328, and xvi. and 358, with portraits. 1879. 21s.

ENGLISH AND FOREIGN PHILOSOPHICAL LIBRARY—*continued.*

    III.—AN ACCOUNT OF THE POLYNESIAN RACE: its Origin and Migrations, and the Ancient History of the Hawaiian People to the Times of Kamehameha I. By Abraham Fornander, Circuit Judge of the Island of Maui, H.I. Vol. I., pp. xvi. and 248. 1877. 7s. 6d.

    IV. and V.—ORIENTAL RELIGIONS, and their Relation to Universal Religion—India. By Samuel Johnson. In 2 vols., pp. viii. and 408; viii. and 402. 1879. 21s.

    VI.—AN ACCOUNT OF THE POLYNESIAN RACE: its Origin and Migration, and the Ancient History of the Hawaiian People to the Times of Kamehameha I. By Abraham Fornander, Circuit Judge of the Island of Maui, H.I. Vol. II., pp. viii. and 400, cloth. 1880. 10s. 6d.

ETHERINGTON.—THE STUDENT'S GRAMMAR OF THE HINDI LANGUAGE. By the Rev. W. Etherington, Missionary, Benares. Second Edition. Crown 8vo, pp. xiv., 255, and xiii., cloth. 1873. 12s.

EYTON.—DOMESDAY STUDIES : AN ANALYSIS AND DIGEST OF THE STAFFORDSHIRE SURVEY. Treating of the Method of Domesday in its Relation to Staffordshire, &c., with Tables, Notes, &c. By the Rev. Robert W. Eyton, late Rector of Ryton, Salop. 4to, pp. vii. and 135, cloth. 1881. £1, 1s.

FABER.—THE MIND OF MENCIUS. See Trübner's Oriental Series.

FALKE.—ART IN THE HOUSE. Historical, Critical, and Æsthetical Studies on the Decoration and Furnishing of the Dwelling. By Jacob von Falke. Vice-Director of the Austrian Museum of Art and Industry at Vienna. Translated from the German. Edited, with Notes, by Charles C. Perkins, M.A. Royal 8vo, pp. xxx. 356, cloth. With Coloured Frontispiece, 60 Plates, and over 150 Illustrations in the Text. 1878. £3.

FARLEY.—EGYPT, CYPRUS, AND ASIATIC TURKEY. By J. Lewis Farley, author of "The Resources of Turkey," &c. 8vo, pp. xvi. and 270, cloth gilt. 1878. 10s. 6d.

FEATHERMAN.—THE SOCIAL HISTORY OF THE RACES OF MANKIND. Vol. V. THE ARAMÆANS. By A. Featherman. Demy 8vo, pp. xvii. and 664, cloth. 1881. £1, 1s.

FENTON.—EARLY HEBREW LIFE: a Study in Sociology. By John Fenton. 8vo, pp. xxiv. and 102, cloth. 1880. 5s.

FERGUSON AND BURGESS.—THE CAVE TEMPLES OF INDIA. By James Ferguson, D.C.L., F.R.S., and James Burgess, F.R.G.S. Impl. 8vo, pp. xx. and 536, with 98 Plates, half bound. 1880. £2, 2s.

FERGUSSON.—CHINESE RESEARCHES. First Part. Chinese Chronology and Cycles. By Thomas Fergusson, Member of the North China Branch of the Royal Asiatic Society. Crown 8vo, pp. viii. and 274, sewed. 1881. 10s. 6d.

FEUERBACH.—THE ESSENCE OF CHRISTIANITY. By Ludwig Feuerbach. Translated from the Second German Edition by Marian Evans, translator of Strauss's "Life of Jesus." Second English Edition. Post 8vo, pp. xx. and 340, cloth. 1881. 7s. 6d.

FICHTE.—J. G. FICHTE'S POPULAR WORKS : The Nature of the Scholar—The Vocation of Man—The Doctrine of Religion. With a Memoir by William Smith, LL.D. Demy 8vo, pp. viii. and 564, cloth. 1873. 15s.

FICHTE.—THE CHARACTERISTICS OF THE PRESENT AGE. By Johann Gottlieb Fichte. Translated from the German by William Smith. Post 8vo, pp. xi. and 271, cloth. 1847. 6s.

FICHTE.—Memoir of Johann Gottlieb Fichte. By William Smith. Second Edition. Post 8vo, pp. 168, cloth. 1848. 4s.

FICHTE.—On the Nature of the Scholar, and its Manifestations. By Johann Gottlieb Fichte. Translated from the German by William Smith. Second Edition. Post 8vo, pp. vii. and 131, cloth. 1848. 3s.

FICHTE. The Science of Knowledge. By J. G. Fichte. Translated from the German by A. E. Kroeger. Crown 8vo, pp. 378, cloth. 1868. 10s.

FICHTE. The Science of Rights. By J. G. Fichte. Translated from the German by A. E. Kroeger. Crown 8vo, pp. 506, cloth. 1869. 10s.

FICHTE.—New Exposition of the Science of Knowledge. By J. G. Fichte. Translated from the German by A. E. Kroeger. 8vo, pp. vi. and 182, cloth. 1869. 6s.

FIELD.—Outlines of an International Code. By David Dudley Field. Second Edition. Royal 8vo, pp. iii. and 712, sheep. 1876. £2, 2s.

FIGANIERE. Elva : A Story of the Dark Ages. By Viscount de Figanière, G.C. St. Anne, &c. Crown 8vo, pp. viii. and 194, cloth. 1878. 5s.

FISCHEL.—Specimens of Modern German Prose and Poetry ; with Notes, Grammatical, Historical, and Idiomatical. To which is added a Short Sketch of the History of German Literature. By Dr. M. M. Fischel, formerly of Queen's College, Harley Street, and late German Master to the Stockwell Grammar School. Crown 8vo, pp. viii. and 280, cloth. 1880. 4s.

FISKE.—The Unseen World, and other Essays. By John Fiske, M.A., LL.B. Crown 8vo, pp. 350. 1876. 10s.

FISKE.—Myths and Myth-Makers ; Old Tales and Superstitions, interpreted by Comparative Mythology. By John Fiske. M.A., LL.B., Assistant Librarian, and late Lecturer on Philosophy at Harvard University. Crown 8vo, pp. 260, cloth. 1873. 10s. 6d.

FITZGERALD.—Australian Orchids. By R. D. Fitzgerald, F.L.S. Folio.—Part I. 7 Plates.—Part II. 10 Plates.—Part III. 10 Plates.—Part IV. 10 Plates.— Part V. 10 Plates. —Part VI. 10 Plates. Each Part, Coloured 21s.; Plain, 10s. 6d.

FITZGERALD.—An Essay on the Philosophy of Self-Consciousness. Comprising an Analysis of Reason and the Rationale of Love. By P. F. Fitzgerald. Demy 8vo, pp. xvi. and 196, cloth. 1882. 5s.

FORJETT. External Evidences of Christianity. By E. H. Forjett. 8vo, pp. 114, cloth. 1874. 2s. 6d.

FORNANDER.—The Polynesian Race. See English and Foreign Philosophical Library, Extra Series, Vols. III. and VI.

FORSTER.—Political Presentments.—By William Forster, Agent-General for New South Wales. Crown 8vo, pp. 122, cloth. 1878. 4s. 6d.

FOULKES. The Daya Bhaga, the Law of Inheritance of the Sarasvati Vilasa. The Original Sanskrit Text, with Translation by the Rev. Thos. Foulkes, F.L.S., M.R.A.S., F.R.G.S., Fellow of the University of Madras, &c. Demy 8vo, pp. xxvi. and 194 162, cloth. 1881. 10s. 6d.

FOX.—Memorial Edition of Collected Works, by W. J. Fox. 12 vols. 8vo, cloth. £3.

FRANKLYN.—Outlines of Military Law, and the Laws of Evidence. By H. B. Franklyn, LL.B. Crown 16mo, pp. viii. and 152, cloth. 1874. 3s. 6d.

FRIEDRICH.—Progressive German Reader, with Copious Notes to the First Part. By P. Friedrich. Crown 8vo, pp. 166, cloth. 1868. 4s. 6d.

FRIEDRICH.—A GRAMMATICAL COURSE OF THE GERMAN LANGUAGE. By P. Friedrich. Second Edition. Crown 8vo, pp. viii. and 102, cloth. 1877. 3s. 6d.

FRIEDRICH.—A GRAMMAR OF THE GERMAN LANGUAGE, WITH EXERCISES. See under DUSAR.

FRIEDERICI.—BIBLIOTHECA ORIENTALIS, or a Complete List of Books, Papers, Serials, and Essays, published in England and the Colonies, Germany and France ; on the History, Geography, Religions, Antiquities, Literature, and Languages of the East. Compiled by Charles Friederici. 8vo, boards. 1876, pp. 86, 2s. 6d. 1877, pp. 100, 3s. 1878, pp. 112, 3s. 6d. 1879, 3s. 1880, 3s.

FRŒMBLING.—GRADUATED GERMAN READER. Consisting of a Selection from the most Popular Writers, arranged progressively ; with a complete Vocabulary for the first part. By Friedrich Otto Frœmbling. Sixth Edition. 12mo, pp. viii. and 306, cloth. 1879. 3s. 6d.

FRŒMBLING.—GRADUATED EXERCISES FOR TRANSLATION INTO GERMAN. Consisting of Extracts from the best English Authors, arranged progressively ; with an Appendix, containing Idiomatic Notes. By Friedrich Otto Frœmbling, Ph.D., Principal German Master at the City of London School. Crown 8vo, pp. xiv. and 322, cloth. With Notes, pp. 66. 1867. 4s. 6d. Without Notes, 4s.

FROUDE.—THE BOOK OF JOB. By J. A. Froude, M.A., late Fellow of Exeter College, Oxford. Reprinted from the *Westminster Review*. 8vo, pp. 38, cloth. 1s.

FRUSTON.—ECHO FRANÇAIS. A Practical Guide to French Conversation. By F. de la Fruston. With a Vocabulary. 12mo, pp. vi. and 192, cloth. 3s.

FRYER.—THE KHYENG PEOPLE OF THE SANDOWAY DISTRICT, ARAKAN. By G. E. Fryer, Major, M.S.C., Deputy Commissioner, Sandoway. With 2 Plates. 8vo pp. 44, cloth. 1875. 3s. 6d.

FRYER.—PÁLI STUDIES. No. I. Analysis, and Páli Text of the Subodhálankara, or Easy Rhetoric, by Sangharakkhita Thera. 8vo, pp. 35, cloth. 1875. 3s. 6d.

FURNIVALL.—EDUCATION IN EARLY ENGLAND. Some Notes used as forewords to a Collection of Treatises on "Manners and Meals in Olden Times," for the Early English Text Society. By Frederick J. Furnivall, M.A. 8vo, pp. 4 and lxxiv., sewed. 1867. 1s.

GALLOWAY.—A TREATISE ON FUEL. Scientific and Practical. By Robert Galloway, M.R.I.A., F.C.S., &c. With Illustrations. Post 8vo, pp. x. and 136, cloth. 1880. 6s.

GALLOWAY.—EDUCATION : SCIENTIFIC AND TECHNICAL ; or, How the Inductive Sciences are Taught, and How they Ought to be Taught. By Robert Galloway, M.R.I.A., F.C.S. 8vo, pp. xvi. and 462, cloth. 1881. 10s. 6d.

GAMBLE.—A MANUAL OF INDIAN TIMBERS : An Account of the Structure, Growth, Distribution, and Qualities of Indian Woods. By J. C. Gamble, M.A., F.L.S. 8vo, pp. xxx. and 522, with a Map, cloth. 1881. 10s.

GARBE.—See AUCTORES SANSKRITI, Vol. III.

GARFIELD.—THE LIFE AND PUBLIC SERVICE OF JAMES A. GARFIELD, Twentieth President of the United States. A Biographical Sketch. By Captain F. H. Mason, late of the 42d Regiment, U.S.A. With a Preface by Bret Harte. Crown 8vo. pp. vi. and 134, cloth. With Portrait. 1881. 2s. 6d.

GARRETT.—A CLASSICAL DICTIONARY OF INDIA : Illustrative of the Mythology, Philosophy, Literature, Antiquities. Arts, Manners, Customs, &c., of the Hindus. By John Garrett, Director of Public Instruction in Mysore. 8vo, pp. x. and 794, cloth. With Supplement, pp. 160. 1871 and 1873. £1, 16s.

GAUTAMA.—The Institutes of. See Auctores Sanskriti, Vol. II.

GAZETTEER of the Central Provinces of India. Edited by Charles Grant, Secretary to the Chief Commissioner of the Central Provinces. Second Edition. With a very large folding Map of the Central Provinces of India. Demy 8vo, pp. clvii. and 582, cloth. 1870. £1, 4s.

GEIGER.—A Peep at Mexico; Narrative of a Journey across the Republic from the Pacific to the Gulf, in December 1873 and January 1874. By J. L. Geiger, F.R.G.S. Demy 8vo, pp. 368, with Maps and 45 Original Photographs. Cloth, 24s.

GEIGER.—Contributions to the History of the Development of the Human Race: Lectures and Dissertations, by Lazarus Geiger. Translated from the Second German Edition, by David Asher, Ph.D. Post 8vo, pp. x.-156, cloth. 1880. 6s.

GELDART.—Faith and Freedom. Fourteen Sermons. By E. M. Geldart, M.A. Crown 8vo, pp. vi. and 168, cloth. 1881. 4s. 6d.

GELDART.—A Guide to Modern Greek. By E. M. Geldart, M.A. Post 8vo, pp. xii and 274, cloth. 1883. 7s. 6d. Key, pp. 28, cloth. 1883. 2s. 6d.

GELDART.—Greek Grammar. See Trübner's Collection.

GEOLOGICAL MAGAZINE (The): or, Monthly Journal of Geology. With which is incorporated "The Geologist." Edited by Henry Woodward, LL.D., F.R.S., F.G.S., &c., of the British Museum. Assisted by Professor John Morris, M.A., F.G.S., &c., and Robert Etheridge, F.R.S., L. & E., F.G.S., &c., of the Museum of Practical Geology. 8vo, cloth. 1866 to 1882. 20s. each.

GHOSE.—The Modern History of the Indian Chiefs, Rajas, Zamindars, &c. By Loke Nath Ghose. 2 vols. post 8vo, pp. xii. and 218, and xviii. and 612, cloth. 1883. 21s.

GILES.—Chinese Sketches.—By Herbert A. Giles, of H.B.M.'s China Consular Service. 8vo, pp. 204, cloth. 1875. 10s. 6d.

GILES.—A Dictionary of Colloquial Idioms in the Mandarin Dialect. By Herbert A. Giles. 4to, pp. 65, half bound. 1873. 28s.

GILES.—Synoptical Studies in Chinese Character. By Herbert A. Giles. 8vo, pp. 118, half bound. 1874. 15s.

GILES.—Chinese without a Teacher. Being a Collection of Easy and Useful Sentences in the Mandarin Dialect. With a Vocabulary. By Herbert A. Giles. 12mo, pp. 60, half bound. 1872. 5s.

GILES.—The San Tzŭ Ching; or, Three Character Classic; and the Ch'Jen Tsu Wen; or, Thousand Character Essay. Metrically Translated by Herbert A. Giles. 12mo, pp. 28, half bound. 1873. 2s. 6d.

GLASS.—Advance Thought. By Charles E. Glass. Crown 8vo, pp. xxxvi. and 188, cloth. 1876. 6s.

GOETHE'S Faust.—See Scoones.

GOETHE'S Minor Poems.—See Selss.

GOLDSTÜCKER.—A Dictionary, Sanskrit and English, extended and improved from the Second Edition of the Dictionary of Professor H. H. Wilson, with the sanction and concurrence. Together with a Supplement, Grammatical Appendices, and an Index, serving as a Sanskrit-English Vocabulary. By Theodore Goldstücker. Parts I. to VI. 4to, pp. 400. 1856-63. 6s. each.

GOLDSTÜCKER.—See AUCTORES SANSKRITI, Vol. I.

GOOROO SIMPLE. Strange Surprising Adventures of the Venerable G. S. and his Five Disciples, Noodle, Doodle, Wiseacre, Zany, and Foozle : adorned with Fifty Illustrations, drawn on wood, by Alfred Crowquill. A companion Volume to " Münchhausen " and " Owlglass," based upon the famous Tamul tale of the Gooroo Paramartan, and exhibiting, in the form of a skilfully-constructed consecutive narrative, some of the finest specimens of Eastern wit and humour. Elegantly printed on tinted paper, in crown 8vo, pp. 223, richly gilt ornamental cover, gilt edges. 1861. 10s. 6d.

GORKOM.—HANDBOOK OF CINCHONA CULTURE. By K. W. Van Gorkom, formerly Director of the Government Cinchona Plantations in Java. Translated by B. D. Jackson, Secretary of the Linnæan Society of London. With a Coloured Illustration. Imperial 8vo, pp. xii. and 292, cloth. 1882. £2.

GOUGH.—The SARVA-DARSANA-SAMGRAHA. See Trübner's Oriental Series.

GOUGH.—PHILOSOPHY OF THE UPANISHADS. See Trübner's Oriental Series.

GOVER.—THE FOLK-SONGS OF SOUTHERN INDIA. By C. E. Gover, Madras. Contents : Canarese Songs ; Badaga Songs ; Coorg Songs ; Tamil Songs ; The Cural ; Malayalam Songs ; Telugu Songs. 8vo, pp. xxviii. and 300, cloth. 1872. 10s. 6d.

GRAY.—DARWINIANA : Essays and Reviews pertaining to Darwinism. By Asa Gray. Crown 8vo, pp. xii. and 396, cloth. 1877. 10s.

GRAY.—NATURAL SCIENCE AND RELIGION : Two Lectures Delivered to the Theological School of Yale College. By Asa Gray. Crown 8vo, pp. 112, cloth. 1880. 5s.

GREEN.—SHAKESPEARE AND THE EMBLEM-WRITERS : An Exposition of their Similarities of Thought and Expression. Preceded by a View of the Emblem-Book Literature down to A.D. 1616. By Henry Green, M.A. In one volume, pp. xvi. 572, profusely illustrated with Woodcuts and Photolith. Plates, elegantly bound in cloth gilt, 1870. Large medium 8vo, £1, 11s. 6d. ; large imperial 8vo. £2, 12s. 6d.

GREEN.—ANDREA ALCIATI, and his Books of Emblems : A Biographical and Bibliographical Study. By Henry Green, M.A. With Ornamental Title, Portraits, and other Illustrations. Dedicated to Sir William Stirling-Maxwell, Bart., Rector of the University of Edinburgh. Only 250 copies printed. Demy 8vo, pp. 360, handsomely bound. 1872. £1, 1s.

GREENE.—A NEW METHOD OF LEARNING TO READ, WRITE, AND SPEAK THE FRENCH LANGUAGE : or, First Lessons in French (Introductory to Ollendorff's Larger Grammar). By G. W. Greene, Instructor in Modern Languages in Brown University. Third Edition, enlarged and rewritten. Fcap. 8vo, pp. 248, cloth. 1869. 3s. 6d.

GREENE.—THE HEBREW MIGRATION FROM EGYPT. By J. Baker Greene, LL.B., M.B., Trin. Coll., Dub. Second Edition. Demy 8vo, pp. xii. and 440, cloth. 1882. 10s. 6d.

GREG.—TRUTH VERSUS EDIFICATION. By W. R. Greg. Fcap. 8vo, pp. 32, cloth. 1869. 1s.

GREG.—WHY ARE WOMEN REDUNDANT ? By W. R. Greg. Fcap. 8vo, pp. 40, cloth. 1869. 1s.

GREG.—LITERARY AND SOCIAL JUDGMENTS. By W. R. Greg. Fourth Edition, considerably enlarged. 2 vols. crown 8vo, pp. 310 and 288, cloth. 1877. 15s.

GREG.—MISTAKEN AIMS AND ATTAINABLE IDEALS OF THE ARTISAN CLASS. By W. R. Greg. Crown 8vo, pp. vi. and 332, cloth. 1876. 10s. 6d.

GREG.—ENIGMAS OF LIFE. By W. R. Greg. Fifteenth Edition, with a postscript. Contents: Realisable Ideals. Malthus Notwithstanding. Non-Survival of the Fittest. Limits and Directions of Human Development. The Significance of Life. De Profundis. Elsewhere. Appendix. Post 8vo, pp. xxii. and 314, cloth. 1883. 10s. 6d.

GREG.—POLITICAL PROBLEMS FOR OUR AGE AND COUNTRY. By W. R. Greg. Contents: I. Constitutional and Autocratic Statesmanship. II. England's Future Attitude and Mission. III. Disposal of the Criminal Classes. IV. Recent Change in the Character of English Crime. V. The Intrinsic Vice of Trade-Unions. VI. Industrial and Co-operative Partnerships. VII. The Economic Problem. VIII. Political Consistency. IX. The Parliamentary Career. X. The Price we pay for Self-government. XI. Vestryism. XII. Direct v. Indirect Taxation. XIII. The New Régime, and how to meet it. Demy 8vo, pp. 342, cloth. 1870. 10s. 6d.

GREG.—THE GREAT DUEL: Its true Meaning and Issues. By W. R. Greg. Crown 8vo, pp. 96, cloth. 1871. 2s. 6d.

GREG.—THE CREED OF CHRISTENDOM. See English and Foreign Philosophical Library, Vols. V. and VI.

GREG.—ROCKS AHEAD; or, The Warnings of Cassandra. By W. R. Greg. Second Edition, with a Reply to Objectors. Crown 8vo, pp. xliv. and 236, cloth. 1874. 9s.

GREG.—MISCELLANEOUS ESSAYS. By W. R. Greg. Crown 8vo, pp. 260, cloth. 1881. 7s. 6d.
> CONTENTS:— Rocks Ahead and Harbours of Refuge. Foreign Policy of Great Britain. The Echo of the Antipodes. A Grave Perplexity before us. Obligations of the Soil. The Right Use of a Surplus. The Great Twin Brothers: Louis Napoleon and Benjamin Disraeli. Is the Popular Judgment in Politics more Just than that of the Higher Orders? Harriet Martineau. Verify your Compass. The Prophetic Element in the Gospels. Mr. Frederick Harrison on the Future Life. Can Truths be Apprehended which could not have been discovered?

GREG.—INTERLEAVES IN THE WORKDAY PROSE OF TWENTY YEARS. By Percy Greg. Fcap. 8vo, pp. 128, cloth. 1875. 2s. 6d.

GRIFFIN.—THE RAJAS OF THE PUNJAB. Being the History of the Principal States in the Punjab, and their Political Relations with the British Government. By Lepel H. Griffin, Bengal Civil Service, Acting Secretary to the Government of the Punjab, Author of "The Punjab Chiefs," &c. Second Edition. Royal 8vo, pp. xvi. and 630, cloth. 1873. £1, 1s.

GRIFFIN.—THE WORLD UNDER GLASS. By Frederick Griffin, Author of "The Destiny of Man," "The Storm King," and other Poems. Fcap. 8vo, pp. 204, cloth gilt. 1879. 3s. 6d.

GRIFFIS.—THE MIKADO'S EMPIRE. Book I. History of Japan, from 660 B.C. to 1872 A.D.—Book II. Personal Experiences, Observations, and Studies in Japan, 1870-1874. By W. E. Griffis, A.M. 8vo, pp. 636, cloth. Illustrated. 1877. 20s.

GRIFFIS.—JAPANESE FAIRY WORLD. Stories from the Wonder-Lore of Japan. By W. E. Griffis. Square 16mo, pp. viii. and 304, with 12 Plates. 1880. 7s. 6d.

GRIFFITH.—The Birth of the War God. See Trübner's Oriental Series.

GRIFFITH.—Yusuf and Zulaikha. See Trübner's Oriental Series.

GRIFFITH.—Scenes from the Ramayana, Meghaduta, &c. Translated by Ralph T. H. Griffith, M.A., Principal of the Benares College. Second Edition. Crown 8vo, pp. xviii. and 244, cloth. 1870. 6s.

Contents.—Preface—Ayodhya—Ravan Doomed--The Birth of Rama—The Heir-Apparent—Manthara's Guile—Dasaratha's Oath—The Step-mother—Mother and Son—The Triumph of Love—Farewell ?—The Hermit's Son—The Trial of Truth—The Forest—The Rape of Sita—Rama's Despair—The Messenger Cloud—Khumbakarna—The Suppliant Dove—True Glory—Feed the Poor—The Wise Scholar.

GRIFFITH.—The Rámáyan of Válmíki. Translated into English Verse. By Ralph T H. Griffith, M.A., Principal of the Benares College. Vol. I., containing Books I. and II., demy 8vo, pp. xxxii. and 440, cloth. 1870. —Vol. II., containing Book II., with additional Notes and Index of Names. Demy 8vo, pp. 504, cloth. 1871. —Vol. III., demy 8vo, pp. 390, cloth. 1872. —Vol. IV., demy 8vo, pp. viii. and 432, cloth. 1873. —Vol. V., demy 8vo, pp. viii. and 360, cloth. 1875. The complete work, 5 vols. £7, 7s.

GROTE.—Review of the Work of Mr. John Stuart Mill entitled "Examination of Sir William Hamilton's Philosophy." By George Grote, Author of the "History of Ancient Greece," "Plato, and the other Companions of Socrates," &c. 12mo, pp. 112, cloth. 1868. 3s. 6d.

GROUT.—Zulu-Land; or, Life among the Zulu-Kafirs of Natal and Zulu-Land, South Africa. By the Rev. Lewis Grout. Crown 8vo, pp. 352, cloth. With Map and Illustrations. 7s. 6d.

GROWSE.—Mathura : A District Memoir. By F. S. Growse, B.C.S., M.A., Oxon, C.I.E., Fellow of the Calcutta University. Second edition, illustrated, revised, and enlarged, 4to, pp. xxiv. and 520, boards. 1880. 42s.

GUBERNATIS.—Zoological Mythology ; or, The Legends of Animals. By Angelo de Gubernatis, Professor of Sanskrit and Comparative Literature in the Instituto di Studii Superorii e di Perfezionamento at Florence, &c. 2 vols. 8vo, pp. xxvi. and 432, and vii. and 442, cloth. 1872. £1, 8s.

This work is an important contribution to the study of the comparative mythology of the Indo-Germanic nations. The author introduces the denizens of the air, earth, and water in the various characters assigned to them in the myths and legends of all civilised nations, and traces the migration of the mythological ideas from the times of the early Aryans to those of the Greeks, Romans, and Teutons.

GULSHAN I. RAZ : The Mystic Rose Garden of Sa'd Ud Din Mahmud Shabis-tari. The Persian Text, with an English Translation and Notes, chiefly from the Commentary of Muhammed Bin Yahya Lahiji. By E. H. Whinfield, M.A., Bar-rister-at-Law, late of H.M.B.C.S. 4to, pp. xvi., 94, 60, cloth. 1880. 10s. 6d.

GUMPACH.—Treaty Rights of the Foreign Merchant, and the Transit System in China. By Johannes von Gumpach. 8vo, pp. xviii. and 421, sewed. 10s. 6d.

HAAS.—Catalogue of Sanskrit and Pali Books in the British Museum. By Dr. Ernst Haas. Printed by permission of the Trustees of the British Museum. 4to, pp. viii. and 188, paper boards. 1876. 21s.

HAFIZ OF SHIRAZ.—Selections from his Poems. Translated from the Persian by Hermann Bicknell. With Preface by A. S. Bicknell. Demy 4to, pp. xx. and 384, printed on fine stout plate-paper, with appropriate Oriental Bordering in gold and colour, and Illustrations by J. R. Herbert, R.A. 1875. £2, 2s.

HAFIZ.—See Trübner's Oriental Series.

HAGEN.—Norica ; or, Tales from the Olden Time. Translated from the German of August Hagen. Fcap. 8vo, pp. xiv. and 374. 1850. 5s.

HAGGARD.—Cetywayo and his White Neighbours ; or, Remarks on Recent Events in Zululand, Natal, and the Transvaal. By H. R. Haggard. Crown 8vo, pp. xvi. and 294. cloth. 1882. 10s. 6d.

HAGGARD.—See "The Vazir of Lankuran."

HAHN.—Tsuni-||Goam, the Supreme Being of the Khoi-Khoi. By Theophilus Hahn, Ph.D., Custodian of the Grey Collection, Cape Town, &c., &c. Post 8vo, pp. xiv. and 154. 1882. 7s. 6d.

HALDEMAN.—Pennsylvania Dutch: A Dialect of South Germany with an Infusion of English. By S. S. Haldeman, A.M., Professor of Comparative Philology in the University of Pennsylvania, Philadelphia. 8vo, pp. viii. and 70, cloth. 1872. 3s. 6d.

HALL.—On English Adjectives in -Able, with Special Reference to Reliable. By FitzEdward Hall, C.E., M A., Hon. D.C.L. Oxon ; formerly Professor of Sanskrit Language and Literature, and of Indian Jurisprudence in King's College, London. Crown 8vo, pp. viii. and 238, cloth. 1877. 7s. 6d.

HALL.—Modern English. By FitzEdward Hall, M.A., Hon. D.C.L. Oxon. Crown 8vo, pp. xvi. and 394, cloth. 1873. 10s. 6d.

HALL.—Sun and Earth as Great Forces in Chemistry. By T. W. Hall, M.D. L.R.C.S.E. Crown 8vo, pp. xii. and 220, cloth. 1874. 3s.

HALL.—The Pedigree of the Devil. By F. T. Hall, F.R.A.S. With Seven Autotype Illustrations from Designs by the Author. Demy 8vo, pp. xvi. and 256, cloth. 1883. 7s. 6d.

HALL.—Arctic Expedition. See Nourse.

HALLOCK.—The Sportsman's Gazetteer and General Guide. The Game Animals, Birds, and Fishes of North America: their Habits and various methods of Capture, &c., &c. With a Directory to the principal Game Resorts of the Country. By Charles Hallock. Fourth Edition. Crown 8vo, cloth. Maps and Portrait. 1878. 15s.

HAM.—The Maid of Corinth. A Drama in Four Acts. By J. Panton Ham. Crown 8vo, pp. 65, sewed. 2s. 6d.

HARDY.—Christianity and Buddhism Compared. By the late Rev. R. Spence Hardy, Hon. Member Royal Asiatic Society. 8vo, pp. 138, sewed. 1875. 7s. 6d.

HARLEY.—The Simplification of English Spelling, specially adapted to the Rising Generation. An Easy Way of Saving Time in Writing, Printing, and Reading. By Dr. George Harley, F.R.S., F.C.S. 8vo. pp. 128, cloth. 1877. 2s. 6d.

HARRISON.—The Meaning of History. Two Lectures delivered by Frederic Harrison, M.A. 8vo, pp. 80, sewed. 1862. 1s.

HARRISON.—Woman's Handiwork in Modern Homes. By Constance Cary Harrison. With numerous Illustrations and Five Coloured Plates, from designs by Samuel Colman, Rosina Emmet, George Gibson, and others. 8vo, pp. xii. and 242, cloth. 1881. 10s.

HARTING.—British Animals Extinct within Historic Times: with some Account of British Wild White Cattle. By J. E. Harting, F.L.S., F.Z.S. With Illustrations by Wolf, Whymper, Sherwin, and others. Demy 8vo, pp. 256, cloth. 1881. 14s. A few copies, large paper, 31s. 6d.

HARTZENBUSCH and LEMMING.—Eco de Madrid. A Practical Guide to Spanish Conversation. By J. E. Hartzenbusch and H. Lemming. Second Edition. Post 8vo, pp. 250, cloth. 1870. 5s.

HASE.—Miracle Plays and Sacred Dramas : An Historical Survey. By Dr. Karl Hase. Translated from the German by A. W. Jackson, and Edited by the Rev. W. W. Jackson, Fellow of Exeter College, Oxford. Crown 8vo, pp. 288. 1880. 9s.

HAUG.—Glossary and Index of the Pahlavi Texts of the Book of Arda Viraf, the Tale of Gosht—J. Fryano, the Hadokht Nask, and to some extracts from the Dinkard and Nirangistan ; prepared from Destur Hoshangji Jamaspji Asa's Glossary to the Arda Viraf Namak, and from the Original Texts, with Notes on Pahlavi Grammar by E. W. West, Ph.D. Revised by M. Haug, Ph.D., &c. Published by order of the Bombay Government. 8vo, pp. viii. and 352, sewed. 1874. 25s.

HAUG.— The Sacred Language, &c., of the Parsis. See Trübner's Oriental Series.

HAUPT.—The London Arbitrageur ; or, The English Money Market, in connection with Foreign Bourses. A Collection of Notes and Formulæ for the Arbitration of Bills, Stocks, Shares, Bullion, and Coins, with all the Important Foreign Countries. By Ottomar Haupt. Crown 8vo, pp. viii. and 196, cloth. 1870. 7s. 6d.

HAWKEN.—Upa-Sastra : Comments, Linguistic, Doctrinal, on Sacred and Mythic Literature. By J. D. Hawken. Crown 8vo, pp. viii. and 288, cloth. 1877. 7s. 6d.

HAZEN.—The School and the Army in Germany and France, with a Diary of Siege Life at Versailles. By Brevet Major-General W. B. Hazen, U.S.A., Col. 6th Infantry. 8vo, pp. 408, cloth. 1872. 10s. 6d.

HEATH.—Edgar Quinet. See English and Foreign Philosophical Library, Vol. XIV.

HEBREW LITERATURE SOCIETY.—Subscription, one guinea per annum. List of publications on application.

HECKER.—The Epidemics of the Middle Ages. Translated by G. B. Babington, M.D., F.R.S. Third Edition, completed by the Author's Treatise on Child-Pilgrimages. By J. F. C. Hecker. 8vo, pp. 384, cloth. 1859. 9s. 6d.
Contents.—The Black Death—The Dancing Mania—The Sweating Sickness—Child Pilgrimages.

HEDLEY.—Masterpieces of German Poetry. Translated in the Measure of the Originals, by F. H. Hedley. With Illustrations by Louis Wanke. Crown 8vo, pp. viii. and 120, cloth. 1876. 6s.

HEINE.—Religion and Philosophy in Germany. See English and Foreign Philosophical Library, Vol. XVIII.

HEINE.—Wit, Wisdom, and Pathos from the Prose of Heinrich Heine. With a few pieces from the " Book of Songs." Selected and Translated by J. Snodgrass. With Portrait. Crown 8vo, pp. xx. and 340, cloth. 1879. 7s. 6d.

HEINE.—Pictures of Travel. Translated from the German of Henry Heine, by Charles G. Leland. 7th Revised Edition. Crown 8vo, pp. 472, with Portrait, cloth. 1873. 7s. 6d.

HEINE.—Heine's Book of Songs. Translated by Charles G. Leland. Fcap. 8vo, pp. xiv. and 240, cloth, gilt edges. 1874. 7s. 6d.

HENDRIK.—MEMOIRS OF HANS HENDRIK, THE ARCTIC TRAVELLER; serving under Kane, Hayes, Hall, and Nares, 1853-76. Written by Himself. Translated from the Eskimo Language, by Dr. Henry Rink. Edited by Prof. Dr. G. Stephens, F.S.A. Crown 8vo, pp. 100, Map, cloth. 1878. 3s. 6d.

HENNELL.—PRESENT RELIGION: As a Faith owning Fellowship with Thought. Vol. I. Part I. By Sara S. Hennell. Crown 8vo, pp. 570, cloth. 1865. 7s. 6d.

HENNELL. PRESENT RELIGION: As a Faith owning Fellowship with Thought. Part II. First Division. Intellectual Effect: shown as a Principle of Metaphysical Comparativism. By Sara S. Hennell. Crown 8vo, pp. 618, cloth. 1873. 7s. 6d.

HENNELL.—PRESENT RELIGION, Vol. III. Part II. Second Division. The Effect of Present Religion on its Practical Side. By S. S. Hennell. Crown 8vo, pp. 68, paper covers. 1882. 2s.

HENNELL.—COMPARATIVISM shown as Furnishing a Religious Basis to Morality. (Present Religion. Vol. III. Part II. Second Division : Practical Effect.) By Sara S. Hennell. Crown 8vo, pp. 220, stitched in wrapper. 1878. 3s. 6d.

HENNELL.—THOUGHTS IN AID OF FAITH. Gathered chiefly from recent Works in Theology and Philosophy. By Sara S. Hennell. Post 8vo, pp. 428, cloth. 1860. 6s.

HENWOOD.—THE METALLIFEROUS DEPOSITS OF CORNWALL AND DEVON : with Appendices on Subterranean Temperature ; the Electricity of Rocks and Veins : the Quantities of Water in the Cornish Mines ; and Mining Statistics. (Vol. V. of the Transactions of the Royal Geographical Society of Cornwall.) By William Jory Henwood, F.R.S., F.G.S. 8vo, pp. x. and 515 ; with 113 Tables, and 12 Plates, half bound. £2, 2s.

HENWOOD.—OBSERVATIONS ON METALLIFEROUS DEPOSITS, AND ON SUBTERRANEAN TEMPERATURE. (Vol. VIII. of the Transactions of the Royal Geological Society of Cornwall.) By William Jory Henwood, F.R.S., F.G.S., President of the Royal Institution of Cornwall. In 2 Parts. 8vo, pp. xxx., vii. and 916 ; with 38 Tables, 31 Engravings on Wood, and 6 Plates. £1, 16s.

HEPBURN.—A JAPANESE AND ENGLISH DICTIONARY. With an English and Japanese Index. By J. C. Hepburn, M.D., LL.D. Second Edition. Imperial 8vo, pp. xxxii., 632, and 201, cloth. £8, 8s.

HEPBURN.—JAPANESE-ENGLISH AND ENGLISH-JAPANESE DICTIONARY. By J. C. Hepburn, M.D., LL.D. Abridged by the Author. Square fcap., pp. vi. and 536, cloth. 1873. 18s.

HERNISZ.—A GUIDE TO CONVERSATION IN THE ENGLISH AND CHINESE LANGUAGES, for the Use of Americans and Chinese in California and elsewhere. By Stanislas Hernisz. Square 8vo, pp. 274, sewed. 1855. 10s. 6d.

HERSHON.—TALMUDIC MISCELLANY. See Trübner's Oriental Series.

HERZEN.—DU DEVELOPPEMENT DES IDÉES REVOLUTIONNAIRES EN RUSSIE. Par Alexander Herzen. 12mo, pp. xxiii. and 144, sewed. 1853. 2s. 6d.

HERZEN.—A separate list of A. Herzen's works in Russian may be had on application.

HILL.—THE HISTORY OF THE REFORM MOVEMENT in the Dental Profession in Great Britain during the last twenty years. By Alfred Hill, Licentiate in Dental Surgery, &c. Crown 8vo, pp. xvi. and 400, cloth. 1877. 10s. 6d.

HILLEBRAND.—FRANCE AND THE FRENCH IN THE SECOND HALF OF THE NINETEENTH CENTURY. By Karl Hillebrand. Translated from the Third German Edition. Post 8vo, pp. xx. and 262, cloth. 1881. 10s. 6d.

HINDOO Mythology Popularly Treated. Being an Epitomised Description of the various Heathen Deities illustrated on the Silver Swami Tea Service presented, as a memento of his visit to India, to H.R.H. the Prince of Wales, K.G., G.C.S.I., by His Highness the Gaekwar of Baroda. Small 4to, pp. 42, limp cloth. 1875. 3s. 6d.

HITTELL.—The Commerce and Industries of the Pacific Coast of North America. By J. S. Hittell, Author of "The Resources of California." 4to, pp. 820. 1882. £1, 10s.

HODGSON.—Essays on the Languages, Literature, and Religion of Nepal and Tibet. Together with further Papers on the Geography, Ethnology, and Commerce of those Countries. By B. H. Hodgson, late British Minister at the Court of Nepál. Royal 8vo, cloth, pp. xii. and 276. 1874. 14s.

HODGSON.— Essays on Indian Subjects. See Trübner's Oriental Series.

HODGSON.—The Education of Girls; and the Employment of Women of the Upper Classes Educationally considered. Two Lectures. By W. B. Hodgson, LL.D. Second Edition. Crown 8vo, pp. xvi. and 114, cloth. 1869. 3s. 6d.

HODGSON.—Turgot: His Life, Times, and Opinions. Two Lectures. By W. B. Hodgson, LL.D. Crown 8vo, pp. vi. and 83, sewed. 1870. 2s.

HOERNLE.—A Comparative Grammar of the Gaudian Languages, with Special Reference to the Eastern Hindi. Accompanied by a Language Map, and a Table of Alphabets. By A. F. Rudolf Hoernle. Demy 8vo, pp. 474, cloth. 1880. 18s.

HOLBEIN SOCIETY.—Subscription, one guinea per annum. List of publications on application.

HOLMES-FORBES.—The Science of Beauty. An Analytical Inquiry into the Laws of Æsthetics. By Avary W. Holmes-Forbes, of Lincoln's Inn, Barrister-at-Law. Post 8vo, cloth, pp. vi. and 200. 1881. 6s.

HOLST.—The Constitutional and Political History of the United States. By Dr. H. von Holst. Translated by J. J. Lalor and A. B. Mason. Royal 8vo. Vol. I. 1750-1833. State Sovereignty and Slavery. Pp. xvi. and 506. 1876. 18s. —Vol. II. 1828-1846. Jackson's Administration—Annexation of Texas. Pp. 720. 1879. £1, 2s.—Vol. III. 1846-1850. Annexation of Texas—Compromise of 1850. Pp. x. and 598. 1881. 18s.

HOLYOAKE.—The Rochdale Pioneers. Thirty-three Years of Co-operation in Rochdale. In two parts. Part I. 1844-1857; Part II. 1857-1877. By G. J. Holyoake. Crown 8vo, pp. 174, cloth. 1882. 2s. 6d.

HOLYOAKE.—The History of Co-operation in England: its Literature and its Advocates. By G. J. Holyoake. Vol. I. The Pioneer Period, 1812-44. Crown 8vo, pp. xii. and 420, cloth. 1875. 6s.—Vol. II. The Constructive Period, 1845-78. Crown 8vo, pp. x. and 504, cloth. 1878. 8s.

HOLYOAKE.—The Trial of Theism accused of Obstructing Secular Life. By G. J. Holyoake. Crown 8vo, pp. xvi. and 256, cloth. 1877. 4s.

HOLYOAKE.—Reasoning from Facts: A Method of Everyday Logic. By G. J. Holyoake. Fcap., pp. xii. and 94, wrapper. 1877. 1s. 6d.

HOPKINS.—Elementary Grammar of the Turkish Language. With a few Easy Exercises. By F. L. Hopkins, M.A., Fellow and Tutor of Trinity Hall, Cambridge. Crown 8vo, pp. 48, cloth. 1877. 3s. 6d.

HOWELLS.—Dr. Breen's Practice: A Novel. By W. D. Howells. English Copyright Edition. Crown 8vo, pp. 272, cloth. 1882. 6s.

C

HOWSE.—A GRAMMAR OF THE CREE LANGUAGE. With which is combined an Analysis of the Chippeway Dialect. By Joseph Howse, F.R.G.S. 8vo, pp. xx. and 324, cloth. 1865. 7s. 6d.

HULME.—MATHEMATICAL DRAWING INSTRUMENTS, AND HOW TO USE THEM. By F. Edward Hulme, F.L.S., F.S.A., Art-Master of Marlborough College, Author of "Principles of Ornamental Art," "Familiar Wild Flowers," "Suggestions on Floral Design," &c. With Illustrations. Second Edition. Imperial 16mo, pp. xvi. and 152, cloth. 1881. 3s. 6d.

HUMBERT.—ON "TENANT RIGHT." By C. F. Humbert. 8vo, pp. 20, sewed. 1875. 1s.

HUMBOLDT.—THE SPHERE AND DUTIES OF GOVERNMENT. Translated from the German of Baron Wilhelm Von Humboldt by Joseph Coulthard, jun. Post 8vo, pp. xv. and 203, cloth. 1854. 5s.

HUMBOLDT.—LETTERS OF WILLIAM VON HUMBOLDT TO A FEMALE FRIEND. A complete Edition. Translated from the Second German Edition by Catherine M. A. Couper, with a Biographical Notice of the Writer. 2 vols. crown 8vo, pp. xxviii. and 592, cloth. 1867. 10s.

HUNT.—THE RELIGION OF THE HEART. A Manual of Faith and Duty. By Leigh Hunt. Fcap. 8vo, pp. xxiv. and 259, cloth. 2s. 6d.

HUNT.—CHEMICAL AND GEOLOGICAL ESSAYS. By Professor T. Sterry Hunt. Second Edition. 8vo, pp. xxii. and 448, cloth. 1879. 12s.

HUNTER.—A COMPARATIVE DICTIONARY OF THE NON-ARYAN LANGUAGES OF INDIA AND HIGH ASIA. With a Dissertation, Political and Linguistic, on the Aboriginal Races. By W. W. Hunter, B.A., M.R.A.S., Hon. Fel. Ethnol. Soc., Author of the "Annals of Rural Bengal," of H.M.'s Civil Service. Being a Lexicon of 144 Languages, illustrating Turanian Speech. Compiled from the Hodgson Lists, Government Archives, and Original MSS., arranged with Prefaces and Indices in English, French, German, Russian, and Latin. Large 4to, toned paper, pp. 230, cloth. 1869. 42s.

HUNTER.—THE INDIAN MUSSULMANS. By W. W. Hunter, B.A., LL.D., Director-General of Statistics to the Government of India, &c., Author of the "Annals of Rural Bengal," &c. Third Edition. 8vo, pp. 219, cloth. 1876. 10s. 6d.

HUNTER.—FAMINE ASPECTS OF BENGAL DISTRICTS. A System of Famine Warnings. By W. W. Hunter, B.A., LL.D. Crown 8vo, pp. 216, cloth. 1874. 7s. 6d.

HUNTER.—A STATISTICAL ACCOUNT OF BENGAL. By W. W. Hunter, B.A., LL.D.. Director-General of Statistics to the Government of India, &c. In 20 vols. 8vo. half morocco. 1877. £5.

HUNTER.—CATALOGUE OF SANSKRIT MANUSCRIPTS (BUDDHIST). Collected in Nepal by B. H. Hodgson, late Resident at the Court of Nepal. Compiled from Lists in Calcutta, France, and England, by W. W. Hunter, C.I.E., LL.D. 8vo, pp. 28, paper. 1880. 2s.

HUNTER.—THE IMPERIAL GAZETTEER OF INDIA. By W. W. Hunter, C.I.E., LL.D., Director-General of Statistics to the Government of India In Nine Volumes. 8vo, pp. xxxiii. and 544, 539, 567, xix. and 716, 509, 513, 555, 537, and xii. and 478, half morocco. With Maps. 1881.

HUNTER.—THE INDIAN EMPIRE: Its History, People, and Products. By W. W. Hunter, C.I.E., LL.D. Post 8vo, pp. 568, with Map, cloth. 1882. 16s.

HUNTER.—AN ACCOUNT OF THE BRITISH SETTLEMENT OF ADEN, IN ARABIA. Compiled by Capt. F. M. Hunter, Assistant Political Resident, Aden. 8vo, pp. xii. and 232, half bound. 1877. 7s. 6d.

HUNTER.—A Statistical Account of Assam. By W. W. Hunter, B.A., LL.D., C.I.E., Director-General of Statistics to the Government of India, &c. 2 vols. 8vo, pp. 420 and 490, with 2 Maps, ha morocco. 1879. 10s.

HUNTER.—A Brief History of the Indian People. By W. W. Hunter, C.I.E., LL.D. Second Edition. Crown 8vo, pp. 222, cloth. With Map. 1883. 3s. 6d.

HURST.—History of Rationalism: embracing a Survey of the Present State of Protestant Theology. By the Rev. John F. Hurst, A.M. With Appendix of Literature. Revised and enlarged from the Third American Edition. Crown 8vo, pp. xvii. and 525, cloth. 1867. 10s. 6d.

HYETT.—Prompt Remedies for Accidents and Poisons : Adapted to the use of the Inexperienced till Medical aid arrives. By W. H. Hyett, F.R.S. A Broadsheet, to hang up in Country Schools or Vestries, Workshops, Offices of Factories, Mines and Docks, on board Yachts, in Railway Stations, remote Shooting Quarters, Highland Manses, and Private Houses, wherever the Doctor lives at a distance. Sold for the benefit of the Gloucester Eye Institution. In sheets, 21½ by 17½ inches, 2s. 6d. ; mounted, 3s. 6d.

HYMANS.—Pupil *Versus* Teacher. Letters from a Teacher to a Teacher. Fcap. 8vo, pp. 92, cloth. 1875. 2s.

IHNE.—A Latin Grammar for Beginners. By W. H. Ihne, late Principal of Carlton Terrace School, Liverpool. Crown 8vo, pp. vi. and 184, cloth. 1864. 3s.

IKHWÁNU-S Safá; or, Brothers of Purity. Translated from the Hindustani by Professor John Dowson, M.R.A.S., Staff College, Sandhurst. Crown 8vo, pp. viii. and 156, cloth. 1869. 7s.

INDIA.—Archæological Survey of Western India. See Burgess.

INDIA.—Publications of the Archæological Survey of India. A separate list on application.

INDIA.—Publications of the Geographical Department of the India Office, London. A separate list, also list of all the Government Maps, on application.

INDIA.—Publications of the Geological Survey of India. A separate list on application.

INDIA OFFICE PUBLICATIONS :—

Aden, Statistical Account of. 5s.
Assam, do. do. Vols. I. and II. 5s. each.
Baden Powell, Land Revenues, &c., in India. 12s.
Bengal, Statistical Account of. Vols. I. to XX. 100s. per set.
  Do. do. do. Vols. VI. to XX. 5s. each.
Bombay Code. 21s.
Bombay Gazetteer. Vol. II. 14s.
  Do. do. Vols. III. to VI. 8s. each.
Burgess' Archæological Survey of Western India. Vols. I. and III. 42s. each.
  Do. do. do. Vol. II. 63s.
  Do. do. do. Vols. IV. and V. 126s.
Burma (British) Gazetteer. 2 vols. 50s.
Catalogue of Manuscripts and Maps of Surveys. 12s.
Chambers' Meteorology (Bombay) and Atlas. 30s.
Cole's Agra and Muttra. 70s.
Cook's Gums and Resins. 5s.
Corpus Inscriptionum Indicarum. Vol. I. 32s.
Cunningham's Archæological Survey. Vols. I. to XIV. 10s. and 12s. each.
  Do. Stupa of Bharut. 63s.

INDIA OFFICE PUBLICATIONS—*continued.*

Egerton's Catalogue of Indian Arms. 2s. 6d.
Ferguson and Burgess, Cave Temples of India. 42s.
    Do.   Tree and Serpent Worship. 105s.
Gamble, Manual of Indian Timbers. 10s.
Hunter's Imperial Gazetteer. 9 vols.
Jaschke's Tibetan-English Dictionary. 30s.
Kurz. Forest Flora of British Burma. Vols. I. and II. 15s. each.
Liotard's Materials for Paper. 2s. 6d.
Markham's Tibet. 21s.
    Do.   Memoir of Indian Surveys. 10s. 6d.
    Do.   Abstract of Reports of Surveys. 1s. 6d.
Mitra (Rajendralala), Buddha Gaya. 60s.
Moir, Torrent Regions of the Alps. 1s.
Mysore and Coorg Gazetteer. Vols. I. and II. 10s. each.
    Do.   do.   Vol. III. 5s.
N. W. P. Gazetteer. Vols. I. and II. 10s. each.
    Do.   do.   Vols. III. to VI. and X. 12s. each.
Oudh   do.   Vols. I. to III. 10s. each.
Pharmacopœia of India, The. 6s.
People of India, The. Vols. I. to VIII. 45s. each.
Raverty's Notes on Afghanistan and Baluchistan. Sections I. and II. 2s. Section III. 5s.
Rajputana Gazetteer. 3 vols. 15s.
Saunders' Mountains and River Basins of India. 3s.
Sewell's Amaravati Tope. 3s.
Smith's (Brough) Gold Mining in Wynaad. 1s.
Trigonometrical Survey, Synopsis of Great. Vols. I. to VI. 10s. 6d. each.
Trumpp's Adi Granth. 52s. 6d.
Watson's Cotton for Trials. Boards, 10s. 6d. Paper, 10s.
    Do.   Rhea Fibre. 2s. 6d.
    Do.   Tobacco. 5s.

INDIAN GAZETTEER.—See GAZETTEER.

INGLEBY.—See SHAKESPEARE.

INMAN.—NAUTICAL TABLES. Designed for the use of British Seamen. By the Rev. James Inman, D.D., late Professor at the Royal Naval College, Portsmouth. Demy 8vo, pp. xvi. and 410, cloth. 1877. 15s.

INMAN.—HISTORY OF THE ENGLISH ALPHABET : A Paper read before the Liverpool Literary and Philosophical Society. By T. Inman, M.D. 8vo, pp. 36, sewed. 1872. 1s.

IN SEARCH OF TRUTH. Conversations on the Bible and Popular Theology, for Young People. By A. M. Y. Crown 8vo, pp. x. and 138, cloth. 1875. 2s. 6d.

INTERNATIONAL NUMISMATA ORIENTALIA (THE).—Royal 4to, in paper wrapper. Part I. Ancient Indian Weights. By E. Thomas, F.R.S. Pp.84, with a Plate and Map of the India of Manu. 9s. 6d.—Part II. Coins of the Urtukí Turkumáns. By Stanley Lane Poole, Corpus Christi College, Oxford. Pp. 44, with 6 Plates. 9s.—Part III. The Coinage of Lydia and Persia, from the Earliest Times to the Fall of the Dynasty of the Achæmenidæ. By Barclay V. Head, Assistant-Keeper of Coins, British Museum. Pp. viii.-56, with 3 Autotype Plates. 10s. 6d.—Part IV. The Coins of the Tuluni Dynasty. By Edward Thomas Rogers. Pp. iv.-22, and 1 Plate. 5s.—Part V. The Parthian Coinage. By Percy Gardner, M.A. Pp. iv.-66, and 8 Autotype Plates. 18s.—Part VI. The Ancient Coins and Measures of Ceylon. By T. W. Rhys Davids. Pp. iv. and 60, and 1 Plate. 10s.—Vol. I., containing the first six parts, as specified above. Royal 4to, half bound. £3, 13s. 6d.

INTERNATIONAL N UMISMATA —*continued.*

Vol. II. COINS OF THE JEWS. Being a History of the Jewish Coinage and Money in the Old and New Testaments. By Frederick W. Madden, M.R.A.S., Member of the Numismatic Society of London, Secretary of the Brighton College, &c., &c. With 279 woodcuts and a plate of alphabets. Royal 4to, pp. xii. and 330, Sewed. 1881. £2.

THE COINS OF ARAKAN, OF PEGU, AND OF BURMA. By Lieut.-General Sir Arthur Phayre, C.B., K.C.S.I., G.C.M.G., late Commissioner of British Burma. Royal 4to, pp. viii. and 48, with Five Autotype Illustrations, wrapper. 1882. 8s. 6d.

JACKSON.—ETHNOLOGY AND PHRENOLOGY AS AN AID TO THE HISTORIAN. By the late J. W. Jackson. Second Edition. With a Memoir of the Author, by his Wife. Crown 8vo, pp. xx. and 324, cloth. 1875. 4s. 6d.

JACKSON.—THE SHROPSHIRE WORD-BOOK. A Glossary of Archaic and Provincial Words, &c., used in the County. By Georgina F. Jackson. Crown 8vo, pp. civ. and 524, cloth. 1881. 31s. 6d.

JACOB.—HINDU PANTHEISM. See Trübner's Oriental Series.

JAGIELSKI.—ON MARIENBAD SPA, and the Diseases Curable by its Waters and Baths. By A. V. Jagielski, M.D., Berlin. Second Edition. Crown 8vo, pp. viii. and 186. With Map. Cloth. 1874. 5s.

JAMISON.—THE LIFE AND TIMES OF BERTRAND DU GUESCLIN. A History of the Fourteenth Century. By D. F. Jamison, of South Carolina. Portrait. 2 vols. 8vo, pp. xvi., 287, and viii., 314, cloth. 1864. £1, 1s.

JAPAN.—MAP OF NIPPON (Japan): Compiled from Native Maps, and the Notes of most recent Travellers. By R. Henry Brunton, M.I.C.E., F.R.G.S., 1880. Size, 5 feet by 4 feet. 20 miles to the inch. In 4 Sheets, £1, 1s.; Roller, varnished, £1, 11s. 6d.; Folded, in Case, £1, 5s. 6d.

JATAKA (THE), together with its COMMENTARY : being tales of the Anterior Births of Gotama Buddha. Now first published in Pali, by V. Fausboll. Text. 8vo. Vol. I., pp. viii. and 512, cloth. 1877. 28s.—Vol. II., pp. 452, cloth. 1879. 28s.—Vol. III. *in preparation.* (For Translation see Trübner's Oriental Series, "Buddhist Birth Stories.")

JENKINS.—A PALADIN OF FINANCE : Contemporary Manners. By E. Jenkins, Author of "Ginx's Baby." Crown 8vo, pp. iv. and 392, cloth. 1882. 7s. 6d.

JENKINS.—VEST-POCKET LEXICON. An English Dictionary of all except familiar Words, including the principal Scientific and Technical Terms, and Foreign Moneys, Weights and Measures; omitting what everybody knows, and containing what everybody wants to know and cannot readily find. By Jabez Jenkins. 64mo, pp. 564, cloth. 1879. 1s. 6d.

JOHNSON.—ORIENTAL RELIGIONS. See English and Foreign Philosophical Library, Extra Series. Vols. IV. and V.

JOLLY.—See NARADÍYA.

JOMINI.—THE ART OF WAR. By Baron de Jomini, General and Aide-de-Camp to the Emperor of Russia. A New Edition, with Appendices and Maps. Translated from the French. By Captain G. H. Mendell, and Captain W. O. Craighill. Crown 8vo, pp. 410, cloth. 1879. 9s.

JORDAN.—ALBUM TO THE COURSE OF LECTURES ON METALLURGY, at the Paris Central School of Arts and Manufactures. By S. Jordan, C.E.M.1. & S.I. Demy 4to, paper. With 140 Plates, Description of the Plates, Numerical Data, and Notes upon the Working of the Apparatus. £4.

JOSEPH.—RELIGION, NATURAL AND REVEALED. A Series of Progressive Lessons for Jewish Youth. By N. S. Joseph. Crown 8vo, pp. xii.-296, cloth. 1879. 3s.

JUVENALIS SATIRÆ. With a Literal English Prose Translation and Notes. By J. D. Lewis, M.A., Trin. Coll. Camb. Second Edition. 8vo, pp. xii. and 230 and 400, cloth. 1882. 12s.

KARCHER.—QUESTIONNAIRE FRANÇAIS. Questions on French Grammar, Idiomatic Difficulties, and Military Expressions. By Theodore Karcher, LL.B. Fourth Edition, greatly enlarged. Crown 8vo, pp. 224, cloth. 1879. 4s. 6d. Interleaved with writing paper, 5s. 6d.

KARDEC.—THE SPIRIT'S BOOK. Containing the Principles of Spiritist Doctrine on the Immortality of the Soul, &c., &c., according to the Teachings of Spirits of High Degree, transmitted through various mediums, collected and set in order by Allen Kardec. Translated from the 120th thousand by Anna Blackwell. Crown 8vo, pp. 512, cloth. 1875. 7s. 6d.

KARDEC.—THE MEDIUM'S BOOK; or, Guide for Mediums and for Evocations. Containing the Theoretic Teachings of Spirits concerning all kinds of Manifestations, the Means of Communication with the Invisible World, the Development of Mediumnimity, &c., &c. By Allen Kardec. Translated by Anna Blackwell. Crown 8vo, pp. 456, cloth. 1876. 7s. 6d.

KARDEC.—HEAVEN AND HELL: or, the Divine Justice Vindicated in the Plurality of Existences. By Allen Kardec. Translated by Anna Blackwell. Crown 8vo, pp. viii. and 448, cloth. 1878. 7s. 6d.

KENDRICK.—GREEK OLLENDORFF. A Progressive Exhibition of the Principles of the Greek Grammar. By Asahel C. Kendrick. 8vo, pp. 371, cloth. 1870. 9s.

KERMODE.—NATAL: Its Early History, Rise, Progress, and Future Prospects as a Field for Emigration. By W. Kermode, of Natal. Crown 8vo, pp. xii. and 228, with Map, cloth. 1883. 3s. 6d.

KEYS OF THE CREEDS (THE). Third Revised Edition. Crown 8vo, pp. 210, cloth. 1876. 5s.

KINAHAN.—VALLEYS AND THEIR RELATION TO FISSURES, FRACTURES, AND FAULTS. By G. H. Kinahan, M.R.I.A., F.R.G.S.I., &c. Dedicated by permission to his Grace the Duke of Argyll. Crown 8vo, pp. 256, cloth, illustrated. 7s. 6d.

KING'S STRATAGEM (The); OR, THE PEARL OF POLAND; A Tragedy in Five Acts. By Stella. Second Edition. Crown 8vo, pp. 94, cloth. 1874. 2s. 6d.

KINGSTON.—THE UNITY OF CREATION. A Contribution to the Solution of the Religious Question. By F. H. Kingston. Crown 8vo, pp. viii. and 152, cloth. 1874. 5s.

KISTNER.—BUDDHA AND HIS DOCTRINES. A Bibliographical Essay. By Otto Kistner. 4to, pp. iv. and 32, sewed. 1869. 2s. 6d.

KLEMM.—MUSCLE BEATING; or, Active and Passive Home Gymnastics, for Healthy and Unhealthy People. By C. Klemm. With Illustrations. 8vo. pp. 60, wrapper. 1878. 1s.

KOHL.—TRAVELS IN CANADA AND THROUGH THE STATES OF NEW YORK AND PENNSYLVANIA. By J. G. Kohl. Translated by Mrs Percy Sinnett. Revised by the Author. Two vols. post 8vo, pp. xiv. and 794, cloth. 1861. £1, 1s.

KRAPF.—DICTIONARY OF THE SUAHILI LANGUAGE. Compiled by the Rev. Dr. L. Krapf, missionary of the Church Missionary Society in East Africa. With an Appendix, containing an outline of a Suahili Grammar. Medium 8vo, pp. xl. and 434, cloth. 1882. 30s.

KRAUS.—CARLSBAD AND ITS NATURAL HEALING AGENTS, from the Physiological and Therapentical Point of View. By J. Kraus, M.D. With Notes Introductory by the Rev. J. T. Walters, M.A. Second Edition. Revised and enlarged. Crown 8vo, pp. 104, cloth. 1880. 5s.

KROEGER.—THE MINNESINGER OF GERMANY. By A. E. Kroeger. Fcap. 8vo, pp. 290, cloth. 1873. 7s.

KURZ.—FOREST FLORA OF BRITISH BURMA. By S. Kurz, Curator of the Herbarium, Royal Botanical Gardens, Calcutta. 2 vols. crown 8vo, pp. xxx., 550, and 614, cloth. 1877. 30s.

LACERDA'S JOURNEY TO CAZEMBE in 1798. Translated and Annotated by Captain R. F. Burton, F.R.G.S. Also Journey of the Pombeiros, &c. Demy 8vo, pp. viii. and 272. With Map, cloth. 1873. 7s. 6d.

LANARI.—COLLECTION OF ITALIAN AND ENGLISH DIALOGUES. By A. Lanari. Fcap. 8vo, pp. viii. and 200, cloth. 1874. 3s. 6d.

LAND.—THE PRINCIPLES OF HEBREW GRAMMAR. By J. P. N. Land, Professor of Logic and Metaphysics in the University of Leyden. Translated from the Dutch, by Reginald Lane Poole, Balliol College, Oxford. Part I. Sounds. Part II. Words. With Large Additions by the Author, and a new Preface. Crown 8vo, pp. xx. and 220, cloth. 1876. 7s. 6d.

LANE.—THE KORAN. See Trübner's Oriental Series.

LANGE.—A HISTORY OF MATERIALISM. See English and Foreign Philosophical Library, Vols. I. to III.

LANGE.—GERMANIA. A German Reading-book Arranged Progressively. By F. K. W. Lange, Ph.D. Part I. Anthology of German Prose and Poetry, with Vocabulary and Biographical Notes. 8vo. pp. xvi. and 216, cloth, 1881, 3s. 6d. Part II. Essays on German History and Institutions, with Notes. 8vo, pp. 124, cloth. Parts I. and II. together. 5s. 6d.

LANGE.—GERMAN PROSE WRITING. Comprising English Passages for Translation into German. Selected from Examination Papers of the University of London, the College of Preceptors, London, and the Royal Military Academy, Woolwich, arranged progressively. with Notes and Theoretical as well as Practical Treatises on themes for the writing of Essays. By F. K. W. Lange, Ph.D., Assistant German Master, Royal Academy, Woolwich; Examiner, Royal College of Preceptors London. Crown 8vo, pp. viii. and 176, cloth. 1881. 4s.

LANGE.—GERMAN GRAMMAR PRACTICE. By F. K. W. Lange, Ph.D. Crown 8vo, pp. viii. and 64, cloth. 1882. 1s. 6d.

LANGE.—COLLOQUIAL GERMAN GRAMMAR. With Special Reference to the Anglo-Saxon Element in the English Language. By F. K. W. Lange, Ph.D., &c. Crown 8vo, pp. xxxii. and 380, cloth. 1882. 4s. 6d.

LASCARIDES.—A COMPREHENSIVE PHRASEOLOGICAL ENGLISH-ANCIENT AND MODERN GREEK LEXICON. Founded upon a manuscript of G. P. Lascarides, and Compiled by L. Myrianthous, Ph.D. 2 vols. 18mo, pp. xi. and 1338, cloth. 1882. £1, 10s.

LATHE (THE) AND ITS USES; or, Instruction in the Art of Turning Wood and Metal, including a description of the most modern appliances for the Ornamentation of Plain and Curved Surfaces, &c. Fifth Edition. With additional Chapters and Index. Illustrated. 8vo, pp. iv. and 316, cloth. 1878. 16s.

LE-BRUN.—MATERIALS FOR TRANSLATING FROM ENGLISH INTO FRENCH; being a short Essay on Translation, followed by a Graduated Selection in Prose and Verse. By L. Le-Brun. Seventh Edition Revised and corrected by Henri Van Laun. Post 8vo, pp. xii. and 204, cloth. 1882. 4s. 6d.

LEE.—ILLUSTRATIONS OF THE PHYSIOLOGY OF RELIGION. In Sections adapted for the use of Schools. Part I. By Henry Lee, F.R.C.S., formerly Professor of Surgery, Royal College of Surgeons, &c. Crown 8vo, pp. viii. and 108, cloth. 1880. 3s. 6d.

LEES.—A PRACTICAL GUIDE TO HEALTH, AND TO THE HOME TREATMENT OF THE COMMON AILMENTS OF LIFE: With a Section on Cases of Emergency, and Hints to Mothers on Nursing, &c. By F. Arnold Lees, F.L.S. Crown 8vo, pp. 334, stiff covers. 1874. 3s.

LEGGE.—THE CHINESE CLASSICS. With a Translation, Critical and Exegetical, Notes, Prolegomena, and copious Indexes. By James Legge, D.D., of the London Missionary Society. In 7 vols. Royal 8vo. Vols. I.-V. in Eight Parts, published, cloth. £2, 2s. each Part.

LEGGE.—THE CHINESE CLASSICS, translated into English. With Preliminary Essays and Explanatory Notes. Popular Edition. Reproduced for General Readers from the Author's work, containing the Original Text. By James Legge, D.D. Crown 8vo, Vol. I. The Life and Teachings of Confucius. Third Edition. Pp. vi. and 338, cloth. 1872. 10s. 6d. Vol. II. The Works of Mencius. Pp. x. and 402, cloth, 12s. Vol. III. The She-King; or, The Book of Poetry. Pp. vi. and 432, cloth. 1876. 12s.

LEGGE.—CONFUCIANISM IN RELATION TO CHRISTIANITY. A Paper read before the Missionary Conference in Shanghai, on May 11th, 1877. By Rev. James Legge, D.D., LL.D., &c. 8vo, pp. 12, sewed. 1877. 1s. 6d.

LEGGE.—A LETTER TO PROFESSOR MAX MÜLLER, chiefly on the Translation into English of the Chinese Terms Tî and Shang Tî. By James Legge, Professor of the Chinese Language and Literature in the University of Oxford. Crown 8vo, pp. 30, sewed. 1880. 1s.

LEIGH.—THE RELIGION OF THE WORLD. By H. Stone Leigh. 12mo, pp. xii. and 66, cloth. 1869. 2s. 6d.

LEIGH.—THE STORY OF PHILOSOPHY. By Aston Leigh. Post 8vo, pp. xii. and 210, cloth. 1881. 6s.

LELAND.—THE BREITMANN BALLADS. The only authorised Edition. Complete in 1 vol., including Nineteen Ballads, illustrating his Travels in Europe (never before printed), with Comments by Fritz Schwackenhammer. By Charles G. Leland. Crown 8vo, pp. xxviii. and 292, cloth. 1872. 6s.

LELAND.—THE MUSIC LESSON OF CONFUCIUS, and other Poems. By Charles G. Leland. Fcap. 8vo, pp. viii. and 168, cloth. 1871. 3s. 6d.

LELAND.—GAUDEAMUS. Humorous Poems translated from the German of Joseph Victor Scheffel and others. By Charles G. Leland. 16mo, pp. 176, cloth 1872. 3s. 6d.

LELAND.—THE EGYPTIAN SKETCH-BOOK. By C. G. Leland. Crown 8vo, pp. viii. and 316, cloth. 1873. 7s. 6d.

LELAND.—THE ENGLISH GIPSIES AND THEIR LANGUAGE. By Charles G. Leland. Second Edition. Crown 8vo, pp. xvi. and 260, cloth. 1874. 7s. 6d.

LELAND.—ENGLISH GIPSY SONGS IN ROMMANY, with Metrical English Translations. By Charles G. Leland, Professor E. H. Palmer, and Janet Tuckey. Crown 8vo, pp. xii. and 276, cloth. 1875. 7s. 6d.

LELAND.— Fu-Sang ; or, The Discovery of America by Chinese Buddhist Priests in the Fifth Century. By Charles G. Leland. Crown 8vo, pp. 232, cloth. 1875. 7s. 6d.

LELAND.—Pidgin-English Sing-Song ; or, Songs and Stories in the China-English Dialect. With a Vocabulary. By Charles G. Leland. Crown 8vo, pp. viii. and 140, cloth. 1876. 5s.

LELAND.—The Gypsies. By C. G. Leland. Crown 8vo, pp. 372, cloth. 1882. 10s. 6d.

LEOPARDI.—See English and Foreign Philosophical Library, Vol. XVII.

LEO.—Four Chapters of North's Plutarch, Containing the Lives of Caius Marcius, Coriolanus, Julius Cæsar, Marcus Antonius, and Marcus Brutus, as Sources to Shakespeare's Tragedies ; Coriolanus, Julius Cæsar, and Antony and Cleopatra ; and partly to Hamlet and Timon of Athens. Photolithographed in the size of the Edition of 1595. With Preface, Notes comparing the Text of the Editions of 1579, 1595, 1603, and 1612 ; and Reference Notes to the Text of the Tragedies of Shakespeare. Edited by Professor F. A. Leo, Ph.D., Vice-President of the New Shakespeare Society ; Member of the Directory of the German Shakespeare Society ; and Lecturer at the Academy of Modern Philology at Berlin. Folio, pp. 22, 130 of facsimiles, half-morocco. Library Edition (limited to 250 copies), £1, 11s. 6d. ; Amateur Edition (50 copies on a superior large hand-made paper), £3, 3s.

LERMONTOFF.—The Demon. By Michael Lermontoff. Translated from the Russian by A. Coudie Stephen. Crown 8vo, pp. 88, cloth. 1881. 2s. 6d.

LESLEY.—Man's Origin and Destiny. Sketched from the Platform of the Physical Sciences. By. J. P. Lesley, Member of the National Academy of the United States, Professor of Geology, University of Pennsylvania. Second (Revised and considerably Enlarged) Edition, crown 8vo, pp. viii. and 142, cloth. 1881. 7s. 6d.

LESSING.—Letters on Bibliolatry. By Gotthold Ephraim Lessing. Translated from the German by the late H. H. Bernard, Ph.D. 8vo, pp. 184, cloth. 1862. 5s.

LESSING.—See English and Foreign Philosophical Library, Extra Series, Vols. I. and II.

LETTERS on the War between Germany and France. By Mommsen, Strauss, Max Müller, and Carlyle. Second Edition. Crown 8vo, pp. 120, cloth. 1871. 2s. 6d.

LEWES.— Problems of Life and Mind. By George Henry Lewes. First Series : The Foundations of a Creed. Vol. I., demy 8vo. Third edition, pp. 488, cloth. 12s.—Vol. II., demy 8vo, pp. 552, cloth. 1875. 16s.

LEWES.—Problems of Life and Mind. By George Henry Lewes. Second Series. The Physical Basis of Mind. 8vo, with Illustrations, pp. 508, cloth. 1877. 16s. Contents.—The Nature of Life ; The Nervous Mechanism ; Animal Automatism ; The Reflex Theory.

LEWES.—Problems of Life and Mind. By George Henry Lewes. Third Series. Problem the First—The Study of Psychology : Its Object, Scope, and Method. Demy 8vo, pp. 200, cloth. 1879. 7s. 6d.

LEWES.—Problems of Life and Mind. By George Henry Lewes. Third Series. Problem the Second—Mind as a Function of the Organism. Problem the Third — The Sphere of Sense and Logic of Feeling. Problem the Fourth—The Sphere of Intellect and Logic of Signs. Demy 8vo, pp. x. and 500, cloth. 1879. 15s.

LEWIS.—See JUVENAL and PLINY.

LIBRARIANS, TRANSACTIONS AND PROCEEDINGS OF THE CONFERENCE OF, held in London, October 1877. Edited by Edward B. Nicholson and Henry R. Tedder. Imperial 8vo, pp. 276, cloth. 1878. £1, 8s.

LIBRARY ASSOCIATION OF THE UNITED KINGDOM, Transactions and Proceedings of the Annual Meetings of the. Imperial 8vo, cloth. FIRST, held at Oxford, October 1, 2, 3, 1878. Edited by the Secretaries, Henry R. Tedder, Librarian of the Athenæum Club, and Ernest C. Thomas, late Librarian of the Oxford Union Society. Pp. viii. and 192. 1879. £1, 8s. SECOND, held at Manchester, September 23, 24, and 25, 1879. Edited by H. R. Tedder and E. C. Thomas. Pp. x. and 184. 1880. £1, 1s.—THIRD, held at Edinburgh, October 5, 6, and 7, 1880. Edited by E. C. Thomas and C. Welsh. Pp. x. and 202. 1881. £1, 1s.

LIEBER.—THE LIFE AND LETTERS OF FRANCIS LIEBER. Edited by T. S. Perry. 8vo, pp. iv. and 440, cloth, with Portrait. 1882. 14s.

LILLIE.—BUDDHA AND EARLY BUDDHISM. By Arthur Lillie, late Regiment of Lucknow. With numerous Illustrations drawn on Wood by the Author. Post 8vo, pp. xiv. and 256, cloth. 1881. 7s. 6d.

LITTLE FRENCH READER (THE). Extracted from "The Modern French Reader." Second Edition. Crown 8vo, pp. 112, cloth. 1872. 2s.

LLOYD AND NEWTON.—PRUSSIA'S REPRESENTATIVE MAN. By F. Lloyd of the Universities of Halle and Athens, and W. Newton, F.R.G.S. Crown 8vo, pp. 648, cloth. 1875. 10s. 6d.

LOBSCHEID.—CHINESE AND ENGLISH DICTIONARY, arranged according to the Radicals. By W. Lobscheid. 1 vol. imperial 8vo, pp. 600, cloth. £2, 8s.

LOBSCHEID.—ENGLISH AND CHINESE DICTIONARY, with the Punti and Mandarin Pronunciation. By W. Lobscheid. Four Parts. Folio, pp. viii. and 2016, boards. £8, 8s.

LONG.—EASTERN PROVERBS. See Trübner's Oriental Series.

LOVETT.—THE LIFE AND STRUGGLES OF WILLIAM LOVETT in his pursuit of Bread, Knowledge, and Freedom ; with some short account of the different Associations he belonged to, and of the Opinions he entertained. 8vo, pp. vi. and 474, cloth. 1876. 5s.

LOVELY.—WHERE TO GO FOR HELP: Being a Companion for Quick and Easy Reference of Police Stations, Fire-Engine Stations, Fire-Escape Stations, &c., &c., of London and the Suburbs. Compiled by W. Lovely, R.N. Third Edition. 18mo, pp. 16, sewed. 1882. 3d.

LOWELL.—THE BIGLOW PAPERS. By James Russell Lowell. Edited by Thomas Hughes, Q.C. A Reprint of the Authorised Edition of 1859, together with the Second Series of 1862. First and Second Series in 1 vol. Fcap., pp. lxviii.-140 and lxiv.-190, cloth. 1880. 2s. 6d.

LUCAS.—THE CHILDREN'S PENTATEUCH : With the Hephterahs or Portions from the Prophets. Arranged for Jewish Children. By Mrs. Henry Lucas. Crown 8vo, pp. viii. and 570, cloth. 1878. 5s.

LUDEWIG.—THE LITERATURE OF AMERICAN ABORIGINAL LANGUAGES. By Hermann E. Ludewig. With Additions and Corrections by Professor Wm. W. Turner. Edited by Nicolas Trübner. 8vo, pp. xxiv. and 258, cloth. 1858. 10s. 6d.

LUKIN.—THE BOY ENGINEERS: What they did, and how they did it. By the Rev. L. J. Lukin. Author of "The Young Mechanic." &c. A Book for Boys; 30 Engravings. Imperial 16mo, pp. viii. and 344, cloth. 1877. 7s. 6d.

LUX E TENEBRIS; OR, THE TESTIMONY OF CONSCIOUSNESS. A Theoretic Essay. Crown 8vo, pp. 376, with Diagram, cloth. 1874. 10s. 6d.

MACCORMAC.—THE CONVERSATION OF A SOUL WITH GOD : A Theodicy. By Henry MacCormac, M.D. 16mo, pp. xvi. and 144, cloth. 1877. 3s. 6d.

MACHIAVELLI.—THE HISTORICAL, POLITICAL, AND DIPLOMATIC WRITINGS OF NICCOLO MACHIAVELLI. Translated from the Italian by C. E. Detmold. With Portraits. 4 vols. 8vo, cloth, pp. xli., 420, 464, 488, and 472. 1882. £3, 3s.

MADDEN.—COINS OF THE JEWS. Being a History of the Jewish Coinage and Money in the Old and New Testaments. By Frederick W. Madden, M.R.A.S. Member of the Numismatic Society of London, Secretary of the Brighton College. &c., &c. With 279 Woodcuts and a Plate of Alphabets. Royal 4to, pp. xii. and 330, cloth. 1881. £2, 2s.

MADELUNG.—THE CAUSES AND OPERATIVE TREATMENT OF DUPUYTREN'S FINGER CONTRACTION. By Dr. Otto W. Madelung. Lecturer of Surgery at the University, and Assistant Surgeon at the University Hospital, Bonn. 8vo, pp. 24, sewed. 1876. 1s.

MAHAPARINIBBANASUTTA.—See CHILDERS.

MAHA-VIRA-CHARITA; or, The Adventures of the Great Hero Rama. An Indian Drama in Seven Acts. Translated into English Prose from the Sanskrit of Bhavabhūti. By John Pickford, M.A. Crown 8vo, cloth. 5s.

MALET.—INCIDENTS IN THE BIOGRAPHY OF DUST. By H. P. Malet, Author of "The Interior of the Earth," &c. Crown 8vo, pp. 272, cloth. 1877. 6s.

MALET.—THE BEGINNINGS. By H. P. Malet. Crown 8vo, pp. xix. and 124, cloth. 1878. 4s. 6d.

MALLESON.—ESSAYS AND LECTURES ON INDIAN HISTORICAL SUBJECTS. By Colonel G. B. Malleson, C.S.I. Second Issue. Crown 8vo, pp. 348, cloth. 1876. 5s.

MANDLEY.—WOMAN OUTSIDE CHRISTENDOM. An Exposition of the Influence exerted by Christianity on the Social Position and Happiness of Women. By J. G. Mandley. Crown 8vo, pp. viii. and 160, cloth. 1880. 5s.

MANIPULUS VOCABULORUM. A Rhyming Dictionary of the English Language. By Peter Levins (1570). Edited, with an Alphabetical Index, by Henry B. Wheatley. 8vo, pp. xvi. and 370, cloth. 1867. 14s.

MANŒUVRES.—A RETROSPECT OF THE AUTUMN MANŒUVRES, 1871. With 5 Plans. By a Recluse. 8vo, pp. xii. and 133, cloth. 1872. 5s.

MARIETTE-BEY.—THE MONUMENTS OF UPPER EGYPT : a translation of the "Itinéraire de la Haute Égypte" of Auguste Mariette-Bey. Translated by Alphonse Mariette. Crown 8vo, pp. xvi. and 262, cloth. 1877. 7s. 6d.

MARKHAM.—QUICHUA GRAMMAR AND DICTIONARY. Contributions towards a Grammar and Dictionary of Quichua, the Language of the Yncas of Peru. Collected by Clements R. Markham, F.S.A. Crown 8vo, pp. 223, cloth. £1, 11s. 6d.

MARKHAM.—OLLANTA: A Drama in the Quichua Language. Text, Translation, and Introduction. By Clements R. Markham, C.B. Crown 8vo, pp. 128, cloth. 1871. 7s. 6d.

MARKHAM. A MEMOIR OF THE LADY ANA DE OSORIO, Countess of Chincon, and Vice-Queen of Peru, A.D. 1629-39. With a Plea for the correct spelling of the Chinchona Genus. By Clements R. Markham, C.B., Member of the Imperial Academy Naturæ Curiosorum, with the Cognomen of Chinchon. Small 4to, pp. xii. and 100. With 2 Coloured Plates, Map, and Illustrations. Handsomely bound. 1874. 28s.

MARKHAM.—A MEMOIR ON THE INDIAN SURVEYS. By Clements R. Markham, C.B., F.R.S., &c., &c. Published by Order of H. M. Secretary of State for India in Council. Illustrated with Maps. Second Edition. Imperial 8vo, pp. xxx. and 481, boards. 1878. 10s. 6d.

MARKHAM.—NARRATIVES OF THE MISSION OF GEORGE BOGLE TO TIBET, and of the Journey of Thomas Manning to Lhasa. Edited with Notes, an Introduction, and Lives of Mr. Bogle and Mr. Manning. By Clements R. Markham, C B., F.R.S. Second Edition. 8vo, pp. clxv. and 362, cloth. With Maps and Illustrations. 1879. 21s.

MARMONTEL.—BELISAIRE. Par Marmontel. Nouvelle Edition. 12mo, pp. xii. and 123, cloth. 1867. 2s. 6d.

MARTIN AND TRÜBNER.—THE CURRENT GOLD AND SILVER COINS OF ALL COUNTRIES, their Weight and Fineness, and their Intrinsic Value in English Money, with Facsimiles of the Coins. By Leopold C. Martin, of Her Majesty's Stationery Office, and Charles Trübner. In 1 vol. medium 8vo, 141 Plates, printed in Gold and Silver, and representing about 1000 Coins, with 160 pages of Text, handsomely bound in embossed cloth, richly gilt, with Emblematical Designs on the Cover, and gilt edges. 1863. £2. 2s.

MARTIN.—THE CHINESE: THEIR EDUCATION, PHILOSOPHY, AND LETTERS. By W. A. P. Martin, D.D., LL.D., President of the Tungwen College, Pekin. 8vo. pp. 320, cloth. 1881. 7s. 6d.

MARTINEAU.—ESSAYS, PHILOSOPHICAL AND THEOLOGICAL. By James Martineau. 2 vols. crown 8vo, pp. iv. and 414—x. and 430, cloth. 1875. £1, 4s.

MARTINEAU.—LETTERS FROM IRELAND. By Harriet Martineau. Reprinted from the *Daily News*. Post 8vo, pp. viii. and 220, cloth. 1852. 6s. 6d.

MATHEWS.—ABRAHAM IBN EZRA'S COMMENTARY ON THE CANTICLES AFTER THE FIRST RECENSION. Edited from the MSS., with a translation, by H. J. Mathews, B.A., Exeter College, Oxford. Crown 8vo, pp. x., 34, and 24, limp cloth. 1874. 2s. 6d.

MAXWELL.—A MANUAL OF THE MALAY LANGUAGE. By W. E. Maxwell, of the Inner Temple, Barrister-at-Law; Assistant Resident, Perak, Malay Peninsula. With an Introductory Sketch of the Sanskrit Element in Malay. Crown 8vo, pp. viii. and 182, cloth. 1882. 7s. 6d.

MAYER.—ON THE ART OF POTTERY: with a History of its Rise and Progress in Liverpool. By Joseph Mayer, F.S.A., F.R.S.N.A., &c. 8vo, pp. 100, boards. 1873. 5s.

MAYERS.—TREATIES BETWEEN THE EMPIRE OF CHINA AND FOREIGN POWERS, together with Regulations for the conduct of Foreign Trade, &c. Edited by W. F. Mayers, Chinese Secretary to H.B.M.'s Legation at Peking. 8vo, pp. 246, cloth. 1877. 25s.

MAYERS -The Chinese Government: a Manual of Chinese Titles, categorically arranged and explained, with an Appendix. By Wm. Fred. Mayers, Chinese Secretary to H.B.M.'s Legation at Peking, &c., &c. Royal 8vo, pp. viii. and 160, cloth. 1878. 30s.

M'CRINDLE.—Ancient India, as Described by Megasthenes and Arrian; being a translation of the fragments of the Indika of Megasthenes collected by Dr. Schwanbeck, and of the first part of the Indika of Arrian. By J. W. M'Crindle, M.A., Principal of the Government- College, Patna, &c. With Introduction, Notes, and Map of Ancient India. Post 8vo, pp. xi. and 224, cloth. 1877. 7s. 6d.

M'CRINDLE.—The Commerce and Navigation of the Erythraean Sea. Being a Translation of the Periplus Maris Erythraei, by an Anonymous Writer, and of Arrian's Account of the Voyage of Nearkhos, from the Mouth of the Indus to the Head of the Persian Gulf. With Introduction, Commentary, Notes, and Index. By J. W. M'Crindle, M.A., Edinburgh, &c. Post 8vo, pp. iv. and 238, cloth. 1879. 7s. 6d.

M'CRINDLE.—Ancient India as Described by Ktesias the Knidian: being a Translation of the Abridgment of his "Indika" by Photios, and of the Fragments of that Work preserved in other Writers. With Introduction, Notes, and Index. By J. W. M'Crindle, M.A., M.R.S.A. 8vo, pp. viii. and 104, cloth. 1882. 6s.

MECHANIC (The Young). A Book for Boys, containing Directions for the use of all kinds of Tools, and for the construction of Steam Engines and Mechanical Models, including the Art of Turning in Wood and Metal. Fifth Edition. Imperial 16mo, pp. iv. and 346, and 70 Engravings, cloth. 1878. 6s.

MECHANIC'S Workshop (Amateur). A Treatise containing Plain and Concise Directions for the Manipulation of Wood and Metals, including Casting, Forging, Brazing, Soldering, and Carpentry. By the Author of "The Lathe and its Uses." Sixth Edition. Demy 8vo, pp. iv. and 148. Illustrated, cloth. 1880. 6s.

MEDITATIONS on Death and Eternity. Translated from the German by Frederica Rowan. Published by Her Majesty's gracious permission. 8vo, pp. 386, cloth. 1862. 10s. 6d.

Ditto. Smaller Edition, crown 8vo, printed on toned paper, pp. 352, cloth. 1863. 6s.

MEDITATIONS on Life and its Religious Duties. Translated from the German by Frederica Rowan. Dedicated to H.R.H. Princess Louis of Hesse. Published by Her Majesty's gracious permission. Being the Companion Volume to "Meditations on Death and Eternity." 8vo, pp. vi. and 370, cloth. 1863. 10s. 6d.

Ditto. Smaller Edition, crown 8vo, printed on toned paper, pp. 338. 1863. 6s.

MEDLICOTT.—A Manual of the Geology of India, chiefly compiled from the observations of the Geological Survey. By H. B. Medlicott, M.A., Superintendent, Geological Survey of India, and W. T. Blanford, A.R.S.M., F.R.S., Deputy Superintendent. Published by order of the Government of India. 2 vols. 8vo, pp. xviii.-lxxx.-818. with 21 Plates and large coloured Map mounted in case, uniform, cloth. 1879. 16s. (For Part III. see Ball.)

MEGHA-DUTA (The). (Cloud-Messenger.) By Kālidāsa. Translated from the Sanskrit into English Verse by the late H. H. Wilson, M.A., F.R.S. The Vocabulary by Francis Johnson. New Edition. 4to, pp. xi. and 180, cloth. 10s. 6d.

MENKE.—ORBIS ANTIQUI DESCRIPTIO: An Atlas illustrating Ancient History and Geography, for the Use of Schools; containing 18 Maps engraved on Steel and Coloured, with Descriptive Letterpress. By D. T. Menke. Fourth Edition. Folio, half bound morocco. 1866. 5s.

MEREDYTH.—ARCA, A REPERTOIRE OF ORIGINAL POEMS, Sacred and Secular. By F. Meredyth, M.A., Canon of Limerick Cathedral. Crown 8vo, pp. 124, cloth. 1875. 5s.

METCALFE.—THE ENGLISHMAN AND THE SCANDINAVIAN. By Frederick Metcalfe, M.A., Fellow of Lincoln College, Oxford; Translator of "Gallus" and "Charicles;" and Author of "The Oxonian in Iceland." Post 8vo, pp. 512, cloth. 1880. 18s.

MICHEL.—LES ÉCOSSAIS EN FRANCE, LES FRANÇAIS EN ÉCOSSE. Par Francisque Michel, Correspondant de l'Institut de France, &c. In 2 vols. 8vo, pp. vii., 547, and 551, rich blue cloth, with emblematical designs. With upwards of 100 Coats of Arms, and other Illustrations. Price, £1, 12s.—Also a Large-Paper Edition (limited to 100 Copies), printed on Thick Paper. 2 vols. 4to, half morocco, with 3 additional Steel Engravings. 1862. £3, 3s.

MICKIEWICZ.—KONRAD WALLENROD. An Historical Poem. By A. Mickiewicz. Translated from the Polish into English Verse by Miss M. Biggs. 18mo, pp. xvi. and 100, cloth. 1882. 2s. 6d.

MILL.—AUGUSTE COMTE AND POSITIVISM. By the late John Stuart Mill, M.P. Third Edition. 8vo, pp. 200, cloth. 1882. 3s. 6d.

MILLHOUSE.—MANUAL OF ITALIAN CONVERSATION. For the Use of Schools. By John Millhouse. 18mo, pp. 126, cloth. 1866. 2s.

MILLHOUSE.—NEW ENGLISH AND ITALIAN PRONOUNCING AND EXPLANATORY DICTIONARY. By John Millhouse. Vol. I. English-Italian. Vol. II. Italian-English. Fourth Edition. 2 vols. square 8vo, pp. 654 and 740, cloth. 1867. 12s.

MILNE.—NOTES ON CRYSTALLOGRAPHY AND CRYSTALLO-PHYSICS. Being the Substance of Lectures delivered at Yedo during the years 1876-1877. By John Milne, F.G.S. 8vo, pp. viii. and 70, cloth. 1879. 3s.

MINOCHCHERJI.—PAHLAVI, GUJÁRATI, AND ENGLISH DICTIONARY. By Jamashji Dastur Minochcherji. Vol. I., with Photograph of Author. 8vo, pp. clxxii. and 168, cloth. 1877. 14s.

MITRA.—BUDDHA GAYA: The Hermitage of Sákya Muni. By Rajendralala Mitra, LL.D., C.I.E., &c. 4to, pp. xvi. and 258, with 51 Plates, cloth. 1879. £3.

MOCATTA.—MORAL BIBLICAL GLEANINGS AND PRACTICAL TEACHINGS, Illustrated by Biographical Sketches Drawn from the Sacred Volume. By J. L. Mocatta. 8vo, pp. viii. and 446, cloth. 1872. 7s.

MODERN FRENCH READER (THE). Prose. Junior Course. Sixth Edition. Edited by Ch. Cassal, LL.D., and Théodore Karcher, LL.B. Crown 8vo, pp. xiv. and 224, cloth. 1879. 2s. 6d.

SENIOR COURSE. Third Edition. Crown 8vo, pp. xiv. and 418, cloth. 1880. 4s.

MODERN FRENCH READER.—A GLOSSARY of Idioms, Gallicisms, and other Difficulties contained in the Senior Course of the Modern French Reader; with Short Notices of the most important French Writers and Historical or Literary Characters, and hints as to the works to be read or studied. By Charles Cassal, LL.D., &c. Crown 8vo, pp. viii. and 104, cloth. 1881. 2s. 6d.

MODERN FRENCH READER. —Senior Course and Glossary combined. 6s.

MORELET. —Travels in Central America, including Accounts of some Regions unexplored since the Conquest. From the French of A. Morelet, by Mrs. M. F. Squier. Edited by E. G. Squier. 8vo, pp. 430, cloth. 1871. 8s. 6d.

MORFIT. —A Practical Treatise on the Manufacture of Soaps. By Campbell Morfit, M.D., F.C.S., formerly Professor of Applied Chemistry in the University of Maryland. With Illustrations. Demy 8vo, pp. xii. and 270, cloth. 1871. £2, 12s. 6d.

MORFIT. —A Practical Treatise on Pure Fertilizers, and the Chemical Conversion of Rock Guanos, Marlstones, Coprolites, and the Crude Phosphates of Lime and Alumina generally into various valuable Products. By Campbell Morfit, M.D., F.C.S., formerly Professor of Applied Chemistry in the University of Maryland. With 28 Plates. 8vo, pp. xvi. and 547, cloth. 1873. £4, 4s.

MORRIS. —A Descriptive and Historical Account of the Godavery District, in the Presidency of Madras. By Henry Morris, formerly of the Madras Civil Service, author of "A History of India, for use in Schools," and other works. With a Map. 8vo, pp. xii. and 390, cloth. 1878. 12s.

MOSENTHAL. —Ostriches and Ostrich Farming. By J. de Mosenthal, late Member of the Legistive Council of the Cape of Good Hope, &c., and James E. Harting, F.L.S., F.Z.S., Member of the British Ornithologist's Union, &c. Second Edition. With 8 full-page illustrations and 20 woodcuts. Royal 8vo, pp. xxiv. and 246, cloth. 1879. 10s. 6d.

MOTLEY. —John Lothrop Motley : a Memoir. By Oliver Wendell Holmes. English Copyright Edition. Crown 8vo, pp. xii. and 275, cloth. 1878. 6s.

MUELLER. —The Organic Constituents of Plants and Vegetable Substances, and their Chemical Analysis. By Dr. G. C. Wittstein. Authorised Translation from the German Original, enlarged with numerous Additions, by Baron Ferd. von Mueller. K.C.M.G., M. & Ph. D., F.R.S. Crown 8vo, pp. xviii. and 332, wrapper. 1880. 14s.

MUELLER. —Select Extra-Tropical Plants readily eligible for Industrial Culture or Naturalisation. With Indications of their Native Countries and some of their Uses. By F. Von Mueller, K.C.M.G., M.D., Ph.D., F.R.S. 8vo, pp. x., 394, cloth. 1880. 8s.

MUHAMMED. —The Life of Muhammed. Based on Muhammed Ibn Ishak. By Abd El Malik Ibn Hisham. Edited by Dr. Ferdinand Wüstenfeld. One volume containing the Arabic Text. 8vo, pp. 1026, sewed. £1, 1s. Another volume, containing Introduction, Notes, and Index in German. 8vo, pp. lxxii. and 266, sewed. 7s. 6d. Each part sold separately.

MUIR. —Extracts from the Coran. In the Original, with English rendering. Compiled by Sir William Muir, K.C.S.I., LL.D., Author of "The Life of Mahomet." Crown 8vo, pp. viii. and 64, cloth. 1880. 3s. 6d.

MUIR. —Original Sanskrit Texts, on the Origin and History of the People of India, their Religion and Institutions. Collected, Translated, and Illustrated by John Muir, D.C.L., LL.D., Ph.D., &c. &c.
Vol. I. Mythical and Legendary Accounts of the Origin of Caste, with an Inquiry into its existence in the Vedic Age. Second Edition, rewritten and greatly enlarged. 8vo, pp. xx. and 532, cloth. 1868. £1, 1s.

MUIR.—ORIGINAL SANSKRIT TEXTS—*continued.*

Vol. II. The Trans-Himalayan Origin of the Hindus, and their Affinity with the Western Branches of the Aryan Race. Second Edition, revised, with Additions. 8vo, pp. xxxii. and 512, cloth. 1871. £1, 1s.

Vol. III. The Vedas: Opinions of their Authors, and of later Indian Writers, on their Origin, Inspiration, and Authority. Second Edition, revised and enlarged. 8vo, pp. xxxii. and 312, cloth. 1868. 16s.

Vol. IV. Comparison of the Vedic with the later representation of the principal Indian Deities. Second Edition, revised. 8vo, pp. xvi. and 524, cloth. 1873. £1, 1s.

Vol. V. Contributions to a Knowledge of the Cosmogony, Mythology, Religious Ideas, Life and Manners of the Indians in the Vedic Age. 8vo, pp. xvi. and 492, cloth. 1870. £1, 1s.

MUIR.—TRANSLATIONS FROM THE SANSKRIT. See Trübner's Oriental Series.

MÜLLER.—OUTLINE DICTIONARY, for the Use of Missionaries, Explorers, and Students of Language. With an Introduction on the proper Use of the Ordinary English Alphabet in transcribing Foreign Languages. By F. Max Müller, M.A. The Vocabulary compiled by John Bellows. 12mo, pp. 368, morocco. 1867. 7s. 6d.

MÜLLER.—LECTURE ON BUDDHIST NIHILISM. By F. Max Müller, M.A. Fcap. 8vo, sewed. 1869. 1s.

MÜLLER.—THE SACRED HYMNS OF THE BRAHMINS, as preserved to us in the oldest collection of religious poetry, the Rig-Veda-Sanhita. Translated and explained, by F. Max Müller, M.A., Fellow of All Souls' College, Professor of Comparative Philology at Oxford, Foreign Member of the Institute of France. &c., &c. Vol. I. Hymns to the Maruts or the Storm-Gods. 8vo, pp. clii. and 264, cloth. 1869. 12s. 6d.

MÜLLER.—THE HYMNS OF THE RIG-VEDA, in the Samhita and Pada Texts. Reprinted from the Editio Princeps. By F. Max Müller, M.A., &c. Second Edition, with the two Texts on Parallel Pages. In two vols. 8vo, pp. 1704, sewed. £1, 12s.

MÜLLER.—A SHORT HISTORY OF THE BOURBONS. From the Earliest Period down to the Present Time. By R. M. Müller, Ph.D., Modern Master at Forest School, Walthamstow, and Author of "Parallèle entre 'Jules César,' par Shakespeare, et 'Le Mort de César,' par Voltaire," &c. Fcap. 8vo, pp. 30, wrapper. 1882. 1s.

MÜLLER.—ANCIENT INSCRIPTIONS IN CEYLON. By Dr. Edward Müller. 2 Vols. Text, crown 8vo, pp. 220, cloth, and Plates, oblong folio, cloth. 1883. 21s.

MULLEY.—GERMAN GEMS IN AN ENGLISH SETTING. Translated by Jane Mulley. Fcap., pp. xii. and 180, cloth. 1877. 3s. 6d.

NÁGÁNANDA; OR, THE JOY OF THE SNAKE WORLD. A Buddhist Drama in Five Acts. Translated into English Prose, with Explanatory Notes, from the Sanskrit of Sri-Harsha-Deva, by Palmer Boyd, B.A. With an Introduction by Professor Cowell. Crown 8vo, pp. xvi. and 100, cloth. 1872. 4s. 6d.

NAPIER.—FOLK LORE: or, Superstitious Beliefs in the West of Scotland within this Century. With an Appendix, showing the probable relation of the modern Festivals of Christmas, May Day, St. John's Day, and Hallowe'en, to ancient Sun and Fire Worship. By James Napier, F.R.S.E., &c. Crown 8vo, pp. vii. and 190, cloth. 1878. 4s.

NARADÍYA DHARMA-SASTRA; OR, THE INSTITUTES OF NARADA. Translated, for the first time, from the unpublished Sanskrit original. By Dr. Julius Jolly, University, Wurzburg. With a Preface, Notes, chiefly critical, an Index of Quotations from Narada in the principal Indian Digests, and a general Index. Crown 8vo, pp. xxxv. and 144, cloth. 1876. 10s. 6d.

NEVILL.—HAND LIST OF MOLLUSCA IN THE INDIAN MUSEUM, CALCUTTA. By Geoffrey Nevill, C.M.Z.S., &c., First Assistant to the Superintendent of the Indian Museum. Part I. Gastropoda, Pulmonata, and Prosobranchia-Neurobranchia. 8vo, pp. xvi. and 338, cloth. 1878. 15s.

NEWMAN.— THE ODES OF HORACE. Translated into Unrhymed Metres, with Introduction and Notes. By F. W. Newman. Second Edition. Post 8vo, pp. xxi. and 247, cloth. 1876. 4s.

NEWMAN.—THEISM, DOCTRINAL AND PRACTICAL; or, Didactic Religious Utterances. By F. W. Newman. 4to, pp. 184, cloth. 1858. 4s. 6d.

NEWMAN.—HOMERIC TRANSLATION IN THEORY AND PRACTICE. A Reply to Matthew Arnold. By F. W. Newman. Crown 8vo, pp. 104, stiff covers. 1861. 2s. 6d.

NEWMAN.—HIAWATHA: Rendered into Latin. With Abridgment. By F. W. Newman. 12mo, pp. vii. and 110, sewed. 1862. 2s. 6d.

NEWMAN.—A HISTORY OF THE HEBREW MONARCHY from the Administration of Samuel to the Babylonish Captivity. By F. W. Newman. Third Edition. Crown 8vo, pp. x. and 354, cloth. 1865. 8s. 6d.

NEWMAN.—PHASES OF FAITH; or, Passages from the History of my Creed. New Edition; with Reply to Professor Henry Rogers, Author of the "Eclipse of Faith." Crown 8vo, pp. viii. and 212, cloth. 1881. 3s. 6d.

NEWMAN.—A HANDBOOK OF MODERN ARABIC, consisting of a Practical Grammar, with numerous Examples, Dialogues, and Newspaper Extracts, in European Type. By F. W. Newman. Post 8vo, pp. xx. and 192, cloth. 1866. 6s.

NEWMAN.—TRANSLATIONS OF ENGLISH POETRY INTO LATIN VERSE. Designed as Part of a New Method of Instructing in Latin. By F. W. Newman. Crown 8vo, pp. xiv. and 202, cloth. 1868. 6s.

NEWMAN.—THE SOUL: Her Sorrows and her Aspirations. An Essay towards the Natural History of the Soul, as the True Basis of Theology. By F. W. Newman. Tenth Edition. Post 8vo, pp. xii. and 162, cloth. 1882. 3s. 6d.

NEWMAN.—MISCELLANIES; chiefly Addresses, Academical and Historical. By F. W. Newman. 8vo, pp. iv. and 356, cloth. 1869. 7s. 6d.

NEWMAN.—THE ILIAD OF HOMER, faithfully translated into Unrhymed English Metre, by F. W. Newman. Royal 8vo, pp. xvi. and 384, cloth. 1871. 10s. 6d.

NEWMAN.—A DICTIONARY OF MODERN ARABIC. 1. Anglo-Arabic Dictionary. 2. Anglo-Arabic Vocabulary. 3 Arabo-English Dictionary. By F. W. Newman. In 2 vols. crown 8vo, pp. xvi. and 376-464, cloth. 1871. £1, 1s.

NEWMAN.—HEBREW THEISM. By F. W. Newman. Royal 8vo, pp. viii. and 172. Stiff wrappers. 1874. 4s. 6d.

NEWMAN.—THE MORAL INFLUENCE OF LAW. A Lecture by F. W. Newman, May 20, 1860. Crown 8vo, pp. 16, sewed. 3d.

NEWMAN.—RELIGION NOT HISTORY. By F. W. Newman. Foolscap, pp. 58, paper wrapper. 1877. 1s.

NEWMAN.—MORNING PRAYERS IN THE HOUSEHOLD OF A BELIEVER IN GOD. By F. W. Newman. Second Edition. Crown 8vo, pp. 80, limp cloth. 1882. 1s. 6d.

NEWMAN.—REORGANIZATION OF ENGLISH INSTITUTIONS. A Lecture by Emeritus Professor F. W. Newman. Delivered in the Manchester Athenæum, October 15, 1875. Crown 8vo, pp. 28, sewed. 1880. 6d.

NEWMAN.—WHAT IS CHRISTIANITY WITHOUT CHRIST? By F. W. Newman, Emeritus Professor of University College, London. 8vo, pp. 28, stitched in wrapper. 1881. 1s.

NEWMAN.—LIBYAN VOCABULARY. An Essay towards Reproducing the Ancient Numidian Language out of Four Modern Languages. By F. W. Newman. Crown 8vo, pp. vi. and 204, cloth. 1882. 10s. 6d.

NEW SOUTH WALES, PUBLICATIONS OF THE GOVERNMENT OF. List on application.

NEW SOUTH WALES.—JOURNAL AND PROCEEDINGS OF THE ROYAL SOCIETY OF. Published annually. Price 10s. 6d. List of Contents on application.

NEWTON.—PATENT LAW AND PRACTICE: showing the mode of obtaining and opposing Grants, Disclaimers, Confirmations, and Extensions of Patents. With a Chapter on Patent Agents. By A. V. Newton. Enlarged Edition. Crown 8vo, pp. xii. and 104, cloth. 1879. 2s. 6d.

NEW ZEALAND INSTITUTE PUBLICATIONS :—

I. TRANSACTIONS AND PROCEEDINGS of the New Zealand Institute. Demy 8vo, stitched. Vols. I. to XIV., 1868 to 1881. £1, 1s. each.

II. AN INDEX TO THE TRANSACTIONS AND PROCEEDINGS of the New Zealand Institute. Vols. I. to VIII. Edited and Published under the Authority of the Board of Governors of the Institute. By James Hector, C.M.G., M.D., F.R.S. Demy, 8vo, 44 pp., stitched. 1877. 2s. 6d.

NEW ZEALAND.—GEOLOGICAL SURVEY. List of Publications on application.

NOIRIT.—A FRENCH COURSE IN TEN LESSONS. By Jules Noirit, B.A. Lessons I.-IV. Crown 8vo, pp. xiv. and 80, sewed. 1870. 1s. 6d.

NOIRIT.—FRENCH GRAMMATICAL QUESTIONS for the use of Gentlemen preparing for the Army, Civil Service, Oxford Examinations, &c., &c. By Jules Noirit. Crown 8vo, pp. 62, cloth. 1870. 1s. Interleaved, 1s. 6d.

NOURSE.—NARRATIVE OF THE SECOND ARCTIC EXPEDITION MADE BY CHARLES F. HALL. His Voyage to Repulse Bay; Sledge Journeys to the Straits of Fury and Hecla, and to King William's Land, and Residence among the Eskimos during the years 1864-69. Edited under the orders of the Hon. Secretary of the Navy, by Prof. J. E. Nourse, U.S.N. 4to, pp. l. and 644, cloth. With maps, heliotypes, steel and wood engravings. 1880. £1, 8s.

NUGENT'S IMPROVED FRENCH AND ENGLISH AND ENGLISH AND FRENCH POCKET DICTIONARY. Par Smith. 24mo, pp. 489 and 320, cloth. 1873. 3s.

NUTT.—TWO TREATISES ON VERBS CONTAINING FEEBLE AND DOUBLE LETTERS. By R. Jehuda Hayug of Fez. Translated into Hebrew from the original Arabic by R. Moses Gikatilia of Cordova, with the Treatise on Punctuation by the same author, translated by Aben Ezra. Edited from Bodleian MSS., with an English translation, by J. W. Nutt, M.A. Demy 8vo, pp. 312, sewed. 1870. 5s.

NUTT.—A SKETCH OF SAMARITAN HISTORY, DOGMA, AND LITERATURE. An Introduction to "Fragments of a Samaritan Targum." By J. W. Nutt, M.A., &c., &c. Demy 8vo, pp. 180, cloth. 1874. 5s.

OEHLENSCHLÄGER.—AXEL AND VALBORG : a Tragedy, in Five Acts, and other Poems. Translated from the Danish of Adam Oehlenschläger by Pierce Butler, M.A., late Rector of Ulcombe, Kent. Edited by Professor Palmer, M.A., of St. John's Coll., Camb. With a Memoir of the Translator. Fcap. 8vo, pp. xii. and 164, cloth. 1874. 5s.

OERA LINDA BOOK (THE).—From a Manuscript of the 13th Century, with the permission of the proprietor, C. Over de Linden of the Helder. The Original Frisian Text as verified by Dr. J. O. Ottema, accompanied by an English Version of Dr. Ottema's Dutch Translation. By W. R. Sandbach. 8vo, pp. xxv. and 254, cloth. 1876. 5s.

OGAREFF.—ESSAI SUR LA SITUATION RUSSE. Lettres à un Anglais. Par N. Ogareff. 12mo, pp. 150, sewed. 1862. 3s.

OLCOTT.—A BUDDHIST CATECHISM, according to the Canon of the Southern Church. By Colonel H. S. Olcott, President of the Theosophical Society. 24mo, pp. 32. 1s.

OLLENDORFF.—METODO PARA APRENDER A LEER, escribir y hablar el Inglés segun el sistema de Ollendorff. Por Ramon Palenzuela y Juan de la Carreño. 8vo, pp. xlvi. and 460, cloth. 1873. 7s. 6d.
KEY to Ditto. Crown 8vo, pp. 112, cloth. 1873. 4s.

OLLENDORFF.—METODO PARA APRENDER A LEER, escribir y hablar el Frances, segun el verdadero sistema de Ollendorff ; ordenado en lecciones progresivas, consistiendo de ejercicios orales y escritos ; enriquecido de la pronunciacion figurada como se estila en la conversacion ; y de un Apéndice abrazando las reglas de la sintáxis, la formacion de los verbos regulares, y la conjugacion de los irregulares. Por Teodoro Simonné, Professor de Lenguas. Crown 8vo, pp. 342, cloth. 1873. 6s.
KEY to Ditto. Crown 8vo, pp. 80, cloth. 1873. 3s. 6d.

OPPERT.—ON THE CLASSIFICATION OF LANGUAGES : A Contribution to Comparative Philology. By Dr. Gustav Oppert, Ph.D., Professor of Sanskrit, Presidency College, Madras. 8vo, paper, pp. viii. and 146. 1883. 7s. 6d.

OPPERT.—LISTS OF SANSKRIT MANUSCRIPTS in Private Libraries of Southern India, Compiled, Arranged, and Indexed by Gustav Oppert, Ph.D., Professor of Sanskrit, Presidency College, Madras. Vol. I. lex 8vo, pp. vii. and 620, cloth. 1883. £1, 1s.

OPPERT.—ON THE WEAPONS, ARMY ORGANISATION, AND POLITICAL MAXIMS OF THE ANCIENT HINDUS ; with special reference to Gunpowder and Firearms. By Dr. Gustav Oppert, Ph.D., Professor of Sanskrit, Presidency College, Madras. 8vo, paper, pp. vi. and 162. 1883. 7s. 6d.

ORIENTAL SERIES.—See TRÜBNER'S ORIENTAL SERIES.

ORIENTAL TEXT SOCIETY'S PUBLICATIONS. A list may be had on application.

ORIENTAL CONGRESS.—REPORT OF THE PROCEEDINGS OF THE SECOND INTERNATIONAL CONGRESS OF ORIENTALISTS HELD IN LONDON, 1874. Royal 8vo, pp. viii. and 68, sewed. 1874. 5s.

ORIENTALISTS.—TRANSACTIONS OF THE SECOND SESSION OF THE INTERNATIONAL CONGRESS OF ORIENTALISTS. Held in London in September 1874. Edited by Robert K. Douglas, Hon. Sec. 8vo, pp. viii. and 456, cloth. 1876. 21s.

OTTÉ.—HOW TO LEARN DANISH (Dano-Norwegian) : a Manual for Students of Danish based on the Ollendorffian system of teaching languages, and adapted for self-instruction. By E. C. Otté. Crown 8vo, pp. xx. and 333, cloth. 1879. 7s. 6d.
Key to above. Crown 8vo, pp. 84, cloth. 3s.

OVERBECK.—CATHOLIC ORTHODOXY AND ANGLO-CATHOLICISM. A Word about the Intercommunion between the English and Orthodox Churches. By J. J. Overbeck, D.D. 8vo, pp. viii. and 200, cloth. 1866. 5s.

OVERBECK.—BONN CONFERENCE. By J. J. Overbeck, D.D. Crown 8vo, pp. 48, sewed. 1876. 1s.

OVERBECK.—A PLAIN VIEW OF THE CLAIMS OF THE ORTHODOX CATHOLIC CHURCH AS OPPOSED TO ALL OTHER CHRISTIAN DENOMINATIONS. By J. J. Overbeck, D.D. Crown 8vo, pp. iv. and 138, wrapper. 1881. 2s. 6d.

OWEN.—Footfalls on the Boundary of Another World. With Narrative Illustrations. By R. D. Owen. An enlarged English Copyright Edition. Post 8vo, pp. xx. and 392, cloth. 1875. 7s. 6d.

OWEN.—The Debatable Land between this World and the Next. With Illustrative Narrations. By Robert Dale Owen. Second Edition. Crown 8vo, pp. 456, cloth. 1874. 7s. 6d.

OWEN.—Threading my Way: Twenty-Seven Years of Autobiography. By R. D. Owen. Crown 8vo, pp. 344, cloth. 1874. 7s. 6d.

OYSTER (The): Where, How, and When to Find, Breed, Cook, and Eat It. Second Edition, with a New Chapter, "The Oyster-Seeker in London." 12mo, pp. viii. and 106, boards. 1863. 1s.

PALESTINE.—Memoirs of the Survey of Western Palestine. Edited by W. Besant, M.A., and E. H. Palmer, M.A., under the Direction of the Committee of the Palestine Exploration Fund. Complete in seven volumes. Demy 4to, cloth, with a Portfolio of Plans, and large scale Map. Second Issue. Price Twenty Guineas.

PALMER.—Leaves from a Word-Hunter's Note-Book. Being some Contributions to English Etymology. By the Rev. A. Smythe Palmer, B.A., sometime Scholar in the University of Dublin. Crown 8vo, pp. xii. and 316, cl. 1876. 7s. 6d.

PALMER.—A Concise Dictionary of the Persian Language. By E. H. Palmer, M.A., of the Middle Temple, Barrister-at-Law, Lord Almoner's Reader, and Professor of Arabic, and Fellow of St. John's College in the University of Cambridge. Square royal 32mo, pp. 726, cloth. 1876. 10s. 6d.

PALMER.—The Song of the Reed, and other Pieces. By E. H. Palmer, M.A., Cambridge. Crown 8vo, pp. 208, cloth. 1876. 5s.

PALMER.—Hindustani, Arabic, and Persian Grammar. See Trübner's Collection.

PALMER.—The Patriarch and the Tsar. Translated from the Russ by William Palmer, M.A. Demy 8vo, cloth. Vol. I. The Replies of the Humble Nicon. Pp. xl. and 674. 1871. 12s.—Vol. II. Testimonies concerning the Patriarch Nicon, the Tsar, and the Boyars. Pp. lxxviii. and 554. 1873. 12s.—Vol. III. History of the Condemnation of the Patriarch Nicon. Pp. lxvi. and 558. 1873. 12s.—Vols. IV., V., and VI. Services of the Patriarch Nicon to the Church and State of his Country, &c. Pp. lxxviii. and 1 to 660; xiv.-661-1028, and 1 to 254; xxvi.-1029-1656, and 1-72. 1876. 36s.

PARKER—Theodore Parker's Celebrated Discourse on Matters Pertaining to Religion. People's Edition. Crown 8vo, pp. 351. 1872. Stitched, 1s. 6d.; cloth, 2s.

PARKER.—Theodore Parker. A Biography. By O. B. Frothingham. Crown 8vo, pp. viii. and 588, cloth, with Portrait. 1876. 12s.

PARKER.—The Collected Works of Theodore Parker, Minister of the Twenty-eighth Congregational Society at Boston, U.S. Containing his Theological, Polemical, and Critical Writings; Sermons, Speeches, and Addresses; and Literary Miscellanies. In 14 vols. 8vo, cloth. 6s. each.
　　Vol. I. Discourse on Matters Pertaining to Religion. Preface by the Editor, and Portrait of Parker from a medallion by Saulini. Pp. 380.
　Vol. II. Ten Sermons and Prayers. Pp. 360.
　Vol. III. Discourses of Theology. Pp. 318.
　Vol. IV. Discourses on Politics. Pp. 312.
　　Vol. V. Discourses of Slavery. I. Pp. 336.
　　Vol. VI. Discourses of Slavery. II. Pp. 323.
　Vol. VII. Discourses of Social Science. Pp. 296.

PARKER.—COLLECTED WORKS—*continued.*

Vol. VIII. Miscellaneous Discourses. Pp. 230.
Vol. IX. Critical Writings. I. Pp. 292.
Vol. X. Critical Writings. II. Pp. 308.
Vol. XI. Sermons of Theism, Atheism, and Popular Theology. Pp. 257.
Vol. XII. Autobiographical and Miscellaneous Pieces. Pp. 356.
Vol. XIII. Historic Americans. Pp. 236.
Vol. XIV. Lessons from the World of Matter and the World of Man. Pp. 352.

PARKER.—MALAGASY GRAMMAR. See Trübner's Collection.

PATERSON.—NOTES ON MILITARY SURVEYING AND RECONNAISSANCE. By Lieut.-Colonel William Paterson. Sixth Edition. With 16 Plates. Demy 8vo, pp. xii. and 146, cloth. 1882. 7s. 6d.

PATERSON.—TOPOGRAPHICAL EXAMINATION PAPERS. By Lieut.-Col. W. Paterson. 8vo, pp. 32, with 4 Plates. Boards. 1882. 2s.

PATERSON.—TREATISE ON MILITARY DRAWING. With a Course of Progressive Plates. By Captain W. Paterson, Professor of Military Drawing at the Royal Military College, Sandhurst. Oblong 4to, pp. xii. and 31, cloth. 1862. £1, 1s.

PATERSON.—THE OROMETER FOR HILL MEASURING, combining Scales of Distances, Protractor, Clinometer, Scale of Horizontal Equivalents, Scale of Shade, and Table of Gradients. By Captain William Paterson. On cardboard. 1s.

PATERSON.—CENTRAL AMERICA. By W. Paterson, the Merchant Statesman. From a MS. in the British Museum, 1701. With a Map. Edited by S. Bannister, M.A. 8vo, pp. 70, sewed. 1857. 2s. 6d.

PATON.—A HISTORY OF THE EGYPTIAN REVOLUTION, from the Period of the Mamelukes to the Death of Mohammed Ali; from Arab and European Memoirs, Oral Tradition, and Local Research. By A. A. Paton. Second Edition. 2 vols. demy 8vo, pp. xii. and 395, viii. and 446, cloth. 1870. 7s. 6d.

PATON.—HENRY BEYLE (otherwise DE STENDAHL). A Critical and Biographical Study, aided by Original Documents and Unpublished Letters from the Private Papers of the Family of Beyle. By A. A. Paton. Crown 8vo, pp. 340, cloth. 1874. 7s. 6d.

PATTON.—THE DEATH OF DEATH; or, A Study of God's Holiness in Connection with the Existence of Evil, in so far as Intelligent and Responsible Beings are Concerned. By an Orthodox Layman (John M. Patton). Revised Edition, crown 8vo, pp. xvi. and 252, cloth. 1881. 6s.

PAULI.—SIMON DE MONTFORT, EARL OF LEICESTER, the Creator of the House of Commons. By Reinhold Pauli. Translated by Una M. Goodwin. With Introduction by Harriet Martineau. Crown 8vo, pp. xvi. and 340, cloth. 1876. 6s.

PETTENKOFER.—THE RELATION OF THE AIR TO THE CLOTHES WE WEAR, THE HOUSE WE LIVE IN, AND THE SOIL WE DWELL ON. Three Popular Lectures delivered before the Albert Society at Dresden. By Dr. Max Von Pettenkofer, Professor of Hygiene at the University of Munich, &c. Abridged and Translated by Augustus Hess, M.D., M.R.C.P., London, &c. Cr. 8vo, pp. viii. and 96, limp cl. 1873. 2s. 6d.

PETRUCCELLI.—PRELIMINAIRES DE LA QUESTION ROMAINE DE M. ED. ABOUT. Par F. Petruccelli de la Gattina. 8vo, pp. xv. and 364, cloth. 1860. 7s. 6d.

PEZZI.—ARYAN PHILOLOGY, according to the most recent researches (Glottologia Aria Recentissima). Remarks Historical and Critical. By Domenico Pezzi. Translated by E. S. Roberts, M.A. Crown 8vo, pp. xvi. and 200, cloth. 1879. 6s.

PHILLIPS. THE DOCTRINE OF ADDAI, THE APOSTLE, now first edited in a complete form in the Original Syriac, with English Translation and Notes. By George Phillips, D.D., President of Queen's College, Cambridge. 8vo, pp. xv. and 52 and 53, cloth. 1876. 7s. 6d.

PHILOLOGICAL SOCIETY, Transactions of, published irregularly. List of publications on application.

PHILOSOPHY (The) of Inspiration and Revelation. By a Layman. With a preliminary notice of an Essay by the present Lord Bishop of Winchester, contained in a volume entitled "Aids to Faith." 8vo, pp. 20, sewed. 1875. 6d.

PICCIOTTO.—Sketches of Anglo-Jewish History. By James Picciotto. Demy 8vo, pp. xi. and 420, cloth. 1875. 12s.

PIESSE. Chemistry in the Brewing-Room : being the substance of a Course of Lessons to Practical Brewers. With Tables of Alcohol, Extract, and Original Gravity. By Charles H. Piesse, F.C.S., Public Analyst. Fcap., pp. viii. and 62, cloth. 1877. 5s.

PIRY.—Le Saint Édit, Étude de Litterature Chinoise. Préparée par A. Théophile Piry, du Service des Douanes Maritimes de Chine. 4to, pp. xx. and 320, cloth. 1879. 21s.

PLAYFAIR.—The Cities and Towns of China. A Geographical Dictionary. By G. M. H. Playfair, of Her Majesty's Consular Service in China. 8vo, pp. 506, cloth. 1879. £1, 5s.

PLINY.—The Letters of Pliny the Younger. Translated by J. D. Lewis, M.A., Trinity College, Cambridge. Post 8vo, pp. vii. and 390, cloth. 1879. 5s.

PLUMPTRE.—King's College Lectures on Elocution ; on the Physiology and Culture of Voice and Speech and the Expression of the Emotions by Language, Countenance, and Gesture. To which is added a Special Lecture on the Causes and Cure of the Impediments of Speech. Being the substance of the Introductory Course of Lectures annually delivered by Charles John Plumptre, Lecturer on Public Reading and Speaking at King's College, London, in the Evening Classes Department. Dedicated by permission to H.R.H. the Prince of Wales. New and greatly Enlarged Illustrated Edition. Post 8vo, pp. xvi. and 488, cloth. 1880. 15s.

PLUMPTRE.—General Sketch of the History of Pantheism. By C. E. Plumptre. Vol. I., from the Earliest Times to the Age of Spinoza ; Vol. II., from the Age of Spinoza to the Commencement of the 19th Century. 2 vols demy 8vo, pp. viii. and 395 ; iv. and 348, cloth. 1881. 18s.

POLE.—The Philosophy of Music. See English and Foreign Philosophical Library, Vol. XI.

PONSARD.—Charlotte Corday. A Tragedy. By F. Ponsard. Edited, with English Notes and Notice on Ponsard, by Professor C. Cassal, LL.D. 12mo, pp. xi. and 133, cloth. 1867. 2s. 6d.

PONSARD.—L'Honneur et L'Argent. A Comedy. By François Ponsard. Edited, with English Notes and Memoir of Ponsard, by Professor C. Cassal, LL.D. Fcap. 8vo, pp. xvi. and 172, cloth. 1869. 3s. 6d.

POOLE.—An Index to Periodical Literature. By W. F. Poole, LL.D., Librarian of the Chicago Public Library. Third Edition, brought down to January 1882. 1 vol., royal 8vo, pp. xxviii. and 1442, cloth. 1883. £3, 13s. 6d. Wrappers, £3, 10s.

PRACTICAL GUIDES :—
France, Belgium, Holland, and the Rhine. 1s.—Italian Lakes. 1s.—Wintering Places of the South. 2s.—Switzerland, Savoy, and North Italy. 2s. 6d.—General Continental Guide. 5s.—Geneva. 1s.—Paris. 1s.—Bernese Oberland. 1s.—Italy. 4s.

PRATT.—A Grammar and Dictionary of the Samoan Language. By Rev. George Pratt, Forty Years a Missionary of the London Missionary Society in Samoa. Second Edition. Edited by Rev. S. J. Whitmee, F.R.G.S. Crown 8vo, pp. viii. and 380, cloth. 1878. 18s.

QUINET.—The Religious Revolution of the Nineteenth Century. From the French of Edgar Quinet. Fcap. 8vo, pp. xl. and 70, parchment. 1881. 1s. 6d.

QUINET.—Edgar Quinet. See English and Foreign Philosophical Library, Vol. XIV.

RAM RAZ.—Essay on the Architecture of the Hindus. By Ram Raz, Native Judge and Magistrate of Bangalore, Corr. Mem. R.A.S. With 48 Plates. 4to, pp. xiv. and 64, sewed. 1834. £2, 2s.

RAMSAY.—Tabular List of all the Australian Birds at present known to the Author, showing the distribution of the species. By E. P. Ramsay, F.L.S., &c., Curator of the Australian Museum, Sydney. 8vo, pp. 36, and Map ; boards. 1878. 5s.

RAND, M'NALLY, & CO.'S Business Atlas of the United States, Canada, and West Indian Islands. With a Complete Reference Map of the World, Ready Reference Index, &c., of all Post Offices, Railroad Stations, and Villages in the United States and Canada. With Official Census. 4to, pp. 212, cloth. 1881. £2, 12s. 6d.

RASK.—Grammar of the Anglo-Saxon Tongue, from the Danish of Erasmus Rask. By Benjamin Thorpe. Third Edition, corrected and improved, with Plate. Post 8vo, pp. vi. and 192. cloth. 1879. 5s. 6d.

RASK.—A Short Tractate on the Longevity ascribed to the Patriarchs in the Book of Genesis, and its relation to the Hebrew Chronology ; the Flood, the Exodus of the Israelites, the Site of Eden, &c. From the Danish of the late Professor Rask, with his manuscript corrections, and large additions from his autograph, now for the first time printed. With a Map of Paradise and the circumjacent Lands. Crown 8vo, pp. 134, cloth. 1863. 2s. 6d.

RATTON.—A Handbook of Common Salt. By J. J. L. Ratton, M.D., M.C., Surgeon, Madras Army. 8vo, pp. xviii. and 282, cloth. 1879. 7s. 6d.

RAVENSTEIN.—The Russians on the Amur; its Discovery, Conquest, and Colonization, with a Description of the Country, its Inhabitants, Productions, and Commercial Capabilities, and Personal Accounts of Russian Travellers. By E. G. Ravenstein, F.R.G.S. With 4 tinted Lithographs and 3 Maps. 8vo, pp. 500, cloth. 1861. 15s.

RAVENSTEIN AND HULLEY.—The Gymnasium and its Fittings. By E. G. Ravenstein and John Hulley. With 14 Plates of Illustrations. 8vo, pp. 32, sewed. 1867. 2s. 6d.

RAVERTY.—Notes on Afghanistan and Part of Baluchistan, Geographical, Ethnographical, and Historical, extracted from the Writings of little known Afghan, and Tajyik Historians, &c., &c., and from Personal Observation. By Major H. G. Raverty, Bombay Native Infantry (Retired). Foolscap folio. Sections I. and II., pp. 98, wrapper. 1880. 2s. Section III., pp. vi. and 218. 1881. 5s.

READE.—The Martyrdom of Man. By Winwood Reade. Fifth Edition. Crown 8vo, pp. viii. and 544, cloth. 1881. 7s. 6d.

RECORD OFFICE.—A Separate Catalogue of the Official Publications of the Public Record Office, on sale by Trübner & Co., may be had on application.

RECORDS OF THE HEART. By Stella, Author of "Sappho," "The King's Stratagem," &c. Second English Edition. Crown 8vo, pp. xvi. and 188, with six steel-plate engravings, cloth. 1881. 3s. 6d.

REDHOUSE.—THE TURKISH VADE-MECUM OF OTTOMAN COLLOQUIAL LANGUAGE: Containing a Concise Ottoman Grammar; a Carefully Selected Vocabulary Alphabetically Arranged, in two Parts, English and Turkish, and Turkish and English; Also a few Familiar Dialogues and Naval and Military Terms. The whole in English Characters, the Pronunciation being fully indicated. By J. W. Redhouse, M.R.A.S. Third Edition. 32mo, pp. viii. and 372, cloth. 1882. 6s.

REDHOUSE. ON THE HISTORY, SYSTEM, AND VARIETIES OF TURKISH POETRY. Illustrated by Selections in the Original and in English Paraphrase, with a Notice of the Islamic Doctrine of the Immortality of Woman's Soul in the Future State. By J. W. Redhouse, Esq., M.R.A.S. 8vo, pp. 62, cloth, 2s. 6d.; wrapper, 1s. 6d. 1879.

REDHOUSE.—THE MESNEVI. See Trübner's Oriental Series.

REEMELIN.—A CRITICAL REVIEW OF AMERICAN POLITICS. By C. Reemelin, of Cincinnati, Ohio. Demy 8vo, pp. xxiv. and 630, cloth. 1881. 14s.

RENAN.—AN ESSAY ON THE AGE AND ANTIQUITY OF THE BOOK OF NABATHÆAN AGRICULTURE. To which is added an Inaugural Lecture on the Position of the Shemitic Nations in the History of Civilisation. By Ernest Renan. Crown 8vo, pp. xvi. and 148, cloth. 1862. 3s. 6d.

RENAN.—THE LIFE OF JESUS. By Ernest Renan. Authorised English Translation. Crown 8vo, pp. xii. and 312, cloth. 2s. 6d.; sewed, 1s. 6d.

RENAN.—THE APOSTLES. By Ernest Renan. Translated from the original French. 8vo, pp. viii. and 288, cloth. 1869. 7s. 6d.

REPORT OF A GENERAL CONFERENCE OF LIBERAL THINKERS, for the discussion of matters pertaining to the religious needs of our time, and the methods of meeting them. Held June 13th and 14th, 1878, at South Place Chapel, Finsbury, London. 8vo, pp. 77, sewed. 1878. 1s.

RHODES.—UNIVERSAL CURVE TABLES FOR FACILITATING THE LAYING OUT OF CIRCULAR ARCS ON THE GROUND FOR RAILWAYS, CANALS, &c. Together with Table of Tangential Angles and Multiples. By Alexander Rhodes, C.E. Oblong 18mo, band, pp. ix. and 104, roan. 1881. 5s.

RHYS.—LECTURES ON WELSH PHILOLOGY. By John Rhys, M.A., Professor of Celtic at Oxford, Honorary Fellow of Jesus College, &c., &c. Second Edition, Revised and Enlarged. Crown 8vo, pp. xiv. and 467, cloth. 1879. 15s.

RICE.—MYSORE AND COORG. A Gazetteer compiled for the Government of India. By Lewis Rice, Director of Public Instruction, Mysore and Coorg. Vol. I. Mysore in General. With 2 Coloured Maps. Vol. II. Mysore, by Districts. With 10 Coloured Maps. Vol. III. Coorg. With a Map. 3 vols. royal 8vo, pp. xii. 670 and xvi.; 544 and xxii.; and 427 and xxvii., cloth. 1878. 25s.

RICE.—MYSORE INSCRIPTIONS. Translated for the Government by Lewis Rice. 8vo, pp. xcii. and 336-xxx., with a Frontispiece and Map, boards. 1879. 30s.

RIDLEY.—KÁMILARÓI, AND OTHER AUSTRALIAN LANGUAGES. By the Rev. William Ridley, B.A. Second Edition, revised and enlarged by the author; with comparative Tables of Words from twenty Australian Languages, and Songs, Traditions, Laws, and Customs of the Australian Race. Small 4to, pp. vi. and 172, cloth. 1877. 10s. 6d.

RIG-VEDA-SANHITA. A Collection of Ancient Hindu Hymns. Constituting the 1st to the 8th Ashtakas, or Books of the Rig-Veda; the oldest authority for the Religious and Social Institutions of the Hindus. Translated from the Original Sanskrit. By the late H. H. Wilson, M.A., F.R.S., &c., &c.
> Vol. I. 8vo, pp. lii. and 348, cloth. 21s.
> Vol. II. 8vo, pp. xxx. and 346, cloth. 1854. 21s.
> Vol. III. 8vo, pp. xxiv. and 525, cloth. 1857. 21s.
> Vol. IV. Edited by E. B. Cowell, M.A. 8vo, pp. 214, cloth. 1866. 14s.
> Vols. V. and VI. in the Press.

RILEY.—MEDIÆVAL CHRONICLES OF THE CITY OF LONDON. Chronicles of the Mayors and Sheriffs of London, and the Events which happened in their Days, from the Year A.D. 1188 to A.D. 1274. Translated from the original Latin of the "Liber de Antiquis Legibus" (published by the Camden Society), in the possession of the Corporation of the City of London; attributed to Arnold Fitz-Thedmar, Alderman of London in the Reign of Henry III.—Chronicles of London, and of the Marvels therein, between the Years 44 Henry III., A.D. 1260, and 17 Edward III., A.D. 1343. Translated from the original Anglo-Norman of the "Croniques de London," preserved in the Cottonian Collection (Cleopatra A. iv.) in the British Museum. Translated, with copious Notes and Appendices, by Henry Thomas Riley, M.A., Clare Hall, Cambridge, Barrister-at-Law. 4to, pp. xii. and 319, cloth. 1863. 12s.

RIOLA.—HOW TO LEARN RUSSIAN: a Manual for Students of Russian, based upon the Ollendorffian System of Teaching Languages, and adapted for Self-Instruction. By Henry Riola, Teacher of the Russian Language. With a Preface by W.R.S. Ralston, M.A. Crown 8vo, pp. 576, cloth. 1878. 12s.
> KEY to the above. Crown 8vo, pp. 126, cloth. 1878. 5s.

RIOLA.—A GRADUATED RUSSIAN READER, with a Vocabulary of all the Russian Words contained in it. By Henry Riola, Author of "How to Learn Russian." Crown 8vo, pp. viii. and 314, cloth. 1879. 10s. 6d.

RIPLEY.—SACRED RHETORIC; or, Composition and Delivery of Sermons. By Henry I. Ripley. 12mo, pp. 234, cloth. 1858. 2s. 6d.

ROCHE.—A FRENCH GRAMMAR, for the use of English Students, adopted for the Public Schools by the Imperial Council of Public Instruction. By A. Roche. Crown 8vo, pp. xii. and 176, cloth. 1869. 3s.

ROCHE.—PROSE AND POETRY. Select Pieces from the best English Authors, for Reading, Composition, and Translation. By A. Roche. Second Edition. Fcap. 8vo, pp. viii. and 226, cloth. 1872. 2s. 6d.

RODD.—THE BIRDS OF CORNWALL AND THE SCILLY ISLANDS. By the late Edward Hearle Rodd. Edited, with an Introduction, Appendix, and Memoir, by J. E. Harting. 8vo, pp. lvi. and 320, with Portrait and Map, cloth. 1880. 14s.

ROGERS.—THE WAVERLEY DICTIONARY: An Alphabetical Arrangement of all the Characters in Sir Walter Scott's Waverley Novels, with a Descriptive Analysis of each Character, and Illustrative Selections from the Text. By May Rogers. 12mo, pp. 358, cloth. 1879. 10s.

ROSS.—ALPHABETICAL MANUAL OF BLOWPIPE ANALYSIS; showing all known Methods, Old and New. By Lieut.-Colonel W. A. Ross, late R.A., Member of the German Chemical Society (Author of "Pyrology, or Fire Chemistry"). Crown 8vo, pp. xii. and 148, cloth. 1880. 5s.

ROSS.—PYROLOGY, OR FIRE CHEMISTRY; a Science interesting to the General Philosopher, and an Art of infinite importance to the Chemist, Metallurgist, Engineer, &c., &c. By W. A. Ross, lately a Major in the Royal Artillery. Small 4to, pp. xxviii. and 346, cloth. 1875. 36s.

ROSS.—CELEBRITIES OF THE YORKSHIRE WOLDS. By Frederick Ross, Fellow of the Royal Historical Society. 12mo, pp. 202, cloth. 1878. 4s.

ROSS.— COREAN PRIMER : being Lessons in Corean on all Ordinary Subjects. Transliterated on the principles of the "Mandarin Primer," by the same author. By Rev. John Ross, Newchwang. 8vo, pp. 90, wrapper. 1877. 10s.

ROSS.—HONOUR OR SHAME? By R. S. Ross. 8vo, pp. 183. 1878. Cloth. 3s. 6d; paper, 2s. 6d.

ROSS.— REMOVAL OF THE INDIAN TROOPS TO MALTA. By R. S. Ross. 8vo, pp. 77, paper. 1878. 1s. 6d.

ROSS—THE MONK OF ST. GALL. A Dramatic Adaptation of Scheffel's "Ekkehard." By R. S. Ross. Crown 8vo, pp. xii. and 218. 1879. 5s.

ROSS.—ARIADNE IN NAXOS. By R. S. Ross. Square 16mo, pp. 200, cloth. 1882. 5s.

ROTH.—NOTES ON CONTINENTAL IRRIGATION. By H. L. Roth. Demy 8vo, pp. 40, with 8 Plates, cloth. 1882. 5s.

ROUGH NOTES OF JOURNEYS made in the years 1868-1873 in Syria, down the Tigris, India, Kashmir, Ceylon, Japan, Mongolia, Siberia, the United States, the Sandwich Islands, and Australasia. Demy 8vo, pp. 624, cloth. 1875. 14s.

ROUSTAING.—THE FOUR GOSPELS EXPLAINED BY THEIR WRITERS. With an Appendix on the Ten Commandments. Edited by J. B. Roustaing. Translated by W. E. Kirby. 3 vols. crown 8vo, pp. 440 456-304, cloth. 1881. 15s.

ROUTLEDGE.—ENGLISH RULE AND NATIVE OPINION IN INDIA. From Notes taken in 1870-74. By James Routledge. 8vo, pp. x. and 338, cloth. 1878. 10s. 6d.

ROWE.—AN ENGLISHMAN'S VIEWS ON QUESTIONS OF THE DAY IN VICTORIA. By C. J. Rowe, M.A. Crown 8vo, pp. 122, cloth. 1882. 4s.

ROWLEY.—ORNITHOLOGICAL MISCELLANY. By George Dawson Rowley, M.A., F.Z.S. Vol. I. Part 1, 15s.—Part 2, 20s.—Part 3, 15s.—Part 4, 20s.
Vol. II. Part 5, 20s.—Part 6, 20s.—Part 7, 10s. 6d.—Part 8, 10s. 6d.—Part 9, 10s. 6d.—Part 10, 10s. 6d.
Vol. III. Part 11, 10s. 6d.—Part 12, 10s. 6d.—Part 13, 10s. 6d.—Part 14, 20s.

ROYAL SOCIETY OF LONDON (THE).—CATALOGUE OF SCIENTIFIC PAPERS (1800-1863), Compiled and Published by the Royal Society of London. Demy 4to, cloth, per vol. £1 ; in half-morocco, £1, 8s. Vol. I. (1867), A to Cluzel. pp. lxxix. and 960; Vol. II. (1868), Coakley—Graydon. pp. iv. and 1012 ; Vol. III. (1869), Greathced—Leze. pp. v. and 1002 ; Vol. IV. (1870), L'Héritier de Brutille—Pozzetti. pp. iv. and 1006 ; Vol. V. (1871), Prang—Tizzani. pp. iv. and 1000 ; Vol. VI. (1872), Tkalee—Zylius. Anonymous and Additions. pp. xi. and 763. Continuation of above (1864-1873) ; Vol. VII. (1877), A to Hyrtl. pp. xxxi. and 1047 ; Vol. VIII. (1879), Ibañez—Zwicky. pp. 1310. A List of the Publications of the Royal Society (Separate Papers from the Philosophical Transactions), on application.

RUNDALL.—A SHORT AND EASY WAY TO WRITE ENGLISH AS SPOKEN. Méthode Rapide et Facile d'Ecrire le Français comme on le Parle. Kurze und Leichte Weise Deutsch zu Schreiben wie man es Spricht. By J. B. Rundall, Certificated Member of the London Shorthand Writers' Association. 6d. each.

RUTHERFORD.—THE AUTOBIOGRAPHY OF MARK RUTHERFORD, Dissenting Minister. Edited by his friend, Reuben Shapcott. Crown 8vo, pp. xii. and 180, boards. 1881. 5s.

RUTTER.—See BUNYAN.

SÂMAVIDHÂNABRÂHMANA (THE) (being the Third Brâhmana) of the Sâma Veda. Edited, together with the Commentary of Sâyana, an English Translation, Introduction, and Index of Words, by A. C. Burnell. Vol. I. Text and Commentary, with Introduction. Demy 8vo, pp. xxxviii. and 104, cloth. 1873. 12s. 6d.

SAMUELSON.—HISTORY OF DRINK. A Review, Social, Scientific, and Political. By James Samuelson, of the Middle Temple, Barrister-at-Law. Second Edition. 8vo, pp. xxviii. and 288, cloth. 1880. 6s.

SAND.—MOLIÈRE. A Drama in Prose. By George Sand. Edited, with Notes, by Th. Karcher, LL.B. 12mo, pp. xx. and 170, cloth. 1868. 3s. 6d.

SARTORIUS.—MEXICO. Landscapes and Popular Sketches. By C. Sartorius. Edited by Dr. Gaspey. With Engravings, from Sketches by M. Rugendas. 4to, pp. vi. and 202, cloth gilt. 1859. 18s.

SATOW.—AN ENGLISH JAPANESE DICTIONARY OF THE SPOKEN LANGUAGE. By Ernest Mason Satow, Japanese Secretary to H.M. Legation at Yedo, and Ishibashi Masakata of the Imperial Japanese Foreign Office. Second Edition. Imperial 32mo, pp. xv. and 416, cloth. 1879. 12s. 6d.

SAVAGE.—THE MORALS OF EVOLUTION. By M. J. Savage, Author of "The Religion of Evolution," &c. Crown 8vo, pp. 192, cloth. 1880. 5s.

SAVAGE.—BELIEF IN GOD; an Examination of some Fundamental Theistic Problems. By M. J. Savage. To which is added an Address on the Intellectual Basis of Faith. By W. H. Savage. 8vo, pp. 176, cloth. 1881. 5s.

SAVAGE.—BELIEFS ABOUT MAN. By M. J. Savage. Crown 8vo, pp. 130, cloth. 1882. 5s.

SAYCE.—AN ASSYRIAN GRAMMAR for Comparative Purposes. By A. H. Sayce, M.A., Fellow and Tutor of Queen s College, Oxford. Crown 8vo, pp. xvi. and 188, cloth. 1872. 7s. 6d.

SAYCE.—THE PRINCIPLES OF COMPARATIVE PHILOLOGY. By A. H. Sayce, M.A. Crown 8vo, pp. 384, cloth. 1874. 10s. 6d.

SCHAIBLE.—AN ESSAY ON THE SYSTEMATIC TRAINING OF THE BODY. By C. H. Schaible, M.D., &c., &c. A Memorial Essay, Published on the occasion of the first Centenary Festival of Frederick L. Jahn, with an Etching by H. Herkomer. Crown 8vo, pp. xviii. and 124, cloth. 1878. 5s.

SCHEFFEL.—MOUNTAIN PSALMS. By J. V. Von Scheffel. Translated by Mrs. F. Brunnow. Fcap., pp. 62, with 6 Plates after designs by A. Von Werner. Parchment. 1882. 3s. 6d.

SCHILLER.—THE BRIDE OF MESSINA. Translated from the German of Schiller in English Verse. By Emily Allfrey. Crown 8vo, pp. viii. and 110, cloth. 1876. 2s.

SCHLAGINTWEIT.—BUDDHISM IN TIBET: Illustrated by Literary Documents and Objects of Religious Worship. By Emil Schlagintweit. LL.D. With a folio Atlas of 20 Plates, and 20 Tables of Native Print in the Text. Roy. 8vo, pp. xxiv. and 404. 1863. £2, 2s.

SCHLEICHER.—A COMPENDIUM OF THE COMPARATIVE GRAMMAR OF THE INDO-EUROPEAN, SANSKRIT, GREEK, AND LATIN LANGUAGES. By August Schleicher. Translated from the Third German Edition, by Herbert Bendall, B.A., Chr. Coll., Camb. 8vo. Part I., Phonology. Pp.184, cloth. 1874. 7s. 6d. Part II., Morphology. Pp. viii. and 104, cloth. 1877. 6s.

SCHULTZ.—UNIVERSAL DOLLAR TABLES (Complete United States). Covering all Exchanges between the United States and Great Britain, France, Belgium, Switzerland, Italy, Spain, and Germany. By C. W. H. Schultz. 8vo, cloth. 1874. 15s.

SCHULTZ.—UNIVERSAL INTEREST AND GENERAL PERCENTAGE TABLES. On the Decimal System. With a Treatise on the Currency of the World, and numerous examples for Self-Instruction. By C. W. H. Schultz. 8vo, cloth. 1874. 10s. 6d.

SCHULTZ.—ENGLISH GERMAN EXCHANGE TABLES. By C. W. H. Schultz. With a Treatise on the Currency of the World. 8vo, boards. 1874. 5s.

SCHWENDLER.—INSTRUCTIONS FOR TESTING TELEGRAPH LINES, and the Technical Arrangements in Offices. Written on behalf of the Government of India, under the Orders of the Director-General of Telegraphs in India. By Louis Schwendler. Vol. I., demy 8vo, pp. 248, cloth. 1878. 12s. Vol. II., demy 8vo, pp. xi. and 268, cloth. 1880. 9s.

SCOONES. FAUST. A Tragedy. By Goethe. Translated into English Verse, by William Dalton Scoones. Fcap., pp. vi. and 230, cloth. 1879. 5s.

SCOTT.—THE ENGLISH LIFE OF JESUS. By Thomas Scott. Crown 8vo, pp. xxviii. and 350, cloth. 1879. 2s. 6d.

SCOTUS.—A NOTE ON MR. GLADSTONE'S "The Peace to Come." By Scotus. 8vo, pp. 106. 1878. Cloth, 2s. 6d; paper wrapper, 1s. 6d.

SELL.—THE FAITH OF ISLAM. By the Rev. E. Sell, Fellow of the University of Madras. Demy 8vo, pp. xiv. and 270, cloth. 1881. 6s. 6d.

SELL.—IHN-I-TAJWID ; OR, ART OF READING THE QURAN. By the Rev. E. Sell, B.D. 8vo, pp. 48, wrappers. 1882. 2s. 6d.

SELSS.—GOETHE'S MINOR POEMS. Selected, Annotated, and Rearranged. By Albert M. Selss, Ph.D. Crown 8vo, pp. xxxi. and 152, cloth. 1875. 3s. 6d.

SERMONS NEVER PREACHED. By Philip Phosphor. Crown 8vo, pp. vi. and 124, cloth. 1878. 2s. 6d.

SEWELL.—REPORT ON THE AMARAVATI TOPE, and Excavations on its Site in 1877. By Robert Sewell, of the Madras C.S., &c. With four plates. Royal 4to, pp. 70, boards. 1880. 3s.

SHADWELL.—A SYSTEM OF POLITICAL ECONOMY. By John Lancelot Shadwell. 8vo, pp. 650, cloth. 1877. 7s. 6d.

SHADWELL.—POLITICAL ECONOMY FOR THE PEOPLE. By John Lancelot Shadwell, Author of "A System of Political Economy." Reprinted from the "Labour News." Fcap., pp. vi. and 154, limp cloth. 1880. 1s. 6d.

SHAKESPEARE'S CENTURIE OF PRAYSE ; being Materials for a History of Opinion on Shakespeare and his Works, culled from Writers of the First Century after his Rise. By C. M. Ingleby. Medium 8vo, pp. xx. and 384. Stiff cover. 1874. £1, 1s. Large paper, fcap. 4to, boards. £2, 2s.

SHAKESPEARE.—HERMENEUTICS ; OR, THE STILL LION. Being an Essay towards the Restoration of Shakespeare's Text. By C. M. Ingleby, M.A., LL.D., of Trinity College, Cambridge. Small 4to, pp. 168, boards. 1875. 6s.

SHAKESPEARE.—THE MAN AND THE BOOK. By C. M. Ingleby, M.A., LL.D. 8vo. Part I. 6s.

SHAKESPEARE.—OCCASIONAL PAPERS ON SHAKESPEARE ; being the Second Part of "Shakespeare : the Man and the Book." By C. M. Ingleby, M.A., LL.D., V.P.R.S.L. Small 4to, pp. x. and 194, paper boards. 1881. 6s.

SHAKESPEARE.—A NEW VARIORUM EDITION OF SHAKESPEARE. Edited by Horace Howard Furness. Royal 8vo. Vol. I. Romeo and Juliet. Pp. xxiii. and 480, cloth. 1871. 18s.—Vol. II. Macbeth. Pp. xix. and 492. 1873. 18s.—Vols. III. and IV. Hamlet. 2 vols. pp. xx. and 474 and 430. 1877. 36s.—Vol. V. King Lear. Pp. vi. and 504. 1880. 18s.

SHAKESPEARE.—CONCORDANCE TO SHAKESPEARE'S POEMS. By Mrs. H. H. Furness. Royal 8vo, cloth. 18s.

SHAKSPERE SOCIETY (THE NEW).—Subscription, One Guinea per annum. List of Publications on application.

SHERRING.—THE SACRED CITY OF THE HINDUS. An Account of Benares in Ancient and Modern Times. By the Rev. M. A. Sherring, M.A., LL.D.; and Prefaced with an Introduction by FitzEdward Hall, D.C.L. With Illustrations. 8vo, pp. xxxvi. and 388, cloth. 21s.

SHERRING. HINDU TRIBES AND CASTES; together with an Account of the Mohamedan Tribes of the North-West Frontier and of the Aboriginal Tribes of the Central Provinces. By the Rev. M. A. Sherring, M.A., LL.B., Lond., &c. 4to. Vol. II. Pp. lxviii. and 376, cloth. 1879. £2, 8s.—Vol. III., with Index of 3 vols. Pp. xii. and 336, cloth. 1881. 32s.

SHERRING.—THE HINDOO PILGRIMS. By Rev. M. A. Sherring, M.A., LL.D. Crown 8vo, pp. 126, cloth. 1878. 5s.

SHIELDS.—THE FINAL PHILOSOPHY; or, System of Perfectible Knowledge issuing from the Harmony of Science and Religion. By Charles W. Shields, D.D., Professor in Princeton College. Royal 8vo, pp. viii. and 610, cloth. 1878. 18s.

SIBREE.—THE GREAT AFRICAN ISLAND. Chapters on Madagascar. A Popular Account of Recent Researches in the Physical Geography, Geology, and Exploration of the Country, and its Natural History and Botany; and in the Origin and Divisions, Customs and Language, Superstitions, Folk-lore, and Religious Beliefs and Practices of the Different Tribes. Together with Illustrations of Scripture and Early Church History from Native Habits and Missionary Experience. By the Rev. James Sibree, jun., F.R.G.S., Author of "Madagascar and its People," &c. 8vo, pp. xii. and 272, with Physical and Ethnological Maps and Four Illustrations, cloth. 1879. 12s.

SIBREE.—FANCY AND OTHER RHYMES. With Additions. By John Sibree, M.A., London. Crown 8vo, pp. iv. and 88, cloth. 1882. 3s.

SIEDENTOPF.—THE GERMAN CALIGRAPHIST. Copies for German Handwriting. By E. Siedentopf. Obl. fcap. 4to, sewed. 1869. 1s.

SIMCOX.—EPISODES IN THE LIVES OF MEN, WOMEN, AND LOVERS. By Edith Simcox. Crown 8vo, pp. 312, cloth. 1882. 7s. 6d.

SIMCOX.—NATURAL LAW. See English and Foreign Philosophical Library, Vol. IV.

SIME.—LESSING. See English and Foreign Philosophical Library, Extra Series, Vols. I. and II.

SIMPSON-BAIKIE.—THE DRAMATIC UNITIES IN THE PRESENT DAY. By E. Simpson-Baikie. Third Edition. Fcap. 8vo, pp. iv. and 108, cloth. 1878. 2s. 6d.

SIMPSON-BAIKIE.—THE INTERNATIONAL DICTIONARY for Naturalists and Sportsmen in English, French, and German. By Edwin Simpson-Baikie. 8vo, pp. iv. and 284, cloth. 1880. 15s.

SINCLAIR.—THE MESSENGER: A Poem. By Thomas Sinclair, M.A. Foolscap 8vo, pp. 174, cloth. 1875. 5s.

SINCLAIR.—LOVE'S TRILOGY: A Poem. By Thomas Sinclair, M.A. Crown 8vo, pp. 150, cloth. 1876. 5s.

SINCLAIR.—THE MOUNT: Speech from its English Heights. By Thomas Sinclair, M.A. Crown 8vo, pp. viii. and 302, cloth. 1877. 10s.

SINGER.—HUNGARIAN GRAMMAR. See Trübner's Collection.

SINNETT.—THE OCCULT WORLD. By A. P. Sinnett. Second Edition. 8vo, pp. xx. and 206, cloth. 1882. 6s.

SMITH.—THE DIVINE GOVERNMENT. By S. Smith, M.D. Fifth Edition. Crown 8vo, pp. xii. and 276, cloth. 1866. 6s.

SMITH.—THE RECENT DEPRESSION OF TRADE. Its Nature, its Causes, and the Remedies which have been suggested for it. By Walter E. Smith, B.A., New College. Being the Oxford Cobden Prize Essay for 1879. Crown 8vo, pp. vi. and 108, cloth. 1880. 3s.

SMYTH.—THE ABORIGINES OF VICTORIA. With Notes relating to the Habits of the Natives of other Parts of Australia and Tasmania. Compiled from various sources for the Government of Victoria. By R. Brough Smyth, F.L.S., F.G.S., &c., &c. 2 vols. royal 8vo, pp. lxxii.-484 and vi.-456, Maps, Plates, and Woodcuts, cloth. 1878. £3, 3s.

SNOW—A THEOLOGICO-POLITICAL TREATISE. By G. D. Snow. Crown 8vo, pp. 180, cloth. 1874. 4s. 6d.

SOLLING.—DIUTISKA: An Historical and Critical Survey of the Literature of Germany, from the Earliest Period to the Death of Goethe. By Gustav Solling. 8vo, pp. xviii. and 368. 1863. 10s. 6d.

SOLLING.—SELECT PASSAGES FROM THE WORKS OF SHAKESPEARE. Translated and Collected. German and English. By G. Solling. 12mo, pp. 155, cloth. 1866. 3s. 6d.

SOLLING.—MACBETH. Rendered into Metrical German (with English Text adjoined). By Gustav Solling. Crown 8vo, pp. 160, wrapper. 1878. 3s. 6d.

SONGS OF THE SEMITIC IN ENGLISH VERSE. By G. E. W. Crown 8vo, pp. iv. and 134, cloth. 1877. 5s.

SOUTHALL.—THE EPOCH OF THE MAMMOTH AND THE APPARITION OF MAN UPON EARTH. By James C. Southall, A.M., LL.D. Crown 8vo, pp. xii. and 430, cloth. Illustrated. 1878. 10s. 6d.

SOUTHALL.—THE RECENT ORIGIN OF MAN, as illustrated by Geology and the Modern Science of Prehistoric Archæology. By James C. Southall. 8vo, pp. 606, cloth. Illustrated. 1875. 30s.

SPANISH REFORMERS OF TWO CENTURIES FROM 1520; Their Lives and Writing, according to the late Benjamin B. Wiffen's Plan, and with the Use of His Materials. Described by E. Boehmer, D.D., Ph.D. Vol. I. With B. B. Wiffen's Narrative of the Incidents attendant upon the Republication of Reformistas Antignos Españoles, and with a Memoir of B. B. Wiffen. By Isaline Wiffen. Royal 8vo, pp. xvi. and 216, cloth. 1874. 12s. 6d. Roxburghe, 15s.

SPEDDING.—THE LIFE AND TIMES OF FRANCIS BACON. Extracted from the Edition of his Occasional Writings, by James Spedding. 2 vols. post 8vo, pp. xx.-710 and xiv.-708, cloth. 1878. 21s.

SPIERS.- THE SCHOOL SYSTEM OF THE TALMUD. By the Rev. B. Spiers. 8vo, pp. 48, cloth. 1882. 2s. 6d.

SPINOZA.--BENEDICT DE SPINOZA: his Life, Correspondence, and Ethics. By R. Willis, M.D. 8vo, pp. xliv. and 648, cloth. 1870. 21s.

SPIRITUAL EVOLUTION. AN ESSAY ON, considered in its bearing upon Modern Spiritualism, Science, and Religion. By J. P. B. Crown 8vo, pp. 156, cloth. 1879. 3s.

SPRUNER.—DR. KARL VON SPRUNER'S HISTORICO-GEOGRAPHICAL HAND-ATLAS, containing 26 Coloured Maps. Obl. cloth. 1861. 15s.

SQUIER.- HONDURAS; Descriptive, Historical, and Statistical. By E. G. Squier, M.A., F.S.A. Cr. 8vo, pp. viii. and 278, cloth. 1870. 3s. 6d.

STATIONERY OFFICE.—PUBLICATIONS OF HER MAJESTY'S STATIONERY OFFICE. List on application.

STEDMAN.—OXFORD: Its Social and Intellectual Life. With Remarks and Hints on Expenses, the Examinations, &c. By Algernon M. M. Stedman, B.A., Wadham College, Oxford. Crown 8vo, pp. xvi. and 309, cloth. 1878. 7s. 6d.

STEELE.—AN EASTERN LOVE STORY. Kusa Játakaya : A Buddhistic Legendary Poem, with other Stories. By Th. Steele. Cr. 8vo, pp. xii. and 260, cl. 1871. 6s.

STENT.—THE JADE CHAPLET. In Twenty-four Beads. A Collection of Songs, Ballads, &c. (from the Chinese). By G. C. Stent, M.N.C.B.R.A.S. Post 8vo, pp. viii. and 168, cloth. 1874. 5s.

STENZLER.—See AUCTORES SANSKRITI, Vol. II.

STOCK.—ATTEMPTS AT TRUTH. By St. George Stock. Crown 8vo, pp. vi. and 248, cloth. 1882. 5s.

STOKES.—GOIDELICA—Old and Early-Middle Irish Glosses: Prose and Verse. Edited by Whitley Stokes. 2d Edition. Med. 8vo, pp. 192, cloth. 1872. 18s.

STOKES.—BEUNANS MERIASEK. The Life of Saint Meriasek, Bishop and Confessor. A Cornish Drama. Edited, with a Translation and Notes, by Whitley Stokes. Med. 8vo, pp. xvi. and 280, and Facsimile, cloth. 1872. 15s.

STOKES.—TOGAIL TROY, THE DESTRUCTION OF TROY. Transcribed from the Facsimile of the Book of Leinster, and Translated, with a Glossarial Index of the Rarer Words, by Whitley Stokes. Crown 8vo, pp. xvi. and 188, paper boards. 1882. 18s.

STOKES.—THREE MIDDLE-IRISH HOMILIES ON THE LIVES OF SAINTS—PATRICK, BRIGIT, AND COLUMBA. Edited by Whitley Stokes. Crown 8vo, pp. xii. and 140, paper boards. 1882. 10s. 6d.

STRANGE.—THE BIBLE ; is it "The Word of God"? By Thomas Lumisden Strange. Demy 8vo, pp. xii. and 384, cloth. 1871. 7s.

STRANGE.—THE SPEAKER'S COMMENTARY. Reviewed by T. L. Strange. Cr. 8vo, pp. viii. and 159, cloth. 1871. 2s. 6d.

STRANGE.—THE DEVELOPMENT OF CREATION ON THE EARTH. By T. L. Strange. Demy 8vo, pp. xii. and 110, cloth. 1874. 2s. 6d.

STRANGE.—THE LEGENDS OF THE OLD TESTAMENT. By T. L. Strange. Demy 8vo, pp. xii. and 244, cloth. 1874. 5s.

STRANGE.—THE SOURCES AND DEVELOPMENT OF CHRISTIANITY. By Thomas Lumisden Strange. Demy 8vo, pp. xx. and 256, cloth. 1875. 5s.

STRANGE.—WHAT IS CHRISTIANITY? An Historical Sketch. Illustrated with a Chart. By Thomas Lumisden Strange. Foolscap 8vo, pp. 72, cloth. 1880. 2s. 6d.

STRANGE.—CONTRIBUTIONS TO A SERIES OF CONTROVERSIAL WRITINGS, issued by the late Mr. Thomas Scott, of Upper Norwood. By Thomas Lumisden Strange. Fcap. 8vo, pp. viii. and 312, cloth. 1881. 2s. 6d.

STRANGFORD.—ORIGINAL LETTERS AND PAPERS OF THE LATE VISCOUNT STRANGFORD UPON PHILOLOGICAL AND KINDRED SUBJECTS. Edited by Viscountess Strangford. Post 8vo, pp. xxii. and 284, cloth. 1878. 12s. 6d.

STRATMANN. THE TRAGICALL HISTORIE OF HAMLET, PRINCE OF DENMARKE. By William Shakespeare. Edited according to the first printed Copies, with the various Readings and Critical Notes. By F. H. Stratmann. 8vo, pp. vi. and 120, sewed. 3s. 6d.

STRATMANN.—A DICTIONARY OF THE OLD ENGLISH LANGUAGE. Compiled from Writings of the Twelfth, Thirteenth, Fourteenth, and Fifteenth Centuries. By F. H. Stratmann. Third Edition. 4to, pp. x. and 662, sewed. 1878. 30s.

STUDIES OF MAN. By a Japanese. Crown 8vo, pp. 124, cloth. 1874. 2s. 6d.

SUYEMATZ.—Genji Monogatari. The Most Celebrated of the Classical Japanese Romances. Translated by K. Suyematz. Crown 8vo, pp. xvi. and 254, cloth. 1882. 7s. 6d.

SWEET.—History of English Sounds, from the Earliest Period, including an Investigation of the General Laws of Sound Change, and full Word Lists. By Henry Sweet. Demy 8vo, pp. iv.-164, cloth. 1874. 4s. 6d.

SYED AHMAD.—A Series of Essays on the Life of Mohammed, and Subjects subsidiary thereto. By Syed Ahmad Khan Bahadur, C.S.I. 8vo, pp. 532, with 4 Tables, 2 Maps, and Plate, cloth. 1870. 30s.

TALBOT.—Analysis of the Organisation of the Prussian Army. By Lieutenant Gerald F. Talbot, 2d Prussian Dragoon Guards. Royal 8vo, pp. 78, cloth. 1871. 3s.

TAYLER.—A Retrospect of the Religious Life of England; or, Church, Puritanism, and Free Inquiry. By J. J. Tayler, B.A. Second Edition. Reissued, with an Introductory Chapter on Recent Development, by James Martineau, LL.D., D.D. Post 8vo, pp. 380, cloth. 1876. 7s. 6d.

TAYLOR.—Prince Deukalion: A Lyrical Drama. By Bayard Taylor. Small 4to, pp. 172. Handsomely bound in white vellum. 1878. 12s.

TECHNOLOGICAL Dictionary of the Terms employed in the Arts and Sciences: Architecture; Civil Engineering; Mechanics; Machine-Making; Shipbuilding and Navigation; Metallurgy; Artillery; Mathematics; Physics; Chemistry; Mineralogy, &c. With a Preface by Dr. K. Karmarsch. Second Edition. 3 vols.

    Vol. I. German-English-French. 8vo, pp. 646. 12s.
    Vol. II. English-German-French. 8vo, pp. 666. 12s.
    Vol. III. French-German-English. 8vo, pp. 618. 12s.

TECHNOLOGICAL DICTIONARY.—A Pocket Dictionary of Technical Terms used in Arts and Manufactures. English-German-French, Deutsch-Englisch-Französisch, Français-Allemand-Anglais. Abridged from the above Technological Dictionary by Rumpf, Mothes, and Unverzagt. With the addition of Commercial Terms. 3 vols. sq. 12mo, cloth, 12s.

TEGNER.—Esaias Tegnèr's Frithiof's Saga. Translated from the Swedish, with Notes, Index, and a short Abstract of the Northern Mythology, by Leopold Hamel. Crown 8vo, pp. vi. and 280, cloth. 1874. 7s. 6d. With Photographic frontispiece, gilt edges, 10s.

THEÂTRE Français Moderne.—A Selection of Modern French Plays. Edited by the Rev. P. H. E. Brette, B.D., C. Cassal, LL.D., and Th. Karcher, LL.B.

    First Series, in 1 vol. crown 8vo, cloth, 6s., containing—

Charlotte Corday. A Tragedy. By F. Ponsard. Edited, with English Notes and Notice on Ponsard, by Professor C. Cassal, LL.D. Pp. xii. and 134. Separately, 2s. 6d.

Diane. A Drama in Verse. By Emile Augier. Edited, with English Notes and Notice on Augier, by Th. Karcher, LL.B. Pp. xiv. and 145. Separately, 2s. 6d.

Le Voyage à Dieppe, A Comedy in Prose. By Wafflard and Fulgence. Edited, with English Notes, by the Rev. P. H. E. Brette, B.D. Pp. 104. Separately, 2s. 6d.

    Second Series, crown 8vo, cloth, 6s., containing—

Molière. A Drama in Prose. By George Sand. Edited, with English Notes and Notice of George Sand, by Th. Karcher, LL.B. Fcap. 8vo, pp. xx. and 170, cloth. Separately, 3s. 6d

Les Aristocraties. A Comedy in Verse. By Etienne Arago. Edited, with English Notes and Notice of Etienne Arago, by the Rev. P. H. E. Brette, B.D. 2d Edition. Fcap. 8vo, pp. xiv. and 236, cloth. Separately, 4s.

THEÁTRE FRANÇAIS MODERNE—*continued.*

Third Series, crown 8vo, cloth, 6s., containing—

LES FAUX BONSHOMMES. A Comedy. By Théodore Barrière and Ernest Capendu. Edited, with English Notes and Notice on Barrière, by Professor C. Cassal, LL.D. Fcap. 8vo, pp. xvi. and 304. 1868. Separately, 4s.

L'HONNEUR ET L'ARGENT. A Comedy. By François Ponsard. Edited, with English Notes and Memoir of Ponsard, by Professor C. Cassal, LL.D. 2d Edition. Fcap. 8vo, pp. xvi. and 171, cloth. 1869. Separately, 3s. 6d.

THEISM —A CANDID EXAMINATION OF THEISM. By Physicus. Post 8vo, pp. xviii. and 198, cloth. 1878. 7s. 6d.

THEOSOPHY AND THE HIGHER LIFE; or, Spiritual Dynamics and the Divine and Miraculous Man. By G. W., M.D , Edinburgh. President of the British Theosophical Society. 12mo, pp. iv. and 138, cloth. 1880. 3s.

THOM.—ST. PAUL'S EPISTLES TO THE CORINTHIANS. An Attempt to convey their Spirit and Significance. By the Rev. J. H. Thom. 8vo, pp. xii. and 408, cloth. 1851. 5s.

THOMAS.—EARLY SASSANIAN INSCRIPTIONS, SEALS, AND COINS, illustrating the Early History of the Sassanian Dynasty, containing Proclamations of Ardeshir Babek, Sapor I., and his Successors. With a Critical Examination and Explanation of the celebrated Inscription in the Hájíábad Cave, demonstrating that Sapor, the Conqueror of Valerian, was a professing Christian. By Edward Thomas. Illustrated. 8vo, pp. 148, cloth. 7s. 6d.

THOMAS.—THE CHRONICLES OF THE PATHAN KINGS OF DEHLI. Illustrated by Coins, Inscriptions, and other Antiquarian Remains. By E. Thomas, F.R.A.S. With Plates and Cuts. Demy 8vo, pp. xxiv. and 467, cloth. 1871. 28s.

THOMAS.—THE REVENUE RESOURCES OF THE MUGHAL EMPIRE IN INDIA, from A.D. 1593 to A.D. 1707. A Supplement to "The Chronicles of the Pathán Kings of Delhi." By E. Thomas, F.R.S. 8vo, pp. 60, cloth. 3s. 6d.

THOMAS.—SASSANIAN COINS. Communicated to the Numismatic Society of London. By E. Thomas, F.R.S. Two Parts, 12mo, pp. 43, 3 Plates and a Cut, sewed. 5s.

THOMAS.—JAINISM; OR, THE EARLY FAITH OF ASOKA. With Illustrations of the Ancient Religions of the East, from the Pantheon of the Indo-Scythians. To which is added a Notice on Bactrian Coins and Indian Dates. By Edward Thomas, F.R.S. 8vo, pp. viii.-24 and 82. With two Autotype Plates and Woodcuts. 1877. 7s. 6d.

THOMAS.—THE THEORY AND PRACTICE OF CREOLE GRAMMAR. By J. J. Thomas. 8vo, pp. viii. and 135, boards. 12s.

THOMAS.—RECORDS OF THE GUPTA DYNASTY. Illustrated by Inscriptions. Written History, Local Tradition, and Coins. To which is added a Chapter on the Arabs in Sind. By Edward Thomas, F.R.S. Folio, with a Plate, pp. iv. and 64, cloth. 14s.

THOMAS.—BOYHOOD LAYS. By William Henry Thomas. 18mo, pp. iv. and 74, cloth. 1877. 2s. 6d.

THOMPSON.—DIALOGUES, RUSSIAN AND ENGLISH. Compiled by A. R. Thompson. sometime Lecturer of the English Language in the University of St. Vladimir, Kieff. Crown 8vo, pp. iv. and 132, cloth. 1882. 5s.

THOMSON.—EVOLUTION AND INVOLUTION. By George Thomson, Author of "The World of Being," &c. Crown 8vo, pp. viii. and 206, cloth. 1880. 5s.

E

THOMSON.—INSTITUTES OF THE LAWS OF CEYLON. By Henry Byerley Thomson, Second Puisne Judge of the Supreme Court of Ceylon. In 2 vols. 8vo, pp. xx. and 647, pp. xx. and 713, cloth. With Appendices, pp. 71. 1866. £2, 2s.

THORBURN.—BANNÚ; OR, OUR AFGHAN FRONTIER. By S. S. Thorburn, F.C.S., Settlement Officer of the Bannú District. 8vo, pp. x. and 480, cloth. 1876. 18s.

THORPE.—DIPLOMATARIUM ANGLICUM ÆVI SAXONICI. A Collection of English Charters, from the reign of King Æthelberht of Kent, A.D. DCV., to that of William the Conqueror. Containing: I. Miscellaneous Charters. II. Wills. III. Guilds. IV. Manumissions and Acquittances. With a Translation of the Anglo-Saxon. By the late Benjamin Thorpe, Member of the Royal Academy of Sciences at Munich, and of the Society of Netherlandish Literature at Leyden. 8vo, pp. xlii. and 682, cloth. 1865. £1, 1s.

THOUGHTS ON LOGIC; or, the S.N.I.X. Propositional Theory. Crown 8vo, pp. iv. and 76, cloth. 1877. 2s. 6d.

THOUGHTS ON THEISM, with Suggestions towards a Public Religious Service in Harmony with Modern Science and Philosophy. Ninth Thousand. Revised and Enlarged. 8vo, pp. 74, sewed. 1882. 1s.

THURSTON.—FRICTION AND LUBRICATION. Determinations of the Laws and Coefficients of Friction by new Methods and with new Apparatus. By Robert H. Thurston, A.M., C.E., &c. Crown 8vo, pp. xvi. and 212, cloth. 1879. 6s. 6d.

TIELE.—See English and Foreign Philosophical Library, Vol. VII. and Trübner's Oriental Series.

TOLHAUSEN.—A SYNOPSIS OF THE PATENT LAWS OF VARIOUS COUNTRIES. By A. Tolhausen, Ph.D. Third Edition. 12mo, pp. 62, sewed. 1870. 1s. 6d.

TONSBERG.—NORWAY. Illustrated Handbook for Travellers. Edited by Charles Tönsberg. With 134 Engravings on Wood, 17 Maps, and Supplement. Crown 8vo, pp. lxx., 482, and 32, cloth. 1875. 18s.

TOPOGRAPHICAL WORKS.—A LIST OF THE VARIOUS WORKS PREPARED AT THE TOPOGRAPHICAL AND STATISTICAL DEPARTMENT OF THE WAR OFFICE may be had on application.

TORRENS.—EMPIRE IN ASIA: How we came by it. A Book of Confessions. By W. M. Torrens, M.P. Med. 8vo, pp. 426, cloth. 1872. 14s.

TOSCANI—ITALIAN CONVERSATIONAL COURSE. A New Method of Teaching the Italian Language, both Theoretically and Practically. By Giovanni Toscani, Professor of the Italian Language and Literature in Queen's Coll., London, &c. Fourth Edition. 12mo, pp. xiv. and 300, cloth. 1872. 5s.

TOSCANI.—ITALIAN READING COURSE. By G. Toscani. Fcap. 8vo, pp. xii. and 160. With table. Cloth. 1875. 4s. 6d.

TOULON.—ITS ADVANTAGES AS A WINTER RESIDENCE FOR INVALIDS AND OTHERS. By an English Resident. The proceeds of this pamphlet to be devoted to the English Church at Toulon. Crown 8vo, pp. 8, sewed. 1873. 6d.

TRIMEN.—SOUTH-AFRICAN BUTTERFLIES; a Monograph of the Extra-Tropical Species. By Roland Trimen, F.L.S., F.Z.S., M.E.S., Curator of the South African Museum, Cape Town. Royal 8vo.   [*In preparation.*

TRÜBNER'S AMERICAN, EUROPEAN, AND ORIENTAL LITERARY RECORD. A Register of the most Important Works published in America, India, China, and the British Colonies. With Occasional Notes on German, Dutch, Danish, French, Italian, Spanish, Portuguese, and Russian Literature. The object of the Publishers in issuing this publication is to give a full and particular account of every publication of importance issued in America and the East. Small 4to 6d. per number. Subscription, 5s. per volume.

TRÜBNER.—TRÜBNER'S BIBLIOGRAPHICAL GUIDE TO AMERICAN LITERATURE : A Classed List of Books published in the United States of America, from 1817 to 1857. With Bibliographical Introduction, Notes, and Alphabetical Index. Compiled and Edited by Nicolas Trübner. In 1 vol. 8vo, half bound, pp. 750. 1859. 18s.

TRÜBNER'S CATALOGUE OF DICTIONARIES AND GRAMMARS OF THE PRINCIPAL LANGUAGES AND DIALECTS OF THE WORLD. Considerably Enlarged and Revised, with an Alphabetical Index. A Guide for Students and Booksellers. Second Edition, 8vo, pp. viii. and 170, cloth. 1882. 5s.

TRÜBNER'S COLLECTION OF SIMPLIFIED GRAMMARS OF THE PRINCIPAL ASIATIC AND EUROPEAN LANGUAGES. Edited by Reinhold Rost, LL.D., Ph.D. Crown 8vo, cloth, uniformly bound.
> I.—HINDUSTANI, PERSIAN, AND ARABIC. By E. H. Palmer, M.A. Pp. 112. 1882. 5s.
> II.—HUNGARIAN. By I. Singer. Pp. vi. and 88. 1882. 4s. 6d.
> III.—BASQUE. By W. Van Eys. Pp. xii. and 52. 1883. 3s. 6d.
> IV.—MALAGASY. By G. W. Parker. Pp. 66, with Plate. 1883. 5s.
> V.—MODERN GREEK. By E. M. Geldart, M.A. Pp. 68. 1883. 2s. 6d.
> VI.—ROUMANIAN. By R. Torceanu. Pp. , 1883.

TRÜBNER'S ORIENTAL SERIES :—
> Post 8vo, cloth, uniformly bound.

> ESSAYS ON THE SACRED LANGUAGE, WRITINGS, AND RELIGION OF THE PARSIS. By Martin Haug, Ph.D., late Professor of Sanskrit and Comparative Philology at the University of Munich. Second Edition. Edited by E. W. West, Ph.D. Pp. xvi. and 428. 1878. 16s.

> TEXTS FROM THE BUDDHIST CANON, commonly known as Dhammapada. With Accompanying Narratives. Translated from the Chinese by S. Beal, B.A., Trinity College, Cambridge, Professor of Chinese, University College, London. Pp. viii. and 176. 1878. 7s. 6d.

> THE HISTORY OF INDIAN LITERATURE. By Albrecht Weber. Translated from the German by J. Mann, M.A., and Dr. T. Zachariae, with the Author's sanction and assistance. 2d Edition. Pp. 368. 1882. 10s. 6d.

> A SKETCH OF THE MODERN LANGUAGES OF THE EAST INDIES. Accompanied by Two Language Maps, Classified List of Languages and Dialects, and a List of Authorities for each Language. By Robert Cust, late of H.M.I.C.S., and Hon. Librarian of R.A.S. Pp. xii. and 198. 1878. 12s.

> THE BIRTH OF THE WAR-GOD: A Poem. By Kálidásá. Translated from the Sanskrit into English Verse, by Ralph T. H. Griffiths, M.A., Principal of Benares College. Second Edition. Pp. xii. and 116. 1879. 5s.

> A CLASSICAL DICTIONARY OF HINDU MYTHOLOGY AND HISTORY, GEOGRAPHY AND LITERATURE. By John Dowson, M.R.A.S., late Professor in the Staff College. Pp. 432. 1879. 16s.

> METRICAL TRANSLATIONS FROM SANSKRIT WRITERS ; with an Introduction, many Prose Versions, and Parallel Passages from Classical Authors. By J. Muir, C.E.I., D.C.L., &c. Pp. xliv.-376. 1879. 14s.

> MODERN INDIA AND THE INDIANS; being a Series of Impressions, Notes, and Essays. By Monier Williams, D.C.L., Hon. LL.D. of the University of Calcutta, Boden Professor of Sanskrit in the University of Oxford. Third Edition, revised and augmented by considerable additions. With Illustrations and Map, pp. vii. and 368. 1879. 14s.

TRÜBNER'S ORIENTAL SERIES—*continued.*

THE LIFE OR LEGEND OF GAUDAMA, the Buddha of the Burmese. With Annotations, the Ways to Neibban, and Notice on the Phongyies, or Burmese Monks. By the Right Rev. P. Bigandet, Bishop of Ramatha, Vicar Apostolic of Ava and Pegu. Third Edition. 2 vols. Pp. xx.-368 and viii.-326. 1880. 21s.

MISCELLANEOUS ESSAYS, relating to Indian Subjects. By B. H. Hodgson, late British Minister at Nepal. 2 vols., pp. viii.-408, and viii.-348. 1880. 28s.

SELECTIONS FROM THE KORAN. By Edward William Lane, Author of an "Arabic-English Lexicon," &c. A New Edition, Revised, with an Introduction. By Stanley Lane Poole. 1p. cxii. and 174. 1879. 9s.

CHINESE BUDDHISM. A Volume of Sketches, Historical and Critical. By J. Edkins, D.D., Author of "China's Place in Philology," "Religion in China," &c., &c. Pp. lvi. and 454. 1880. 18s.

THE GULISTAN ; OR, ROSE GARDEN OF SHEKH MUSHLIU'D-DIN SADI OF SHIRAZ. Translated for the first time into Prose and Verse, with Preface and a Life of the Author, from the Atish Kadah, by E. B. Eastwick, F.R.S., M.R.A.S. 2d Edition. Pp. xxvi. and 244. 1880. 10s. 6d.

A TALMUDIC MISCELLANY ; or, One Thousand and One Extracts from the Talmud, the Midrashim, and the Kabbalah. Compiled and Translated by P. J. Hershon. With a Preface by Rev. F. W. Farrar, D.D., F.R.S., Chaplain in Ordinary to Her Majesty, and Canon of Westminster. With Notes and Copious Indexes. Pp. xxviii. and 362. 1880. 14s.

THE HISTORY OF ESARHADDON (Son of Sennacherib), King of Assyria, B.C. 681-668. Translated from the Cuneiform Inscriptions upon Cylinders and Tablets in the British Museum Collection. Together with Original Texts, a Grammatical Analysis of each word, Explanations of the Ideographs by Extracts from the Bi-Lingual Syllabaries, and List of Eponyms, &c. By E. A. Budge, B.A., M.R.A.S., Assyrian Exhibitioner, Christ's College, Cambridge. Post 8vo, pp. xii. and 164, cloth. 1880. 10s. 6d.

BUDDHIST BIRTH STORIES; or, Jātaka Tales. The oldest Collection of Folk-Lore extant : being the Jātakatthavannanā, for the first time edited in the original Pali, by V. Fausböll, and translated by T. W. Rhys Davids. Translation. Vol. I. Pp. cxvi. and 348. 1880. 18s.

THE CLASSICAL POETRY OF THE JAPANESE. By Basil Chamberlain, Author of "Yeigio Henkaku, Ichiran." Pp. xii. and 228. 1880. 7s. 6d.

LINGUISTIC AND ORIENTAL ESSAYS. Written from the year 1846-1878. By R. Cust, Author of "The Modern Languages of the East Indies." Pp. xii. and 484. 1880. 18s.

INDIAN POETRY. Containing a New Edition of "The Indian Song of Songs," from the Sanskrit of the Gita Govinda of Jayadeva ; Two Books from "The Iliad of India" (Mahábhárata) ; "Proverbial Wisdom" from the Shlokas of the Hitopadésa, and other Oriental Poems. By Edwin Arnold, M.A., C.S.I., &c., &c. Pp. viii. and 270. 1881. 7s. 6d.

THE RELIGIONS OF INDIA. By A. Barth. Authorised Translation by Rev. J. Wood. Pp. xx. and 310. 1881. 16s.

HINDU PHILOSOPHY. The Sānkhya Kārikā of Iswara Krishna. An Exposition of the System of Kapila. With an Appendix on the Nyaya and Vaiseshika Systems. By John Davies, M.A., M.R.A.S. Pp. vi. and 151. 1881. 6s.

TRÜBNER'S ORIENTAL SERIES—*continued.*

A MANUAL OF HINDU PANTHEISM. The Vedantasara. Translated with Copious Annotations. By Major G. A. Jacob, Bombay Staff Corps, Inspector of Army Schools. With a Preface by E. B. Cowell, M.A., Professor of Sanskrit in the University of Cambridge. Pp. x. and 130. 1881. 6s.

THE MESNEVÍ (usually known as the Mesneviyi Sherîf, or Holy Mesneví) of Mevlâná (Our Lord) Jelâlu-'d-Din Muhammed, Er-Rûmî. Book the First. Together with some Account of the Life and Acts of the Author, of his Ancestors, and of his Descendants. Illustrated by a selection of Characteristic Anecdotes as collected by their Historian Mevlâná Shemsu-'d-Dîn Ahmed, El Eflâkî El Arifí. Translated, and the Poetry Versified by James W. Redhouse, M.R.A.S., &c. Pp. xvi. and 136; vi. and 290. 1881. £1, 1s.

EASTERN PROVERBS AND EMBLEMS ILLUSTRATING OLD TRUTHS. By the Rev. J. Long, Member of the Bengal Asiatic Society, F.R.G.S. Pp. xv. and 280. 1881. 6s.

THE QUATRAINS OF OMAR KHAYYÁM. A New Translation. By E. H. Whinfield, late of H.M. Bengal Civil Service. Pp. 96. 1881. 5s.

THE MIND OF MENCIUS; or, Political Economy Founded upon Moral Philosophy. A Systematic Digest of the Doctrines of the Chinese Philosopher Mencius. The Original Text Classified and Translated, with Comments, by the Rev. E. Faber, Rhenish Mission Society. Translated from the German, with Additional Notes, by the Rev. A. B. Hutchinson, Church Mission, Hong Kong. Author in Chinese of " Primer Old Testament History," &c., &c. Pp. xvi. and 294. 1882. 10s. 6d.

YÚSUF AND ZULAIKHA. A Poem by Jami. Translated from the Persian into English Verse. By R. T. H. Griffith. Pp. xiv. and 304. 1882. 8s. 6d.

TSUNI-∥ GOAM: The Supreme Being of the Khoi-Khoi. By Theophilus Hahn, Ph.D., Custodian of the Grey Collection, Cape Town, Corresponding Member of the Geographical Society, Dresden; Corresponding Member of the Anthropological Society, Vienna, &c., &c. Pp. xii. and 154. 1882. 7s. 6d.

A COMPREHENSIVE COMMENTARY TO THE QURÁN. To which is prefixed Sale's Preliminary Discourse, with Additional Notes and Emendations. Together with a Complete Index to the Text, Preliminary Discourse, and Notes. By Rev. E. M. Wherry, M.A., Lodiana. Vol. I. Pp. xii. and 392. 1882. 12s. 6d.

HINDU PHILOSOPHY. THE BHAGAVAD GÍTÁ; or, The Sacred Lay. A Sanskrit Philosophical Lay. Translated, with Notes, by John Davies, M.A. Pp. vi. and 208. 1882. 8s. 6d.

THE SARVA-DARSANA-SAMGRAHA; or, Review of the Different Systems of Hindu Philosophy. By Madhava Acharya. Translated by E. B. Cowell, M.A., Cambridge, and A. E. Gough, M.A., Calcutta. Pp. xii. and 282. 1882. 10s. 6d.

TIBETAN TALES. Derived from Indian Sources. Translated from the Tibetan of the Kay-Gyur. By F. Anton von Schiefner. Done into English from the German, with an Introduction. By W. R. S. Ralston, M.A. Pp. lxvi. and 368. 1882. 14s.

LINGUISTIC ESSAYS. By Carl Abel, Ph.D. Pp. viii. and 265. 1882. 9s.

THE INDIAN EMPIRE: Its History, People, and Products. By W. W. Hunter, C.I.E., LL.D. Pp. 568. 1882. 16s.

TRUBNER'S ORIENTAL SERIES— *continued.*

HISTORY OF THE EGYPTIAN RELIGION. By Dr. C. P. Tiele, Leiden. Translated by J. Ballingal. Pp. xxiv. and 230. 1882. 7s. 6d.

THE PHILOSOPHY OF THE UPANISHADS. By A. E. Gough, M.A., Calcutta. Pp. xxiv.-268. 1882. 9s.

UDANAVARGA. A Collection of Verses from the Buddhist Canon. Compiled by Dharmatrâta. Being the Northern Buddhist Version of Dhammapada. Translated from the Tibetan of Bkah-hgyur, with Notes, and Extracts from the Commentary of Pradjnavarman, by W. Woodville Rockhill. Pp. 240. 1883. 9s.

The following works are in preparation :—

MANAVA—DHARMA—CASTRA; or, Laws of Manu. A New Translation, with Introduction, Notes, &c. By A. C. Burnell, Ph.D., C.I.E., Foreign Member of the Royal Danish Academy, and Hon. Member of several learned societies.

THE APHORISMS OF THE SANKHYA PHILOSOPHY OF KAPILA. With Illustrative Extracts from the Commentaries. By the late J. R. Ballantyne. Second Edition, edited by Fitzedward Hall.

BUDDHIST RECORDS OF THE WESTERN WORLD, being the Si-Yu-Ki by Hwen Thsang. Translated from the original Chinese, with Introduction, Index, &c. By Samuel Beal, Trinity College, Cambridge, Professor of Chinese, University College, London. In 2 vols.

UNGER.—A SHORT CUT TO READING : The Child's First Book of Lessons. Part I. By W. H. Unger. Fourth Edition. Cr. 8vo, pp. 32, cloth. 1873. 5d. In folio sheets. Pp. 44. Sets A to D, 10d. each ; set E, 8d. 1873. Complete, 4s.
SEQUEL to Part I. and Part II. Fourth Edition. Cr. 8vo, pp. 64, cloth. 1873. 6d. Parts I. and II. Third Edition. Demy 8vo, pp. 76, cloth. 1873. 1s. 6d.

UNGER.—W. H. UNGER'S CONTINUOUS SUPPLEMENTARY WRITING MODELS, designed to impart not only a good business hand, but correctness in transcribing. Oblong 8vo, pp. 40, stiff covers. 1874. 6d.

UNGER.—THE STUDENT'S BLUE BOOK: Being Selections from Official Correspondence, Reports, &c. ; for Exercises in Reading and Copying Manuscripts, Writing, Orthography, Punctuation, Dictation, Précis, Indexing, and Digesting, and Tabulating Accounts and Returns. Compiled by W. H. Unger. Folio, pp. 100, paper. 1875. 4s.

UNGER.—TWO HUNDRED TESTS IN ENGLISH ORTHOGRAPHY, or Word Dictations. Compiled by W. H. Unger. Foolscap, pp. viii. and 200, cloth. 1877. 1s. 6d. plain, 2s. 6d. interleaved.

UNGER.—THE SCRIPT PRIMER : By which one of the remaining difficulties of Children is entirely removed in the first stages, and, as a consequence, a considerable saving of time will be effected. In Two Parts. By W. H. Unger. Part I. 12mo, pp. xvi. and 44, cloth. 5d. Part II., pp. 59, cloth. 5d.

UNGER.—PRELIMINARY WORD DICTATIONS ON THE RULES FOR SPELLING. By W. H. Unger. 18mo, pp. 44, cloth. 4d.

URICOECHEA.—MAPOTECA COLOMBIANA : Catalogo de Todos los Mapas, Planos, Vistas, &c., relativos a la América-Española, Brasil, e Islas adyacentes. Arreglada cronologicamente i precedida de una introduccion sobre la historia cartografica de América. Por el Doctor Ezequiel Uricoechea, de Bogóta, Nueva Granada. 8vo, pp. 232, cloth. 1860. 6s.

URQUHART.—ELECTRO-MOTORS. A Treatise on the Means and Apparatus employed in the Transmission of Electrical Energy and its Conversion into Motive-power. For the Use of Engineers and Others. By J. W. Urquhart, Electrician. Crown 8vo, cloth, pp. xii. and 178, illustrated. 1882. 7s. 6d.

VAITANA SUTRA.—See AUCTORES SANSKRITI, Vol. III.

VALDES.—LIVES OF THE TWIN BROTHERS, JUÁN AND ALFONSO DE VALDÉS. By E. Boehmer, D.D. Translated by J. T. Betts. Crown 8vo. pp. 32, wrappers. 1882. 1s.

VALDES.—SEVENTEEN OPUSCULES. By Juán de Valdés. Translated from the Spanish and Italian, and edited by John T. Betts. Crown 8vo, pp. xii. and 188, cloth. 1882. 6s.

VALDES.—JUÁN DE VALDÉS' COMMENTARY UPON THE GOSPEL OF ST. MATTHEW. With Professor Boehmer's "Lives of Juán and Alfonso de Valdés." Now for the first time translated from the Spanish, and never before published in English. By John T. Betts. Post 8vo, pp. xii. and 512-30, cloth. 1882. 7s. 6d.

VALDES.—SPIRITUAL MILK; or, Christian Instruction for Children. By Juán de Valdés. Translated from the Italian, edited and published by John T. Betts. With Lives of the twin brothers, Juán and Alfonso de Valdés. By E. Boehmer, D.D. Fcap. 8vo, pp. 60, wrappers. 1882. 2s.

VALDES.—THREE OPUSCULES: an Extract from Valdés' Seventeen Opuscules. By Juán de Valdés. Translated, edited, and published by John T. Betts. Fcap. 8vo, pp. 58, wrappers. 1881. 1s. 6d.

VALDES.—JUAN DE VALDÉS' COMMENTARY UPON OUR LORD'S SERMON ON THE MOUNT. Translated and edited by J. T. Betts. With Lives of Juán and Alfonso de Valdés. By E. Boehmer, D.D. Crown 8vo, pp. 112, boards. 1882. 2s. 6d.

VALDES.—JUÁN DE VALDÉS' COMMENTARY UPON THE EPISTLE TO THE ROMANS. Edited by J. T. Betts. Crown 8vo, pp. xxxii. and 296, cloth. 1883. 6s.

VAN CAMPEN.—THE DUTCH IN THE ARCTIC SEAS. By Samuel Richard Van Campen, author of "Holland's Silver Feast." 8vo. Vol. I. A Dutch Arctic Expedition and Route. Third Edition. Pp. xxxvii. and 263, cloth. 1877. 10s. 6d. Vol. II. *in preparation.*

VAN DE WEYER.—CHOIX D'OPUSCULES PHILOSOPHIQUES, HISTORIQUES, POLITIQUES ET LITTÉRAIRES de Sylvain Van de Weyer, Précédés d'Avant propos de l'Éditeur, Roxburghe style. Crown 8vo. PREMIÈRE SÉRIE. Pp. 374. 1863. 10s. 6d.--DEUXIÈME SÉRIE. Pp. 502. 1869. 12s.—TROISIÈME SÉRIE. Pp. 391. 1875. 10s. 6d.—QUATRIÈME SÉRIE. Pp. 366. 1876. 10s. 6d.

VAN EYS.—BASQUE GRAMMAR. See Trübner's Collection.

VAN LAUN.—GRAMMAR OF THE FRENCH LANGUAGE By H. Van Laun. Parts I. and II. Accidence and Syntax. 13th Edition. Cr. 8vo, pp. 151 and 120, cloth. 1874. 4s. Part III. Exercises. 11th Edition. Cr. 8vo, pp. xii. and 285, cloth. 1873. 3s. 6d.

VAN LAUN.—LEÇONS GRADUÉES DE TRADUCTION ET DE LECTURE; or, Graduated Lessons in Translation and Reading, with Biographical Sketches, Annotations on History, Geography, Synonyms and Style, and a Dictionary of Words and Idioms. By Henri Van Laun. 4th Edition. 12mo, pp. viii. and 400, cloth. 1868. 5s.

VARDHAMANA'S GANARATNAMAHODADHI. See AUCTORES SANSKRITI, Vol. IV.

VAZIR OF LANKURAN: A Persian Play. A Text-Book of Modern Colloquial Persian. Edited, with Grammatical Introduction, Translation, Notes, and Vocabulary, by W. H. Haggard, late of H.M. Legation in Teheran, and G. le Strange. Crown 8vo, pp. 230, cloth. 1882. 10s. 6d.

VELASQUEZ AND SIMONNÉ'S NEW METHOD TO READ, WRITE, AND SPEAK THE SPANISH LANGUAGE. Adapted to Ollendorff's System. Post 8vo, pp. 558, cloth. 1880. 6s.

    KEY. Post 8vo, pp. 174, cloth. 4s.

VELASQUEZ.—A DICTIONARY OF THE SPANISH AND ENGLISH LANGUAGES. For the Use of Young Learners and Travellers. By M. Velasquez de la Cadena. In Two Parts. I. Spanish-English. II. English-Spanish. Crown 8vo, pp. viii. and 846, cloth. 1878. 7s. 6d.

VELASQUEZ.—A PRONOUNCING DICTIONARY OF THE SPANISH AND ENGLISH LANGUAGES. Composed from the Dictionaries of the Spanish Academy, Terreos, and Salva, and Webster, Worcester, and Walker. Two Parts in one thick volume. By M. Velasquez de la Cadena. Roy. 8vo, pp. 1280, cloth. 1873. £1, 4s.

VELASQUEZ.—NEW SPANISH READER : Passages from the most approved authors, in Prose and Verse. Arranged in progressive order. With Vocabulary. By M. Velasquez de la Cadena. Post 8vo, pp. 352, cloth. 1866. 6s.

VELASQUEZ.—AN EASY INTRODUCTION TO SPANISH CONVERSATION, containing all that is necessary to make a rapid progress in it. Particularly designed for persons who have little time to study, or are their own instructors. By M. Velasquez de la Cadena. 12mo, pp. 150, cloth. 1863. 2s. 6d.

VERSES AND VERSELETS. By a Lover of Nature. Foolscap 8vo, pp. viii. and 88, cloth. 1876. 2s. 6d.

VICTORIA GOVERNMENT.—PUBLICATIONS OF THE GOVERNMENT OF VICTORIA. *List in preparation.*

VOGEL.— ON BEER. A Statistical Sketch. By M. Vogel. Fcap. 8vo, pp. xii. and 76, cloth limp. 1874. 2s.

WAFFLARD and FULGENCE.— LE VOYAGE À DIEPPE. A Comedy in Prose. By Wafflard and Fulgence. Edited, with Notes, by the Rev. P. H. E. Brette, B.D. Cr. 8vo, pp. 104, cloth. 1867. 2s. 6d.

WAKE.—THE EVOLUTION OF MORALITY. Being a History of the Development of Moral Culture. By C. Staniland Wake. 2 vols. crown 8vo, pp. xvi.-506 and xii.-474, cloth. 1878. 21s.

WALLACE.—ON MIRACLES AND MODERN SPIRITUALISM ; Three Essays. By Alfred Russel Wallace, Author of "The Malay Archipelago," "The Geographical Distribution of Animals," &c., &c. Second Edition, crown 8vo, pp. viii. and 236, cloth. 1881. 5s.

WANKLYN and CHAPMAN.—WATER ANALYSIS. A Practical Treatise on the Examination of Potable Water. By J. A. Wanklyn, and E. T. Chapman. Fifth Edition. Entirely rewritten. By J. A. Wanklyn, M.R.C.S. Crown 8vo, pp. x. and 182, cloth. 1879. 5s.

WANKLYN.—MILK ANALYSIS ; a Practical Treatise on the Examination of Milk and its Derivatives, Cream, Butter, and Cheese. By J. A. Wanklyn, M.R.C.S., &c. Crown 8vo, pp. viii. and 72, cloth. 1874. 5s.

WANKLYN.—TEA, COFFEE, AND COCOA. A Practical Treatise on the Analysis of Tea, Coffee, Cocoa, Chocolate, Maté (Paraguay Tea), &c. By J. A. Wanklyn, M.R.C.S., &c. Crown 8vo, pp. viii. and 60, cloth. 1874. 5s.

WAR OFFICE.— A LIST OF THE VARIOUS MILITARY MANUALS AND OTHER WORKS PUBLISHED UNDER THE SUPERINTENDENCE OF THE WAR OFFICE may be had on application.

WARD.—ICE : A Lecture delivered before the Keswick Literary Society, and published by request. To which is appended a Geological Dream on Skiddaw. By J. Clifton Ward, F.G.S. 8vo, pp. 28, sewed. 1870. 1s.

WARD.—ELEMENTARY NATURAL PHILOSOPHY; being a Course of Nine Lectures, specially adapted for the use of Schools and Junior Students. By J. Clifton Ward, F.G.S. Fcap. 8vo, pp. viii. and 216, with 154 Illustrations, cloth. 1871. 3s. 6d.

WARD.—ELEMENTARY GEOLOGY: A Course of Nine Lectures, for the use of Schools and Junior Students. By J. Clifton Ward, F.G.S. Fcap. 8vo, pp. 292, with 120 Illustrations, cloth. 1872. 4s. 6d.

WATSON.—INDEX TO THE NATIVE AND SCIENTIFIC NAMES OF INDIAN AND OTHER EASTERN ECONOMIC PLANTS AND PRODUCTS, originally prepared under the authority of the Secretary of State for India in Council. By John Forbes Watson, M.D. Imp. 8vo, pp. 650, cloth. 1868. £1, 11s. 6d.

WEBER.—THE HISTORY OF INDIAN LITERATURE. By Albrecht Weber. Translated from the Second German Edition, by J. Mann, M.A., and T. Zachariae, Ph.D., with the sanction of the Author. Second Edition, post 8vo, pp. xxiv. and 360, cloth. 1882. 10s. 6d.

WEDGWOOD.—THE PRINCIPLES OF GEOMETRICAL DEMONSTRATION, reduced from the Original Conception of Space and Form. By H. Wedgwood, M.A. 12mo, pp. 48, cloth. 1844. 2s.

WEDGWOOD.—ON THE DEVELOPMENT OF THE UNDERSTANDING. By H. Wedgwood, A.M. 12mo, pp. 133, cloth. 1848. 3s.

WEDGWOOD.—THE GEOMETRY OF THE THREE FIRST BOOKS OF EUCLID. By Direct Proof from Definitions Alone. By H. Wedgwood, M.A. 12mo, pp. 104, cloth. 1856. 3s.

WEDGWOOD.—ON THE ORIGIN OF LANGUAGE. By H. Wedgwood, M.A. 12mo, pp. 165, cloth. 1866. 3s. 6d.

WEDGWOOD.—A DICTIONARY OF ENGLISH ETYMOLOGY. By H. Wedgwood. Third Edition, revised and enlarged. With Introduction on the Origin of Language. 8vo, pp. lxxii. and 746, cloth. 1878. £1, 1s.

WEDGWOOD.—CONTESTED ETYMOLOGIES IN THE DICTIONARY OF THE REV. W. W. SKEAT. By H. Wedgwood. Crown 8vo, pp. viii. and 194, cloth. 1882. 5s.

WEISBACH.—THEORETICAL MECHANICS: A Manual of the Mechanics of Engineering and of the Construction of Machines; with an Introduction to the Calculus. Designed as a Text-book for Technical Schools and Colleges, and for the use of Engineers, Architects, &c. By Julius Weisbach, Ph.D., Oberbergrath, and Professor at the Royal Mining Academy at Freiberg, &c. Translated from the German by Eckley B. Coxe, A.M., Mining Engineer. Demy 8vo, with 902 woodcuts, pp. 1112, cloth. 1877. 31s. 6d.

WELLER—AN IMPROVED DICTIONARY; English and French, and French and English. By E. Weller. Royal 8vo, pp. 384 and 340, cloth. 1864. 7s. 6d.

WEST and BÜHLER.—A DIGEST OF THE HINDU LAW OF INHERITANCE AND PARTITION, from the Replies of the Sástris in the Several Courts of the Bombay Presidency. With Introduction, Notes, and Appendix. Edited by Raymond West and J. G. Bühler. Second Edition. Demy 8vo, 674 pp., sewed. 1879. £1, 11s. 6d.

WETHERELL.—THE MANUFACTURE OF VINEGAR, its Theory and Practice; with especial reference to the Quick Process. By C. M. Wetherell, Ph.D., M.D. 8vo, pp. 30, cloth. 7s. 6d.

WHEELDON.—ANGLING RESORTS NEAR LONDON: The Thames and the Lea. By J. P. Wheeldon, Piscatorial Correspondent to "Bell's Life." Crown 8vo, pp. viii. and 218. 1878. Paper, 1s. 6d.

WHEELER. The History of India from the Earliest Ages. By J. Talboys Wheeler. Demy 8vo, cloth. Vol. I. containing the Vedic Period and the Maha Bhárata. With Map. Pp. lxxv. and 576, cl. 1867, o. p. Vol. II. The Ramayana. and the Brahmanic Period. Pp. lxxxviii. and 680, with 2 Maps, cl. 21s. Vol. III. Hindu, Buddhist, Brahmanical Revival. Pp. xxiv.-500. With 2 Maps, 8vo, cl. 1874. 18s. This volume may be had as a complete work with the following title, "History of India; Hindu, Buddhist, and Brahmanical." Vol. IV. Part I. Mussulman Rule. Pp. xxxii.-320. 1876. 14s. Vol. IV., Part II., completing the History of India down to the time of the Moghul Empire. Pp. xxviii. and 280. 1881. 12s.

WHEELER. Early Records of British India : A History of the English Settlements in India, as told in the Government Records, the works of old Travellers, and other Contemporary Documents, from the earliest period down to the rise of British Power in India. By J. Talboys Wheeler, late Assistant Secretary to the Government of India in the Foreign Department. Royal 8vo, pp. xxxii. and 392, cloth. 1878. 15s.

WHEELER.—The Foreigner in China. By L. N. Wheeler, D.D. With Introduction by Professor W. C. Sawyer, Ph.D. 8vo, pp. 268, cloth. 1881. 6s. 6d.

WHERRY.—A Comprehensive Commentary to the Qurán. To which is prefixed Sale's Preliminary Discourse, with additional Notes and Emendations. Together with a complete Index to the Text, Preliminary Discourse, and Notes. By Rev. E. M. Wherry, M.A., Lodiana. 3 vols. post 8vo, cloth. Vol. I. Pp. xii. and 392. 1882. 12s. 6d.

WHINFIELD.—Quatrains of Omar Khayyam. See Trübner's Oriental Series.

WHINFIELD.—See Gulshan I. Raz.

WHIST.—Short Rules for Modern Whist, Extracted from the "Quarterly Review" of January 1871. Printed on a Card, folded to fit the Pocket. 1878. 6d.

WHITNEY.—Language and the Study of Language : Twelve Lectures on the Principles of Linguistic Science. By W. D. Whitney. Third Edition. Crown 8vo, pp. xii. and 504, cloth. 1870. 10s. 6d.

WHITNEY.—Language and its Study, with especial reference to the Indo-European Family of Languages. Seven Lectures by W. D. Whitney, Instructor in Modern Languages in Yale College. Edited with Introduction, Notes, Tables, &c., and an Index, by the Rev. R. Morris, M.A., LL.D. Second Edition. Crown 8vo, pp. xxii. and 318, cloth. 1880. 5s.

WHITNEY.—Oriental and Linguistic Studies. By W. D. Whitney. First Series. Crown 8vo, pp. x. and 420, cloth. 1874. 12s. Second Series. Crown 8vo, pp. xii. and 434. With chart, cloth. 1874. 12s.

WHITNEY.—A Sanskrit Grammar, including both the Classical Language and the older Dialects of Veda and Brahmana. By William Dwight Whitney, Professor of Sanskrit and Comparative Philology in Yale College, Newhaven, &c., &c. 8vo, pp. xxiv. and 486. 1879. Stitched in wrapper, 10s. 6d; cloth, 12s.

WHITWELL.— Iron Smelter's Pocket Analysis Book. By Thomas Whitwell, Member of the Institution of Mechanical Engineers, &c. Oblong 12mo, pp. 152, roan. 1877. 5s.

WILKINSON.—The Saint's Travel to the Land of Canaan. Wherein are discovered Seventeen False Rests short of the Spiritual Coming of Christ in the Saints, with a Brief Discovery of what the Coming of Christ in the Spirit is. By R. Wilkinson. Printed 1648; reprinted 1874. Fcap. 8vo, pp. 208, cloth. 1s. 6d.

WILLIAMS.—THE MIDDLE KINGDOM. A Survey of the Geography, Government, Education, &c., of the Chinese Empire. By S. W. Williams. New Edition. 2 vols. 8vo. [*In preparation.*]

WILLIAMS.—A SYLLABIC DICTIONARY OF THE CHINESE LANGUAGE; arranged according to the Wu-Fang Yuen Yin, with the pronunciation of the Characters as heard in Pekin, Canton, Amoy, and Shanghai. By S. Wells Williams, LL.D. 4to, pp. 1336. 1874. £5, 5s.

WILLIAMS.—MODERN INDIA AND THE INDIANS. See Trübner's Oriental Series.

WILSON.—WORKS OF THE LATE HORACE HAYMAN WILSON, M.A., F.R.S., &c.

Vols. I. and II. Essays and Lectures chiefly on the Religion of the Hindus, by the late H. H. Wilson, M.A., F.R.S., &c. Collected and Edited by Dr. Reinhold Rost. 2 vols. demy 8vo, pp. xiii. and 399, vi. and 416, cloth. 21s.

Vols. III., IV., and V. Essays Analytical, Critical, and Philological, on Subjects connected with Sanskrit Literature. Collected and Edited by Dr. Reinhold Rost. 3 vols. demy 8vo, pp. 408, 406, and 390, cloth. 36s.

Vols. VI., VII., VIII., IX., and X. (2 parts). Vishnu Puráná, a System of Hindu Mythology and Tradition. Translated from the original Sanskrit, and Illustrated by Notes derived chiefly from other Puránás. By the late H. H. Wilson. Edited by FitzEdward Hall, M.A., D.C.L., Oxon. Vols. I. to V. (2 parts). Demy 8vo, pp. cxl. and 200, 344, 346, 362, and 268, cloth. £3, 4s. 6d.

Vols. XI. and XII. Select Specimens of the Theatre of the Hindus. Translated from the original Sanskrit. By the late H. H. Wilson, M.A., F.R.S. Third corrected Edition. 2 vols. demy 8vo, pp. lxxi. and 384, iv. and 418, cloth. 21s.

WISE.—COMMENTARY ON THE HINDU SYSTEM OF MEDICINE. By T. A. Wise, M.D. 8vo, pp. xx. and 432, cloth. 1845. 7s. 6d.

WISE.—REVIEW OF THE HISTORY OF MEDICINE. By Thomas A. Wise. 2 vols. demy 8vo, cloth. Vol. I., pp. xcviii. and 397. Vol. II., pp. 574. 10s.

WISE.—FACTS AND FALLACIES OF MODERN PROTECTION. By Bernhard Ringrose Wise, B.A., Scholar of Queen's College, Oxford (Being the Oxford Cobden Prize Essay for 1878.) Crown 8vo, pp. vii. and 120, cloth. 1879. 2s. 6d.

WITHERS.—THE ENGLISH LANGUAGE AS PRONOUNCED. By G. Withers. Royal 8vo, pp. 84, sewed. 1874. 1s.

WOOD. CHRONOS. Mother Earth's Biography. A Romance of the New School. By Wallace Wood, M.D. Crown 8vo, pp. xvi. and 334, with Illustration, cloth. 1873. 6s.

WOMEN.—THE RIGHTS OF WOMEN. A Comparison of the Relative Legal Status of the Sexes in the Chief Countries of Western Civilisation. Crown 8vo, pp. 104, cloth. 1875. 2s. 6d.

WRIGHT.—FEUDAL MANUALS OF ENGLISH HISTORY, a series of Popular Sketches of our National History compiled at different periods, from the Thirteenth Century to the Fifteenth, for the use of the Feudal Gentry and Nobility. Now first edited from the Original Manuscripts. By Thomas Wright, M.A., F.S.A., &c. Small 4to, pp. xxix. and 184, cloth. 1872. 15s.

WRIGHT.—THE HOMES OF OTHER DAYS. A History of Domestic Manners and Sentiments during the Middle Ages. By Thomas Wright, M.A., F.S.A. With Illustrations from the Illuminations in Contemporary Manuscripts and other Sources. Drawn and Engraved by F. W. Fairholt, F.S.A. Medium 8vo, 350 Woodcuts, pp. xv. and 512, cloth. 1871. 21s.

WRIGHT. A Volume of Vocabularies, illustrating the Condition and Manners of our Forefathers, as well as the History of the forms of Elementary Education, and of the Languages spoken in this Island from the Tenth Century to the Fifteenth. Edited by Thomas Wright, M.A., F.S.A., &c., &c. [*In the Press.*

WRIGHT.—The Celt, the Roman, and the Saxon; a History of the Early Inhabitants of Britain down to the Conversion of the Anglo-Saxons to Christianity. Illustrated by the Ancient Remains brought to light by Recent Research. By Thomas Wright, M.A., F.S.A., &c., &c. Third Corrected and Enlarged Edition. Cr. 8vo, pp. xiv. and 562. With nearly 300 Engravings. Cloth. 1875. 14s.

WRIGHT. Mental Travels in Imagined Lands. By H. Wright. Crown 8vo, pp. 184, cloth. 1878. 5s.

WYLD.—Clairvoyance; or, the Auto-Noetic Action of the Mind. By George Wyld, M.D. Edin. 8vo, pp. 32, wrapper. 1883. 1s.

YOUNG.—Labour in Europe and America. A Special Report on the Rates of Wages, the Cost of Subsistence, and the Condition of the Working Classes in Great Britain, Germany, France, Belgium, and other Countries of Europe, also in the United States and British America. By Edward Young, Ph.D. Royal 8vo, pp. vi. and 864, cloth. 1876. 10s. 6d.

YOUNG MECHANIC (THE).—See Mechanic.

ZELLER.—Strauss and Renan. An Essay by E. Zeller. Translated from the German. Post 8vo, pp. 110, cloth. 1866. 2s. 6d.

PERIODICALS

PUBLISHED AND SOLD BY TRÜBNER & CO.

AMATEUR MECHANICS.—Monthly, 6d.

ANTHROPOLOGICAL Institute of Great Britain and Ireland (Journal of).—Quarterly, 5s.

ARCHITECT (American) and Building News.—Contains General Architectural News, Articles on Interior Decoration, Sanitary Engineering, Construction, Building Materials, &c., &c. Four full-page Illustrations accompany each Number. Weekly. Annual Subscription, £1, 11s. 6d. Post free.

ASIATIC SOCIETY (Royal) of Great Britain and Ireland (Journal of).—Irregular.

BIBLICAL ARCHÆOLOGICAL SOCIETY (Transactions of).—Irregular.

BIBLIOTHECA SACRA.—Quarterly, 4s. 6d. Annual Subscription, 18s. Post free.

BRITISH ARCHÆOLOGICAL ASSOCIATION (Journal of).—Quarterly, 8s.

BRITISH HOMŒOPATHIC SOCIETY (Annals of).—Half-yearly, 2s. 6d.

BROWNING SOCIETY'S PAPERS. Irregular.

CALCUTTA REVIEW.—Quarterly, 8s. 6d. Annual Subscription, 34s. Post free.

CALIFORNIAN.—A Monthly Magazine devoted to the Literature, Art, Music, Politics, &c., of the West. 1s. 6d. Annual Subscription, 18s. Post free.

CAMBRIDGE PHILOLOGICAL SOCIETY (TRANSACTIONS OF).—Irregular.

ENGLISHWOMAN'S REVIEW.—Social and Industrial Questions. Monthly, 6d.

GEOLOGICAL MAGAZINE, or Monthly Journal of Geology, 1s. 6d. Annual Subscription, 18s. Post free.

GLASGOW, GEOLOGICAL SOCIETY OF (TRANSACTIONS OF).—Irregular.

INDEX MEDICUS.—A Monthly Classified Record of the Current Medical Literature of the World. Annual Subscription, 30s. Post free.

INDIAN ANTIQUARY.—A Journal of Oriental Research in Archæology, History, Literature, Languages, Philosophy, Religion, Folklore, &c. Annual Subscription, £2. Post free.

LIBRARY JOURNAL.—Official Organ of the Library Associations of America and of the United Kingdom. Monthly, 1s. 6d. Annual Subscription, 20s. Post free.

MANCHESTER QUARTERLY.—1s. 6d.

MATHEMATICS (AMERICAN JOURNAL OF).—Quarterly, 7s. 6d. Annual Subscription, 24s. Post free.

ORTHODOX CATHOLIC REVIEW.—Irregular.

PHILOLOGICAL SOCIETY (TRANSACTIONS AND PROCEEDINGS OF).—Irregular.

PSYCHICAL RESEARCH (SOCIETY OF).—PROCEEDINGS.

PUBLISHERS' WEEKLY.—THE AMERICAN BOOK-TRADE JOURNAL. Annual Subscription, 18s. Post free.

SCIENTIFIC AMERICAN.—WEEKLY. Annual subscription, 18s. Post free.

SUPPLEMENT to ditto.—WEEKLY. Annual subscription, 24s. Post free.

SCIENCE AND ARTS (AMERICAN JOURNAL OF).—Monthly, 2s. 6d. Annual Subscription, 30s.

SPECULATIVE PHILOSOPHY (JOURNAL OF).—Quarterly, 4s. Annual Subscription, 16s. Post free, 17s.

SUNDAY REVIEW.—Organ of the Sunday Society for Opening Museums and Art Galleries on Sunday.—Quarterly, 1s. Annual Subscription, 4s. 6d. Post free.

TRÜBNER'S AMERICAN, EUROPEAN, AND ORIENTAL LITERARY RECORD.—A Register of the most Important Works Published in America, India, China, and the British Colonies. With occasional Notes on German, Dutch, Danish, French, Italian, Spanish, Portuguese, and Russian Literature. Subscription for 12 Numbers, 5s. Post free.

TRÜBNER & CO.'S MONTHLY LIST of New and Forthcoming Works, Official and other Authorised Publications, and New American Books. Post free.

WESTMINSTER REVIEW.—Quarterly, 6s. Annual Subscription, 22s. Post free.

WOMAN'S SUFFRAGE JOURNAL.—Monthly, 1d.

TRÜBNER & CO.'S CATALOGUES.

Any of the following Catalogues sent per Post on receipt of Stamps.

Agricultural Works. 2d.

Arabic, Persian, and Turkish Books, printed in the East. 1s.

Assyria and Assyriology. 1s.

Bibliotheca Hispano-Americana. 1s. 6d.

Brazil, Ancient and Modern Books relating to. 2s. 6d.

British Museum, Publications of Trustees of the. 1d.

Dictionaries and Grammars of Principal Languages and Dialects of the World. 5s.

Educational Works. 1d.

Egypt and Egyptology. 1s.

Guide Books. 1d.

Important Works, published by Trübner & Co. 2d.

Linguistic and Oriental Publications. 2d.

Medical, Surgical, Chemical, and Dental Publications. 2d.

Modern German Books. 2d.

Monthly List of New Publications. 1d.

Pali, Prakrit, and Buddhist Literature. 1s.

Portuguese Language, Ancient and Modern Books in the. 6d.

Sanskrit Books. 2s. 6d.

Scientific Works. 2d.

Semitic, Iranian, and Tatar Races. 1s.

TRÜBNER'S
COLLECTION OF SIMPLIFIED GRAMMARS
OF THE
PRINCIPAL ASIATIC AND EUROPEAN LANGUAGES.

EDITED BY REINHOLD ROST, LL.D., PH.D.

The object of this Series is to provide the learner with a concise but practical Introduction to the various Languages, and at the same time to furnish Students of Comparative Philology with a clear and comprehensive view of their structure. The attempt to adapt the somewhat cumbrous grammatical system of the Greek and Latin to every other tongue has introduced a great deal of unnecessary difficulty into the study of Languages. Instead of analysing existing locutions and endeavouring to discover the principles which regulate them, writers of grammars have for the most part constructed a framework of rules on the old lines, and tried to make the language of which they were treating fit into it. Where this proves impossible, the difficulty is met by lists of exceptions and irregular forms, thus burdening the pupil's mind with a mass of details of which he can make no practical use.

In these Grammars the subject is viewed from a different standpoint; the structure of each language is carefully examined, and the principles which underlie it are carefully explained; while apparent discrepancies and so-called irregularities are shown to be only natural euphonic and other changes. All technical terms are excluded unless their meaning and application is self-evident; no arbitrary rules are admitted; the old classification into declensions, conjugations, &c., and even the usual *paradigms* and tables, are omitted. Thus reduced to the simplest principles, the Accidence and Syntax can be thoroughly comprehended by the student on one perusal, and a few hours' diligent study will enable him to analyse any sentence in the language.

NOW READY.
Crown 8vo, cloth, uniformly bound.

I.—**Hindustani, Persian, and Arabic.** By the late E. H. Palmer, M.A. Pp. 112. 5s.

II.—**Hungarian.** By I. SINGER, of Buda-Pesth. Pp. vi. and 88. 4s. 6d.

III.—Basque. By W. Van Eys. Pp. xii. and 52. 3s. 6d.

IV.—Malagasy. By G. W. Parker. Pp. 66. 5s.

V.—Modern Greek. By E. M. Geldart, M.A. Pp. 68. 2s. 6d.

VI.—Roumanian. by M. Torceanu. Pp.

The following are in preparation :—

SIMPLIFIED GRAMMARS OF

Russian, Polish, Bohemian, Bulgarian and Serbian, by Mr. Morfil, of Oxford.

Assyrian, by Prof. Sayce.

Hebrew, by Dr. Ginsburg.

Pali.

Danish, by Miss Otté.

Cymric and Gaelic, by H. Jenner, of the British Museum.

Turkish, by J. W. Redhouse, M.R.A.S.

Malay, by W. E. Maxwell, of the Inner Temple, Barrister-at-Law.

Finnic, by Prof. Otto Donner, of Helsingfors.

Swedish, by W. Sturzen-Becker, of Stockholm.

Mr. Trübner is making arrangements with competent Scholars for the early preparation of Grammars of **Albanian, Siamese, Burmese, Japanese, Chinese,** *and* **Icelandic.**

LONDON : TRÜBNER & CO., LUDGATE HILL.

PRINTED BY BALLANTYNE, HANSON AND CO.
EDINBURGH AND LONDON.

www.ingramcontent.com/pod-product-compliance
Lightning Source LLC
Chambersburg PA
CBHW020607030726
47497CB00007B/2116